A Recognizable Image

By William Carlos Williams

The Autobiography of William Carlos Williams
The Build-up
Collected Earlier Poems
Collected Later Poems
The Embodiment of Knowledge
The Farmers' Daughters
Imaginations
Interviews with William Carlos Williams
In the American Grain
In the Money
I Wanted to Write a Poem
Kora in Hell: Improvisations*
Many Loves and Other Plays
Paterson, Books 1–5
Pictures from Brueghel and Other Poems
A Recognizable Image: WCW on Art and Artists
Selected Essays
Selected Poems
A Voyage to Pagany
White Mule
The William Carlos Williams Reader

*City Lights Books

Frontispiece: Emanuel Romano, *Portrait of William Carlos Williams.*
Courtesy of the Gotham Book Mart Gallery, New York.

A RECOGNIZABLE IMAGE:

William Carlos Williams
on Art and Artists

Edited with an introduction and notes by

Bram Dijkstra

A NEW DIRECTIONS BOOK

Manufactured in the United States of America
First published clothbound by New Directions in 1978
Published simultaneously in Canada by McClelland & Stewart, Ltd.

Library of Congress Cataloging in Publication Data

Williams, William Carlos, 1883–1963.
   A recognizable image.
   (A New Directions Book)
   1. Art—Addresses, essays, lectures.
I. Dijkstra, Bram. II. Title.
N7445.2.w54   1978   704.9'2   78-16919
ISBN 0-8112-0704-8

New Directions Books are published for James Laughlin
by New Directions Publishing Corporation,
333 Sixth Avenue, New York 10014

ACKNOWLEDGMENTS:

Grateful acknowledgment is made to the editors and publishers of the following in which versions of some of these essays first appeared: *Art News, The Black Mountain Review, Catalog of the John Marin Memorial Exhibition* (Art Galleries of the University of California, Los Angeles), *Columbia Review and Morningside, Contact, El Crepusculo, Form, The Freeman,* "G" Gallery Broadsheet (New York), *The General Magazine and Historical Chronicle, The Illustrated Leaves of Grass* (ed. Howard Chapnick, Grosset & Dunlop, Inc.), *Life and Letters Today, The Little Review, The New Republic, Now, Poetry Taos Annual, Sheeler Retrospective* (Museum of Modern Art Catalogue), *The Tiger's Eye, View,* and *Women: A Collaboration of Artists and Writers* (Samuel Kootz Editions, New York).

Thanks are also due for permission to reprint these essays: "The American Spirit in Art" first published in the *Proceedings of the American Academy of Arts and Letters and the National Institute of Arts and Letters,* Second Series, No. 2 (reprinted by permission of the American Academy and Institute of Arts and Letters); "Brancusi" first appeared in *Arts,* November 1955, and "E. E. Cummings's Paintings and Poems" in *Arts Digest,* December 1, 1954 (both reprinted by permission of *Arts Magazine).*

Permission to quote from these copyrighted sources is also gratefully acknowledged: E. E. Cummings, "nonsun blob a," from *Complete Poems 1913–1962* (Copyright 1944 by E. E. Cummings;

Acknowledgments

renewed 1972 by Nancy T. Andrews), reprinted by permission of Harcourt Brace Jovanovich, Inc. and MacGibbon & Kee, Ltd./ Granada Publishing Ltd.; Marianne Moore, "Nevertheless," from the *Collected Poems of Marianne Moore* (Copyright 1944 by Marianne Moore, renewed 1972 by Marianne Moore), reprinted by permission of Macmillan Publishing Co., Inc. and Faber and Faber, Ltd.; Wallace Stevens, "Anecdote of the Jar," from *The Collected Poems of Wallace Stevens* (Copyright 1954 by Wallace Stevens), reprinted by permission of Alfred A. Knopf, Inc.

Special thanks are due: to the Collection of American Literature, Beinecke Rare Book and Manuscript Library, Yale University, and the Poetry Collection, The Lockwood Memorial Library, State University of New York at Buffalo, for the use of manuscript materials; and to the Whitney Museum of American Art for their invaluable assistance.

Contents

List of Illustrations

Introduction

THE CENTRAL importance of the visual in William Carlos Williams's poetry is strikingly emphasized in a short article he wrote for *The Columbia Review* in 1937. "Think," he wrote, "of the poem as an object, an apple that is red and good to eat—or a plum that is blue and sour—or better yet, a machine for making bolts."[1] In 1929, to the question "what is your strongest characteristic?" posed by the editors of *The Little Review,* he had replied: "my sight. I like most my ability to be drunk with a sudden realization of value in things others never notice."[2] In discussing the work of Charles Sheeler he stated categorically: "The moment sight ceases art ceases."

With Williams's emphasis on sight came, not surprisingly, an abiding, life-long interest in the visual arts. His mother had been a painter, and he, too, had tried his hand at it in his youth—although he soon gave it up, probably because his work toward a medical degree required most of his attention. Ever practical about his limitations, he took up poetry instead, because painting was "messy, cumbersome." One can—and Williams frequently did—scribble poems in an unoccupied moment during the long duty hours as an intern, or between appointments as a baby doctor—but setting up an easel, getting out your paints, mixing them, and doing all the other cumbersome things a painter has to do to get started on a picture, simply won't do under similar circumstances.

In deciding to focus on poetry, however, Williams by no means chose to abandon practicing a *visual* art. He believed that poetry pursued the same goals as painting "in this world of images."[3] The poet's job was to express "the meaning of an apple," and that meaning was "not something for a child to eat or for a pie but something more closely related to Cézanne who painted them."[4] Although a good deal has been written now about the close

1

connections between Williams's poetry and the visual arts,[5] some
critics, caught in the essentially non-visual world of writing as such,
still tend to be skeptical about the claim that he was very largely
trying to do in words what the painters were doing with paint on
canvas. Such critics point out that the world of language is
fundamentally different from that of sight. While they may be at
least partially correct, there is absolutely no indication that
Williams shared that conviction. "For poet read—artist, painter,"[6]
he declared at one point. Early in 1921 he had wanted to call a
collection of his poetry *Picture Poems,* changing his mind only at the
last moment to have it published under the title *Sour Grapes,*[7] a title
which, in light of his initial intention, and his proclivity for seeing
poems as fruit, should perhaps be seen as more literally intended,
and to some extent as more self-deprecating (these poems are
"unripe") than has generally been the case.

Almost thirty years later, during a reading at the Metropolitan
Museum of Art in New York, he still saw his poems primarily as
pictures:

> In the course of seeking technical improvements in the use of his
> medium, something he must do if he is to remain alive and
> effective—the artist inadvertently, perhaps, records a few pieces:
> portraits, landscapes or what not to please his public or patron.
> That's the way it has gone for the last few hundred years.
> Let me take advantage of this drift and present some figures of
> men and women to you, mostly anonymous.
> As T. S. Eliot said to me the only time I saw him, Williams,
> you've given us some good characters in your work, let's have more
> of them.—That's what I shall follow tonight—at least at the start.
> You may, looking at the pictures, gather whatever there is else to
> find in the text as we go along.[8]

That Williams was not merely lured into comparisons and figures
of speech by his surroundings at the time of his reading, but was
moved instead by a genuine sense of solidarity with the painters
whose work hung on the walls around him, can be seen from what
he said to Walter Sutton in an interview which took place not long
before he died. When Sutton asked him whether he and the
painters spoke the same language, Williams replied: "Yes, very

1. William Carlos Williams, *Passaic River*. Collection of American Literature, Beinecke Rare Book and Manuscript Library, Yale University (Norman Holmes Pearson "Art for the Wrong Reason" Collection.)

2. Paul Cézanne, *Still Life with Apples* (1895–98). Oil on canvas, 27″ × 36½″. Collection, The Museum of Modern Art, New York (Lillie P. Bliss Collection).

Photograph by Soichi Sunami

close—And as I've grown older, I've attempted to fuse the poetry and painting to make it the same thing—."[9] Emphasizing that design, structure, was the key to the fusion of the two media, he made it clear that for him "the meaning of the poem can be grasped by attention to the design." For Williams the identification of a poem as a composition of sharply, visually, delineated objects and events was a sufficient justification of its existence, as it is commonly accepted to be in a painting. Again it is Cézanne who proves to have been the catalyst for the poet's conception of poetic structure: "I was tremendously involved in an appreciation of Cézanne. He was a designer. He put it down on the canvas so that there would be a meaning without saying anything at all. Just the relation of the parts to themselves. In considering a poem, I don't care whether it is finished or not; if it is put down with a good relation to the parts, it becomes a poem. And the meaning of the poem can be grasped by attention to the design."

In the interview with Sutton, Williams again stressed an aspect of his formation as a poet, which, although he insisted upon it repeatedly in his published reminiscences, continues to be shrugged off with what can only be characterized as a somewhat parochial skepticism by some literary critics, namely that it was more specifically the painters who provided him with the impetus to develop new forms of poetry than his fellow poets:

> Because of my interest in painting, the Imagists appealed to me. It was an image that I was seeking, and when Pound came along with his drive for the image it appealed to me very strongly. Poetry and the image were linked in my mind. And it was very natural for me to speak of poetry as an image and write down a poem as an image and to leave it to the natural intelligence of a man. . . . If an image were set down on canvas, it was both a poem and a picture at the same time, and it was a very fertile thing to me to deal with. . . . When I found Pound talking of the image I accepted it as a poem. . . . I've always admired painters; my best friends have been painters. Charles Demuth is one of my earliest friends, and when I went to Philadelphia to study medicine, I ate in the same boarding house that he did. . . . The image of a painting identified a man as a poet to me.[10]

Each of the many articles in this collection documents, in one way or another, the nature and importance of Williams's fascination with all things visual. But the role of the images created by art, and their function in providing what might be called the furniture of his imagination, is perhaps best indicated in his delightful narrative "Effie Deans." There he remarks: "I love pictures. Nine times out of ten when I go into a house and have to wait a moment or two for whoever it is to appear, I find interesting ones to look at, in the plainest households sometimes." Watercolors, still lifes, old chromolithographs, paintings, calendar pictures, all had the power to fascinate him and frequently found their way into his poems. As he points out in "Effie Deans," his being a physician gave him many special opportunities to feed his fancy, for "a physician often comes upon delightful *objets d'art* inauspiciously lighting the days and years of some obscure household in almost any suburban town." Proceeding to construct his own *musée imaginaire* out of the various objects and pictures he had encountered on his rounds, he offers us, in fact, a brisk and yet detailed insight into the visual sources of many of his poems. For these visible remains of human creativity, we realize, form part of an archive of images stored away in his mind for possible future use in his own creative work. After all, since Williams believed that in matters of technique, of design, and emotional intention, the artistic goals of painters and poets were the same, there was nothing to hold him back from trying to do in words what the painters were doing on canvas, or, for that matter, from trying to turn a striking picture into a poem.

Of course it should be remembered in this context that when Williams constructed a poem from an image he had taken from painting or photography, or when he described a painting in one of his articles, he often did so from memory. Fascinated as he was with the visual nature of things, the innumerable pictures "fastened" by others which he had stored in his memory, would often spontaneously materialize as part of a poem or prose piece he was writing. But during that process of storage, these images, over the years, rarely remained unaltered. His active imagination would most often take hold of the image which had originally caught his attention, and remold it by adding or subtracting details. Thus, as the original image became less clear in his mind, the remembered image would become substantially his own creation, even if structurally and conceptually it might initially have been inspired by a specific painting. So strong, in fact, was the visual bent of Williams's imagination, that at times he would recall what had initially been a nonpictorial stimulus as if it were a picture he had seen somewhere. An interesting instance of this tendency is recorded by Charles Norman in his biography of E. E. Cummings. In the article, included in this volume, which Williams wrote on Cummings's paintings and poems, he described a painting of Cummings's which he remembered as being in the possession of Marianne Moore: "A box of strawberries, pure and simple, painted with realistic but poetic insight, the very scent and taste of the berries, even the feel of them in the mouth when crushed by the tongue against the inside of the cheek is there." Norman comments on this description: "There is, alas, no such picture as 'the box of strawberries' mentioned by Williams. Miss Moore owns a picture of a rose. What Dr. Williams recollected subconsciously was a poem by Miss Moore which begins:

> you've seen a strawberry
> that's had a struggle; yet
> was, where the fragments met,
>
> a hedgehog or a star-
> fish for the multitude
> of seeds.[11]

"Effie Deans" is an outline of the wide range of visual impulses to which Williams responded with enthusiasm throughout his life. But when he reminisced about the liberating impact of painting on his poetry, he usually returned to the exciting first decades of the twentieth century, when the European modernist painters first set progressively-minded American artists reeling under the impact of what seemed to them an onslaught of daring innovations. There is no room to enter here upon a discussion of Williams's involvement in the avant-garde movements of that period, but it is altogether fitting that this collection of Williams's writings on art and artists should open with his, logically rather confused, but characteristically enthusiastic "Vortex" of 1915.

This manifesto, which has remained unpublished until now, was inspired by an equally jejeune, but far more destructively focused and belligerent "Vortex" by the sculptor Gaudier-Brzeska, written "from the trenches" in France, and published in the second issue of Wyndham Lewis's *Blast*. Williams's "Vortex" demonstrates both the complex tracery of influences which the modernist movements were beginning to exert on his work, and the already solid grid of personal conceptions through which these influences had to pass to become part of his intellectual world. His "Vortex" is, indeed, in embryo form, a statement of what was to become the foundation of his poetic theory, his insistence upon the crucial link between "local consciousness" and the universality of "true" art. When, for example, he declared, "I deny—affirm my independence from—the accident of time and space," he in essence alluded to his belief, which would remain with him throughout his long career as a poet, that artists could transcend the "tyranny" of time, and reach the realm of timeless—universal—experience, by insisting on the structural and perceptual integrity of their work. At the same time his assertion that as a poet he would use "whatever I find in my view," was, in effect, a declaration that the sources of the "universal" were in particular objects. Objects whose participation in timelessness and hence universality was affirmed precisely through their manifestation as time-and-place bound "particular" entities, were brought under the transfixing scrunity of the artist, whose perception of their essential qualities served to "liberate" them from their timebound identity by entering them into the universal reality of the world of art. For, Williams argued in his "Vortex," it was in the structural organization of objects, and in the poet's perception of their visual presence, of their existence as "an arrangement of appearances, of planes," that their significance as universal representants of certain supra-individual human emotional states was revealed. Much later, in discussing the paintings of Marsden Hartley, he would assert the same principle more pointedly: "Unless you paint pure nothing, you paint a place—and in that place you will reveal all places in the world."

Objects, in this manner, became a link between the person and universal states of being, the means whereby the person, through the mediating work of the artist, came to recognize the nature and universality of his own emotions. Thus this very early, fragmentary manuscript already announced that it was to be the visual presence of an object which would determine its meaning for Williams; for, he argued, without the planes and surfaces which constitute its visual presence, an object "does not exist," can have no "substance." What Williams called the "apposition of planes," is the conjunction of those surfaces which constitute the visual field of experience. It was, he believed, this visual field which organizes the conceptual patterns of the perceiver.

At the same time, however, Williams showed, in his remark that he would begin by taking "whatever character my environment has presented and turning it to my purpose," that he was at least to some extent aware that the artist in "transferring" an object from local experience to the world of art, was, while "affirming his existence," also imposing a preconditioned perceptual organization on that object. In his "Vortex" however, Williams did not resolve— or for that matter even set out to resolve—the considerable contradiction in focus between these features of his incipient theory of perception. Nor did this contradiction ever disappear from his later theoretical writings, which are largely further explorations of these, to him, crucial themes. He remained throughout his life concerned, as he had been in his "Vortex," with establishing a link between the universality of the emotions which spoke to him out of the structural configurations of the objects surrounding him, and the seemingly contradictory local specificity of those objects. In arguing that what counted for the artist was to "liberate" the universal structures of experience, the design embedded in the objects of a given locality, Williams in fact established a ground rule for the mode of expression which was to preoccupy him consistently from that point on. Williams's later formulations of this theory centered on his motto that "the local is the only universal," and it is this motto, as yet not as compactly worded, which underlies the declaration in his "Vortex," that "I will express my emotions in the appearance: surfaces, sounds, smells, touch of the place in which I happen to be. I will not make an effort to leave that place for I deny that I am dependent on any place."

As becomes clear from Williams's comments on the goals of his magazine *Contact*, he saw one's immediate environment, one's "locality," as the only source of that universal experience which, he thought, "great" art expresses. Such universal experience was communicable only on the basis of an authentic perception of the objects of the material world, which, he reasoned, could only stem from an accurate representation of the things we know, the things with which we are intimately familiar: the "sensual accidents" bred out of "the local conditions which confront us." This was what established "the essential contact between words and the locality that breeds them." However, while the materials which were to make up authentic expression could be found in one's immediate environment, nothing held back the artist in his search for methods to come to an authentic expression of his locality, from utilizing such progressive means of expression as might have been developed by artists in other environments. At the same time he must recognize that even these means of expression were at least partially responsive only to the conditions prevalent in the locality in which they were first developed. Hence, Williams argued, the American artist could profit from, for example, "this French Orchid," Dadaism, in constructing his own means of expression, but only as long as he realized that "the American contour is not particularly dadaesque" and that the Dada method, or any other, would have to be modified substantially to fit into the American context. In an unpublished notation he once remarked: "Picasso will not leave Paris because he has the brains to know that if he came to America he would have to be affected by it and paint that way—and he doesn't wish to at his age."[12] To fail to enter into such a process of modification, to merely copy the styles developed in Paris without adapting them to the particular requirements of the artist's immediate environment, to try to paint Parisian pictures in New York was, Williams asserted, the unenlightened response of truly provincial minds. The styles of painting generally grouped under the heading "Regionalism," too, were in his eyes the products of artists who were imitators, copiers, artists who simply used mechanically learned methods to express the surface eccentricities of a particular locality. Painters of what is called the American Scene Movement of the Thirties, such as Thomas Hart Benton and James Steuart Curry, clearly belonged to the latter group as far as Williams was concerned, trying once more to fashion art from anecdote, from the outward peculiarities of a group of people or a place, without giving thought to their inner contact with the material objects of their environment. It is not, Williams pointed out in "French Painting," the botanical characteristics of a tree which make it, or the picture one might paint of it, "American," but the impression created by the shape and color of it in the artist's "sensual being—his whole body (not his eyes) his body, his mind, his memory, his place." It should therefore be self-evident that it is less than fruitful to try to discuss Williams's work as if he were a "regional poet," or, for that matter, to associate him with the aspirations of the Regionalist painters, as some critics have recently been tempted to do. Williams was completely out of sympathy with their provincialism, and his disdain for their work is amply demonstrated in the absence of any significant reference to them in his voluminous writings. In 1932, in the second incarnation of his magazine *Contact*, he himself said all that was needed to lay this issue to rest: "Always, at this point, some blank idiot cries out, 'Regionalism'! Good God is there no intelligence left on earth. Shall we never differentiate the regional in letters from the objective immediacy of our hand to mouth, eye to brain existence?"[13]

Williams's lack of interest for most American painters who tried consciously to depict things that were "typically American" was directly linked to his continued emphasis, throughout his life, on the primacy of the European Modernist artists. His relentless insistence on the need to find a means of expression appropriate to the American environment makes it easy to be misled into believing that he was an American chauvinist in matters of art. The contrary was clearly the case. Only a relatively small number of his essays on art deal with specifically American artists, and these are usually concerned with the work of friends closely linked to his early years as a member of the New York avant-garde movement grouped around Alfred Stieglitz: Sheeler, Demuth, Hartley, Marin, Stieglitz himself, these are the American artists whose names one most frequently encounters in the pages of this collection, as one does in any of Williams's other works. They were instrumental in helping him develop his basic tenets about art and its relationship to the artist's immediate environment, and the poet felt an inalienable sense of kinship with their mode of expression. Otherwise, aside from his clear enthusiam for the American primitive painters and the photography of Walker Evans, and an occasional reference to a Ben Shahn, Robert Motherwell, or a nineteenth-century forerunner such as Samuel Morse, there is little to show that American painting occupied his attention in any special way. Probably this paucity of references to American artists was at least partially due to his belief that the "American idiom" in painting as well as poetry was still in the process of being forged, but it was certainly also due to his visual eclecticism, which made it possible for him to appreciate a good image when, or wherever he might find it. If a painting by Romare Bearden struck his fancy, it was not the nationality of the artist, but the force of the image he had created which counted for him.

This explains why Williams's focus in these pages is almost entirely on the principal exponents of European Modernist movements such as Cubism, Dadaism and Surrealism, or, as he grew older, the perennial classics of European painting. For Williams the last one hundred years of French painting were an enduring inspiration, and he time and again referred to it as one of the standards of excellence in artistic expression. He believed it to have been "one of the cleanest, most alert and fecund avenues of human endeavor, a positive point of intelligent insistence from which work may depart in any direction." Cézanne and Picasso (French, for Williams, because he painted in Paris) are the artists he most frequently mentioned as exemplary workers in the realm of the imagination. Braque, Duchamp, Gris, Matisse and a number of others follow close behind. Competing with these artists are the great names of Western European art: Rembrandt, El Greco, Michelangelo, Brueghel, Bosch. That Williams was in no way favorably disposed toward a policy of special pleading on behalf of the inherent virtues of American artists can be seen from his scathing denunciation, in "The Neglected Artist," of the spiritual poverty of the Americans as a result of "their history of divorce from the hereditary cultures of Europe."

In fact, when we move away from a consideration of Williams's involvement in the immediate technical aspects of Modernist experimentation, the conservative cast of his thought becomes more and more apparent. Such features make this collection of Williams's writings on art and artists especially valuable and interesting—for, whenever he discussed poetry *per se,* he considered himself called upon to appear in the robes of a tireless searcher after poetic experimentation, and to emphasize the immediate, technical aspects of his craft. But in discussing the visual arts he felt more free to indulge in theoretical generalizations and speculation, and to reveal his beliefs about the relationship of art to "life"—and to politics.

Art had early become for him the privileged realm of transcendent experience, the one steadfast oasis of hope and regenerative promise in a rather grim near-desert of everyday experience. When he was in his twenties and searching for "Meaning," he had found the first stirrings of it in the movements of Isadora Duncan, movements which seemed to him representative of a profoundly new concept of things. Unfortunately the tools of classical versification had proved hardly the means for Williams to immortalize his rapture, and the maudlin sonnet he wrote to Duncan in response to his ecstatic experience shows how direly he needed to break away from traditional means of expression. Williams was very much aware of this and instinctively turned to sources other than literature. In 1908 he wrote to his brother Edgar: "I have been trying to get out and see the city this year and trying to get out and get my share of the good things the city is giving away. I have visited the Metropolitan Museum frequently and with a catalogue I'll soon be able to distinguish a few of the leading characteristics of the principal schools of painting."[14] Experiences such as these strengthened him in his belief in the intimate interaction of the arts, and in his own mission to further what he came to consider the supreme function of art as a catalyst of human experience.

Williams learned to see art as the ideal vehicle for progress in the human condition, the harbinger of a future which was to be more beautiful than the present because it was inevitably to be molded by the ever evolving shapes of art. Early in 1909 he wrote: "This is the province of art, to influence the best and as we learn the better and better to influence each other with beauty so shall we perhaps grow to help others and perhaps who can tell in the end we may help many. Art is intrinsic it is not a plaything, it is an everyday affair and does not need a museum for its exposition; it should breathe in the common places and inspire us at the moments of decision in our work and play."[15] Williams never really changed his mind about this all-important function of art. That is why, when the Armory Show came and liberated him from the traditional formal structures of literature, he joyfully joined in the iconoclasm and irreverence of the European painters and sculptors, while, at the same time never permitting himself to indulge in the pose of world-weary skepticism about the function of art which so often accompanied their experiments. He was awed by Duchamp's creativity, but the painter's apparent lack of respect for art frightened him. He saw Dadaism as an important movement toward change, but refused to go along with it when it began to try to "bury" art.

Still, he learned much from Dada: irreverence toward the formal expectations of the reader, a sense of hilarity in attempting to *épater le bourgeois* by naming the unnameable, the shock of sudden shifts of subject matter, and so on. But in contrast to what was common among the European Dadaists, we find in Williams's work anything but a negative focus toward the possibilities of art as such to elevate human consciousness. Instead he managed to appropriate the Dada influence and make it part of his own conception of art as a catalyst of human experience, as the very center of life, as the means whereby the pointless gestures of every day experience, imposed by mundane necessity, could be turned into a playground for the imagination.

No wonder, then, that to attack art came, in Williams's eyes to be to attack the meaning of life itself. Thus when, in 1920, in *The Freeman,* Harold Stearns derided what he considered to be the various naivetés of the sophisticates, and included in his list of their foibles "an exaggerated emphasis on the importance of art," Williams clearly felt personally attacked. Stearns remarked that where art was concerned, "except for the lucky few caught in the right generations, most of us are doomed to live in fallow periods, periods that live on impassioned recollection of the past or rosy hopefulness about the future."[16] Williams's response, "What Every Artist Knows," therefore became an emphatic justification of the "secret periods" of art, which, he maintained, were anything but fallow. Instead they were periods of gestation, periods of invisible growth, absolutely essential to the cause of progress. Stearns's contention that "of all the illusions which revolt the soul, the illusion of progress is the most trying, the illusion that mere chronology in time works automatically toward moral ends,"[17] infuriated Williams, for it called into question the very basis of his own concept of the ongoing function of art as the central determinant of humanist progress: without art, he believed, there could be no progress, and, more importantly, without a belief in progress there could be no belief in the saving grace of art.

It is in fact Williams's belief in progress through art which underlies his lifelong quest for the "new." To "make it new" in art was to contribute to the development of artistic expression, and hence to work toward the transcendent function of art in the molding of human consciousness. This is why Williams, as he made clear in his "Comment on Contact," came to equate experimentation and creativity, innovation and authenticity—a very questionable shortcut in logic, but one central to his thought.

In *Rome,* the rather chaotic but fascinating record of his intellectual and emotional reaction to what he saw in Europe in 1924, to be published in *The Iowa Review,* the poet, in the context of a heavily, and explicitly, sexually focused passage, associated the creative process closely with the tensions of unfulfilled physical desire: "The poem is the blood coursing full of Madonnas,"[18] he wrote—a statement which perfectly expresses the tension between the ideal and the real which informed all his thinking about art, and which at the same time reflects the mixture of religious fervor and erotic energy which he never failed to muster in its defense. As the artist became the world's savior ("the artist must save us, he is the only one who can," he would declare in his piece on the photographer Walker Evans), he more and more came to see art itself as the

Madonna whose purity needed to be defended against the incursions of contaminating influences. During the turbulent years of the Thirties, with their emphasis on the social responsibilities of the artist, this inevitably precipitated his participation in the controversy concerning the relationship between art and politics.

Williams's writings on that subject show him to be, surely to no one's surprise, firmly against the concept that the artist should subordinate his personality or his art to the demands of collective political action. For Williams the artist's role was more exalted than that; it could not be encompassed by the banal exigencies of immediate social concerns. To subordinate one's imagination to the limitations of political consciousness, he thought, was to consent to "doing less than he is capable of as an artist." It is therefore rather amusing to see him, a staunch defender of the individual talent who believed that "art is amoral in its conceptions," try to square his notions about the primacy of art into a romanticized radical framework—as in his notes concerning his proposed editorship of *Blast* ("A Magazine of Proletarian Fiction"), which tried to represent a Marxist point of view. These notes are an elaboration of his contention, in his "Notes on Art" of a few years earlier, that art is amoral because it transcends the limitations of social theory, and hence the realm of moral theory as well. As an intuitive expression of aesthetic and structural excellence, art was a record of the artist's insight into realities which were beyond the realm of politics. For, although Williams asserted that there is "no absolute in art and no absolute end toward which art is directed," and saw the "spirit of good" as lying beyond art, there can be no doubt that he regarded art as the medium whereby that spirit of good could be most closely approximated. Hence, moral concerns being of a lower order of understanding, their introduction into his creations would simply weaken the impact of the artist's perceptions. Art should serve a political cause only if it could encompass that cause without compromising the artist's "sight," his integrity of vision. It should never allow itself to *be* encompassed by such a cause, for then it would inevitably end up being dragged down to lower standards. Art should be, Williams indicated in "The Neglected Artist," an "asylum," a "haven," a separate world of more perfect structures than the real world of affairs, to which the banker, the politician, the physician might repair, when necessary, "to refresh and engage their minds and emotions." Williams tried to reassure us that this curious world of rest and recuperation for the professional classes was not a "bland Elysium," but there is little in what he says to make us believe otherwise. To those of his readers who tend to see him primarily as an exponent of "hard-edged realism" in poetry, the fact that Williams harbored notions such as these may come as a shock. But if one keeps in mind that he saw in the objects of nature organic equivalents to universal states of being, it should become clear that from his point of view there was nothing to keep the "real" from expressing the ideal.

Williams's lofty conception of the function of art and its elevation above the mundane world of affairs allowed him to make statements about the role of the artist in society which came perilously close to those the partisans of "pure science" have come to use to justify their abdication of responsibility for the destructive uses to which society has put their various discoveries. It is not the artist's concern "to what end he is working: his concern is to work and to work well," Williams contended, for example. True, he apparently subsequently thought better of including that remark in his essay, perhaps appalled by his own frankness, but there can be no doubt that it represents the point of view underlying the whole of his conception of the relationship of art to society.

For Williams, justification for such a position lay in his belief in the "essential individualism of artists." It is ironic that the poet of the local, the poet of place and "contact," who time and again emphasized that there was no way in which the artist could escape the influence of his immediate environment on his mode of expression, should have allowed himself to see politics (which is, after all, only the visible tip of an immense iceberg of ideological manipulation imposed on the person by his social environment) as incapable of sullying the individual perceptions of the artist. Williams clearly did not have, or did not permit himself to have, the slightest suspicion that the "drastic compulsions" of the artist might themselves have been modulated by unconsciously assimilated forms of ideological indoctrination. In "The Neglected Artist" he reiterated the notion that painting and politics don't go together, that to work in the realm of art is "to approach the world indirectly." In other words, for Williams art was not, after all, expressive of life immediately lived, but rather an abstraction from life, a rarified, selective depiction of life. Somehow, Williams believed, the artist was able to pierce through all the layers of untruth surrounding the objects of experience and restore them to their pristine universality. Why it should have been that the artist was given this unusual dispensation from involvement in the societal patterns of delusion, Williams never managed to clarify successfully, but it is clear that he regarded the special quality which guarded the artist from contamination by "political imperatives" as a factor of what he called in "The Poet in Time of Confusion," that "first excellence of the arts, their marvelously complex and superbly efficient eyes." Thus, once again, it is through his sight that the artist proved what Williams finally came to see as the aristocracy of his individual being: "By our eyes we shall prove ourselves better men than those who would block perception," he insisted. The artist's sight was indeed a sight into the universals of right and wrong: "The work of art is valuable and keeps its universality, through variations in time and locality, by the inability of anyone to put a lie in that form which is accurate to the day and make it live."

The artist was dangerous to the politicians because he could see through the politician's aggressive "movie screen on which appear his unfleshed desires, what he would like to have us believe and accept of him." The artist's sight, Williams continued, is like "a beam of light" probing the bare stage of reality behind the screen. It is a striking image and a tempting one, but in its assumption of the matter of course nature of the artist's ability to see through political sham, it does little to clear up the often frantic support given by these very artists, "great" and not so great alike, to some of the most destructive political movements imaginable. Thus when Pound went on the radio in support of the Fascists, and Williams felt called upon, at about the same time that he wrote "The Poet in Time of Confusion," to attack Pound for this political stance, he did so primarily in terms of Pound's ability as a poet, as a "see-er," criticizing, and it must be said by no means inaccurately, the limitations of his old friend's visual judgment:

> The French laughed at him. Old sock. He was still posing, still considering the relics of Remy de Gourmont and lingering over the decayed salon not so very long since frequented by Mallarmé, when a world, the world of Céline, of the painters especially, a world that through lack of primary education and training he had no means of approaching, a world of tone and pigment he was disbarred from by physical deficiency itself was fairly bursting about him. Where will you find a whisper of these things in his writings? Look and see. You will find nothing.
>
> Why? I believe Pound to be as color blind as he is tone deaf. It was the great period of Picasso's supremacy, of Braque, of Juan Gris, Matisse and some of the others. Do you find any inkling of it in what Pound was writing those days? Show it to me and I'll show you that all his comments are literary banter. Picasso snubbed him. Gertrude Stein put him aside after a few words. And who among all these people do you think Pound picked as his champion? Picabia, a purely literary figure, Picabia and Léger. His war against England quickly petered out there and he had to take another jump to save himself. Ah, this time he found it.
>
> Briefly Pound missed the major impact of his age, the social impetus which underlies every effort on that front, largely through his blindness and intense egotism; he is a complete reactionary. Really he can't learn and as a result has been left sadly in the rear.[19]

In other words, only good artists could see behind the screen, because they were visually oriented, while bad artists dealt in non-visual abstractions, in "literary banter." For Williams, clearly, sight and insight were one and the same thing.

That such a judgment is in itself "political" by implication, because it assigns specific social values to various modes of conceptualization, must have occurred to Williams from time to time, especially when he set up the artist as the true revolutionary, the person who was to lead society to a recognition of "truth." But at the same time he was unwilling to recognize the larger ramifications of the artist as political figure, which such a realization implies. Instead he continued to find a way out of politics by pointing to the inevitable position of the "true" artist as an unappreciated prophet whose voice was lost as that of a nightingale in a thunderstorm. The unaltered perception of "objective reality" was a universal, "Truth," and he therefore equated the artist's attempts to record his perception of that objective reality with objectivity, the revelation of the universal in the particular. But while he recognized that the "bad" artist's perception of objective reality was impaired by a "faulty" kind of sight which also caused such an artist to make faulty political choices, he did not at all contemplate the possibility that what he considered the "good" artist's "unaltered" perception of objective reality simply represented another manipulated mode of the conceptualization of that reality.

In his theory of the artist's function, then, Williams, as so many others, did not take into account that all acts of visual perception are contaminated by conceptualization, since all perception is the coming to consciousness of aspects of the relationship between self and other. This recognition of relationship is, in any human being born and bred within reach of other human beings, a factor of the processes of communication, based on the categorization of objects according to methods of classification traditionally established within a specific perceptual community and hence accepted as objective facts by the perceiver. Since all communication is based on the categorization, and therefore, the conceptualization of relationship, the initial visual perceptions of social beings are inevitably conceptualizations of relationship rather than "pure," "unaltered," perceptions of the object seen. Williams failed to recognize that no one's sight, as a consequence, is "unimpaired." Ideological manipulation has structured our perceptions long before we come to intellectual consciousness. Therefore any belief in the inherent purity of our visual perception is itself an ideologically determined delusion. Only a careful and relentless process of critical reexamination of the assumptions which underlie our mode of visual perception can begin to remove our sight from the bounds of such manipulation. Williams was not prepared to engage in a critical reexamination of this kind, and relied instead on his theory concerning the objective truth of sight to escape from political responsibility. In the end, therefore, no matter how loudly he might proclaim that Symbolism was dead,[20] there really was very little which separated his "sight is truth" theory from the "art for art's sake" position of the Symbolists.

Williams's concept of the social function of art was ultimately that art should be an "example" which, through its superior modulation of the objects of experience, might shame the world into mending its ways—as he implied in "The Neglected Artist":

> The whole Renaissance was a rule of so many tyrants. It was they who hired the masters to work for them. The great artists of the time did not stop to attack such men. They were their friends. Instead they made masterpieces. And in their work lies a depth of understanding which must ultimately do away with all tyrants and cruelty, all violence of which art is the antithesis.

Williams knew that he was in effect advocating an "Ivory Tower" position: "We need the world of the artists to remain intact, that to it we may *go*, as the monks and Popes of the Quattrocento went for confirmation and the verification of their faiths which only great art affords." At the time that he wrote "The Neglected Artist" he was apparently still rather uncomfortable with that fact, as is evident from his unwillingness to voice these opinions directly. Instead he put most of them into the mouth of a "visiting artist." Hence it is also this visiting artist who is made responsible for the shortsighted opinion that Van Gogh's *Potato Eaters* is a bad picture because "peasants are happy people"—but there is unfortunately nothing in the article which would indicate that Williams disagreed with this sentiment. Presumably the wasted, misshapen, exhausted peasants Van Gogh depicted did not represent the "higher truth" of art. "They are not that way," we are told, "that is perverse, empty."

A bit abruptly, but not really unexpectedly, we are here confronted with a mentality still completely locked into the aesthetic expectations of high Victorian academic art, when peasants or workers could only be shown in the vigor of young man- or womanhood, and in the presumably glowing enjoyment of healthy labor in the service of the bourgeoisie. Ironically it is this manner of representation, which, when it became associated with the socialist realism of the Soviets, came to be seen as a descent into propaganda. Yet, if we browse through Williams's poetry, it is true that the portraits of peasants or workers we encounter tend to be those of specimens of robust, healthy, "earthy" humanity not far removed from those "noble savages of labor" one encounters in Victorian

art. The fact that in his various drafts of "The Neglected Artist"
Williams showed rather a lack of concern about which remarks to
attribute to himself and which to have spoken by the artist, shifting
some sections to various parts of the essay at will, and attributing
the remarks contained in them to whoever happened to be
"speaking" at the time, indicates that it is reasonable to hold the
poet responsible for these opinions. Thus the visiting painter's
remark about Van Gogh's peasants helps to explain the absence of
portrayals of serious poverty and economic depression in
Williams's poetry—something which is often overlooked in the
presence of his numerous representations of persons courageously
struggling with illness or mental depression, an area of reality with
which he was too intimately connected as a physician to allow
himself to glamorize.

In the speech on "Credit Monopoly," written in the same year as
"The Neglected Artist," Williams continued to develop his ideas
about the limits of the artist's immediate social responsibilities.
Partially inspired by Pound's enthusiasm for Major C. H. Douglas
and the latter's efforts to construct economic theories which could
serve as an antidote to Marxist attacks upon individualism, he began
by acknowledging his debt to Douglas's notions about Social
Credit, proceeding, characteristically, to excise most of the references to the major in his later drafts. It is actually not clear how
familiar Williams was with Douglas's ideas. Reed Whittemore
suggests that Williams may only have read a short outline of the
Social Credit ideas written by Pound for *The New English Weekly*.
Mike Weaver, on the other hand, documents a considerable
involvement on the poet's part in actions inspired by the movement.[21] In any case, there is little evidence in Williams's talk of any
thoroughgoing familiarity with the details of Douglas's concepts,
but the poet could certainly sympathize with the major's attempts
to rescue individualism and the structures of capitalist economic
practice from the speculative excesses of the times, and back to the
primrose path of a massive productive capacity. Already in 1924, in
Rome, Williams had expressed his enthusiasm for the basic premises of American commerce:

Gluttony breeds scheming and scheming sharpens wit. So the typical American genius is he who can get the most with the least work. This is obvious logic.

So we have a class of witty men who are able to drill the lesser gluttons, men who "organize," great rulers of natural aptitude who are able to bring bananas in quantity from Central America, nectarines from Cape Town and pearls, sables etc. coffee, rubber, tea, ivory, anything from the various hot and cold and temperate and deep and difficult places of the earth.

This is the natural history of America. The plain solution is to let this natural and beneficial tendency go free.

Nor must it be imagined that it will cramp intellectual development, science or art. Science, art and intellectual development depend entirely on clarity and thrive under it. Only befuddled lackwit cramps gentle pleasures. Clear, strong worldy action gives the intelligence free reign.[22]

"Men of affairs," as long as they upheld what he saw as the true American spirit, the principle of personal liberty above all else, stood very high in Williams's estimation. Social Credit, which he thought advocated that the state should provide free credit to enterprising individuals to stimulate the development of essential industries, presumably causing the necessities of life to be widely and cheaply available to all, was therefore just the kind of system that could appeal to him. It allowed him to formulate a conspiracy in which a few evil creditors could be blamed for the economic ills of the capitalist system ("a mysterious hand of credit seeking to gain management over the controls"), while the system itself, and "the desirability of preserving individual freedom under the law" could remain unquestioned.

As we have already seen, the artist was, for Williams, *the* type of the rugged individual. Repelled by "the petty tyranny already forced on me by those advocating a dictatorship by a mass group of the labor forces," he intended to sail between the Scylla of usury and the Charybdis of Marxism, and, he hoped, alight safely in the harbor of "free expression for the artist." The contradiction he recognized, but ultimately decided to ignore,was that even though he believed that all "creative power" was vested in the individual, and individualism should therefore be steadfastly defended, and its restriction rejected, he also understood that individualism was a root cause of monopoly and antisocial behavior. His "Credit Monopoly" speech is his attempt at a solution, although it turned out to be neither a very convincing, nor a very original one. Still, the speech is a faithful reflection of Williams's political focus. It furthermore clarifies some of the—largely unconscious—ideological motivations for Williams's ongoing artistic desire to "make it new."

As the material relationships of human beings changed—the result of inevitable material progress—so, he argued, did the means of expression (which were for him, as we have already seen, directly linked to the immediate objects of perception). Consequently, what was "truth" in the work of artists of past generations, became "a lie every twenty years, and must be reborn in a new form every generation," although the artist must always recognize that in effecting this rebirth he was still trying to recreate, and, if possible, to increase, the same glories which engaged the artists of former times. It is clear that Williams was trying to think in what he considered dialectical terms, but the irony is that in his scheme the "new" is inexorably linked to an aesthetic universal, a constant value of transcendent experience to which the "new" affords simply an up-to-date, and perhaps an improved, mode of access. As a result, Williams's search for the new never became representative of a search for more effective structures of interpersonal relationship, or qualitatively better social values, upon which a more humanely integrated society might be structured. Instead it remained merely a reflection of his desire to utilize contemporary materials for the efficient expression of a group of abstract categories of humanist sentiment whose presence had already, in ages past, served as a harmless counterpoint to the prevailing forces of political and social oppression.

Thus, no matter how loudly Williams might protest, as he does in his article on Sheeler, that the world of the artist is "the world in which men meet and work with pick and shovel, talk and write long winded books. It is the same world we go to war in," he in actuality never chose to confront that world in other than its visual textures, in its surface modulations. How an artist could express that world and yet not be part of it, not be influenced by the ideological structures which had shaped that world, even in his negative responses to it, is a question Williams chose to ignore in his rejection of the political dimension of art. Consequently he leaves the reader, in his pieces on art and politics, with an uncomfortable sense of having been the victim of a trick of magic, a bit of rapid doublethink. However, in this case, it must be said, the magician was among those deceived by his own tricks. As a result of his emphasis on the artist's need to remain "of his time" and use the images of the moment, Williams was in fact demonstrating one aspect of the manner in which society exerts ideological control over its artists. By driving the artist away from genuine historical consciousness and into an artificial "avant-gardist" rebellion against immediately preceding periods, it sets up a Manichean system of dualist perceptual structures in which the reversal of an existing pattern is equated with novelty, and in which novelty is equated with progressive insight. Williams, in his theoretical desire to "make it new," was following, in the realm of art, exactly the same impulses which drive other Americans to buy a new car every year. In his dogged pursuit of the new, and his persistent disdain for the past, which made him declare in his late note on Henry Niese that "a man will not and cannot tolerate the past" and made him lace the other articles in this collection with exhortations to break "the tyranny of the past" and its "narrow confines," Williams was forever refuting his own assertion that "you can't use great art as propaganda—or any art. It will resist it." *In the American Grain* and his other writings on historical subjects do not contradict that hostility to the past, for rather than being an exploration of the actual historical forces which served to shape the development of American social configurations, these writings feature imaginative recreations of "great individuals" whose personalities have managed to escape the past to become part of the eternal present of art. Williams had a rather narrow concept of the significance of "events," of the impersonal aspects of history: "Are lives to be twisted forcibly about events, the mere accidents of geography and climate? It is an obscenity which few escape—save at the hands of the stylist, literature, in which alone humanity is protected against

tyrannous designs," he remarked in *In the American Grain*. And he
made it clear that what he most resented about history was its
"pretension" that past and present were extensions of each other,
were connected:

> If history could be that which annihilated all memory of past things
> from our minds it would be a useful tyranny.
>
> But since it lives in us practically day by day we should fear it. But
> if it is, as it may be, a tyranny over the souls of the dead—and so the
> imaginations of the living—where lies our greatest well of inspira-
> tion, our greatest hope of freedom (since the future is totally blank,
> if not black) we should guard it doubly from the interlopers.[23]

The interlopers, of course, are theories about the significance of
history, delineations of "generic patterns," which take our attention away from the "great personalities" whom we should celebrate
because they have managed to transcend the tyranny of the past.
Tradition—the American grain—was personality for Williams; it
had nothing to do with the past as such. By turning the past into a
creation of the individual imagination, into an extension of the
American "moment" and the artist's "local consciousness," he tried
to make even history "new."

In his "Letter Touching the Comintern upon Censorship in the
Arts," Williams came perhaps closest to resolving the contradic-
tions inherent in the inopportune conjunction of his belief in the
primacy of the individual, his desire for freedom from political
manipulation, and his insistence that the artist should be the
embodiment of his time and place. For when he pointed out in this
piece that Darwin (as any other "individual") was "bound to
'discover' the elements with which the *Zeitgeist* had confronted his
world," and that his insight was limited to a synthesis of fragments
of understanding "which he shared in common with all others," he
clearly indicated that he understood that the person is dependent on
what might be called "social knowledge" to express his "indi-
viduality." But when, at the same time, he insisted "that it is only
the individual who can advance 'beyond his day,' formulate the
thoughts about him, remake the world," he still refused to recognize that such "individual" advances, given his remarks about

Darwin, were unlikely to be anything more than felicitous formulations of ideas whose basic structure and legitimacy had already been
determined within the context of the socioeconomic exigencies of
his society. In the last analysis, therefore, such advances were
anything but independent, unmediated efforts on the part of lone
individuals. Williams's profound distrust of the past and his
continued longing for the new provided him with the smoke screen
he needed to avoid countenancing this basic consideration. Still, in
this "Letter Touching the Comintern," with its heavily qualified
stand in favor of some forms of censorship in the service of
progressive social ideas, and its assertion that, after all, "some sort of
censorship is always operative in the arts," he came closer to
relinquishing his belief in individualism as the only hope for
humanity than at any other point in his career as a writer.

Williams, of course, realized perfectly well that there was an
intimate relationship between art and politics. But he was not
willing to admit that this put responsibility for the latent political
content of the work he produced squarely on his own shoulders.
Instead he preferred to see the relationship between art and politics
as one in which the artist, in order to better "reflect" the fullness of
social experience in his time, made "the factors that make physics,
government, economics workable" discoverable in his art—as he
would indicate in his piece on "Art and Social Organization." In his
desire to secure total freedom of expression for the artist, he simply
imposed a form of self-censorship over any consideration which
might lead him to contemplate the possibility that all that is new
might not *ipso facto* be progressive, or that what he—or another—
considered great art might not be part of a universally valid
pantheon of masterpieces, but might instead be selected by means
of categories of evaluation which were themselves intimately tied to
the perceptual structures (and therefore the conceptual limitations)
of the dominant ideology.

Williams's connections with left-wing political movements, or
for that matter, any political movements in general, never were
more than skin deep. His main concern was to be an efficient
transmitter of the many minute modulations of experience which,
together, formed the essence of "the American spirit" of his time.

And that spirit was far from progressive. Therefore, precisely because he was so successful in making his "moment" live in his work, we cannot expect that work to reflect an unusually progressive conception of social relationships. His work did what in "Art and the Social Organization" he insisted all good art should do: "rest solidly on the social base of its time"—that is its merit, and that is also, unavoidably, its limitation.

In any case, as should become clear from Williams's writings on art and politics, there was nothing "Communist" or Marxist in Williams's dislike for the structures of American government in the Thirties. Such ideas central to Williams's point of view, as his insistence on the primacy of the individual, or his notion that cultures are basically self-contained—as he argues in "The American Spirit in Art"—and that there is no valid historical continuity, but only a timeless, universal subject matter to art, should be a sufficient indication of the fundamental incompatibility of Williams's beliefs and Marxism. What is more, his criticisms of the state were entirely focused upon the very narrow topic of the government's official treatment of the arts—and of artists. Williams's social concerns simply did not go any further than that—concern for the condition of the poor, the exploited, the economically oppressed, is completely absent from his considerations. Freedom meant for him solely the freedom of the artist to express himself as he wished—preferably with a government subsidy. He resented the political consciousness of other artists in the Thirties, which had once again made publication of his poetry difficult, unless he were willing to introduce material of a clear-cut sociocritical nature into his work. The Social Credit philosophy presented itself as a means of escape from what he saw as the public neglect of his work, which, in its turn, seemed to him due to the vagaries of political factionalism. Social Credit would step in and reward excellence and make opportunities for the dissemination of works of art available to all. Hopes such as these rather than a real involvement with the pertinent social problems of the period lay behind Williams's "political" writings of the Thirties. They may have the relative merit of being less abrasive and destructive of genuine social progress than those of his friend Ezra Pound, but they give no greater indication of political perspicacity than Pound's. They are most interesting, and can best be read, as statements about Williams's aesthetic preoccupations, as reflections upon the transcendent magic of art. For it is to the theme of art as a haven from the high seas of everyday experience, to the theme of art as an oasis of insight in a desert of human mutual misunderstanding, that Williams returns time and again—to that, and to the theme of the glory of the lone individual, of the magnificent inventions of the artist: "All the great additions to knowledge, all great acts, have originated in the head of one man or one woman," he never failed to insist.

Against the pressures urging him toward greater political involvement, Williams entrenched himself by championing his notions concerning the messianic role of the artist in society. The final step in his apotheosis of the artist came in "Midas," where he declared:

> War elevates the artist, the builder, the thinker to the peaks of the stars, trebles his significance. In times of peace he is, at best, a humdrum worker not because he must be so but because he is perpetually laboring under weights to inflame and to magnify. But in times of war—helplessly split off in the cyclotron of the times—he becomes inevitably king of men by contrast. By his very existence, beyond himself, the elements win new significance, woman blossoms from her imposed shell, man, older than the stones, rears himself and reaches out into the unknown.

There is, it must be said, an exhilaration of rather dubious merit in Williams's position here, another aspect of his tendency to let his social consciousness take shape primarily in terms of the position of the artist in society, in terms of what society can do for the artist, rather than the other way around. Although it is clear that what Williams was trying to say was that when the world descends into barbarism it is all the more important for the artist to preserve and even advance "culture," yet the net effect of his exaggerated conception concerning the importance of the artist in time of war was to negate the seriousness of his claim in the paragraph preceding this paean that "one of the purposes of the Death among us is to terrify the world, to use a destructive ideology to push our culture so far back that it will take a full generation, another crop of flesh and mind, before it can begin to regenerate. Then to thrust another war upon us that will again drive the mind from its advances, this shuttle to go on in perpetuity." In fact, it would seem that in the scheme of things which Williams set up in "Midas," war, far from having a depressive effect on "thought" and "the arts," actually served as a stimulus to creative activity. Later in the article, for example, he declared: "War releases energy. Energy can be used to transmute and create. Thus war by releasing energy indirectly serves in the creation of values. Or may be made to serve if we are prepared to seize the advantage from it." In the published version of "Midas" Williams deleted this passage. He had perhaps become aware of the intolerably "constructive" significance his remarks gave to war, or he may have realized that his sentiments were dangerously close to those of the Futurists, who had supported the fascism he was arguing against. But Futurism, especially in terms of its Bergsonian glorification of action, had indeed made a lasting impression on Williams, and thought processes are not as easily removed from the mind as paragraphs are from an article. It is indeed striking how much Williams's "Midas," in its often far-fetched comparisons and its exaggerated emotional language, resembles the Futurist manifestos of the 1910s. But where the Futurists tended to disparage bourgeois reverence for art, Williams once again hoisted the flag for art as the one central glory of existence.

From what Williams wrote in "Midas," one could easily be left with the impression that, although war serves as a stimulus to art, the barbarians nevertheless, mistakenly, use war primarily as a tool to obstruct the progress of the arts. All wars, he seemed to argue, are wars against art, a notion which itself is the expression of an incredible hubris concerning the actual function of art in society, representative of his fundamental unwillingness to recognize the unromanticized, bleak exploitation of actually having to be a part of that world in which people "work with pick and shovel," and become cannon fodder for reasons quite other than the advancement or obstruction of the arts.

By the time he came to write his "The American Spirit in Art," Williams had given up all pretense of concern with sociopolitical considerations and had without further qualification returned to seeing art as the only solution to the world's problems. In fact he now allowed his fierce attempts to convince the world of the importance of art to take on a stridency which easily overstepped the bounds of reason. "The artist is the most important individual in the world," he said. "If England is destroyed by Russian bombs it will hardly be a matter of importance to history, so long as the works of Shakespeare are not lost." Williams's arguments in "The American Spirit in Art," based on a rough-and-ready interpretation of Toynbee, went on to elevate the American artist to the position of the world's savior, since the "drift of time" had selected America to be the locus for the next step in the transcendence of obsolete modes of expression. The article is a rousing utopian statement of all the wonderful things which will happen to us if only we make certain to continue the pursuit of new form in art. That this "new form" closely corresponded to the processes of object delineation advocated by Williams in both art and literature goes without saying.

It is probably primarily because he maintained throughout his creative years a separate, and very prosaic, profession and was never a "full-time" artist that Williams succeeded in maintaining so steadfastly the amateur's awe for the "miraculous" nature of art. Had he been more completely involved in the problems of art as a profession, his enthusiasm would most likely have been less inordinate. In any case, considering his grandiose conception of the role of the artist in the world, it is not surprising that Williams came to dislike the image he was developing in the Thirties and Forties as a writer of "small" lyrical observations, who, in his work, tried to transcribe the emotive beauty of a flower or a mountain and was satisfied to leave the grander themes to greater poets. Instead, as we have seen, he saw himself as extracting from these small subjects the centrally important equivalences, the universal essences which could expose the beauties of the mind, "the far greater mountains, the far greater depths of the imagination." Thus, while the subjects of his poetry might be the minor occurrences of daily experience, his conception of their importance was anything but modest—and it is very likely that at least one of his motivations for writing *Paterson* was to call attention to what he saw as the monumental significance of his perceptions about the universal implications of "local" experience.

The "Axioms" which Williams wrote in 1943 were again specifically concerned with this favorite topic, the importance of place, of the artist's immediate milieu. Alfred Stieglitz had been a major influence on Williams's development of the concept of "contact," and while it is true that Williams had clearly been much impressed by John Dewey's essay "Americanism and Localism" in the June, 1920, issue of *The Dial,* as some critics have emphasized, this essay actually only reinforced impulses which had already been part of his conceptual world for many years, and which had been given their first and most significant formulation by Stieglitz and the artists and critics who had gathered around the photographer in the early years of the century. The "Axioms" make it very clear that even late in life Williams associated the concept of place primarily with Stieglitz. Not only did he refer to Stieglitz's gallery "An American Place" in the "Axioms," but he also specifically acknowledged the ongoing influence of Stieglitz's ideas on him in a note to Stieglitz, handwritten on a copy of the "Axioms." The note reads: "Inspired by the prose commentaries in your last issue—" a reference, most likely, to the extensive selection of anecdotes and writings by Stieglitz published in Dorothy Norman's *Twice a Year* in 1942. At first Williams probably intended to send this copy of his notes to Stieglitz. However, his characteristic "on second thought" hesitation to acknowledge his indebtedness to others seems to have intervened at this point, and, taking another copy of his "Axioms," he wrote on it instead: "Haven't seen you recently but thought you might be interested"—sending this copy to the photographer and keeping the one with the more revelatory note for his own files.

As a matter of fact the question of influences on Williams takes on an importance of considerably more significance to an immediate understanding of his work than is the case with many other writers of his stature. Highly impulsive by nature, and often uncertain of his own opinions, he frequently depended on the judgment of others for direction in the focus of his ideas. Many of his opinions are ones which he took uncritically, and largely unaltered, from others. His article on Nicolas Calas's interpretation of Hieronymus Bosch's *The Garden of Earthly Delights* is a good example of this tendency. Conscious of the extremely tenuous nature of some of Calas's explanations of the details of Bosch's great painting, Williams nevertheless showed himself uncritically willing to "see" what Calas made visible to him. Many of the "clues" to Bosch's intentions Calas found in the painting simply are not there—yet for Williams they were, because Calas had seen them. And because of this it is ultimately not Williams's own, unmediated understanding of Bosch which confronts us in his poetry, in *Paterson,* for example, but an understanding filtered through the eyes of Nicolas Calas.

Calas's influence on Williams was minor, but the influence of Otto Weininger, the man who many years earlier had helped shape his conceptions about women, was an all-pervasive and enduring one. Weininger, the fanatic young Viennese philosopher, whose *Sex and Character* Williams read not long after its translation into English in 1906, radically influenced the poet's notions about sex roles. It is Weininger who was ultimately behind many of the aspects of Williams's aesthetic least likely to endear him to feminists. Perhaps to counter a certain tendency towards what he saw as "effeminacy" in his own character, Williams resolutely insisted on the "manly" nature of artistic creativity. To write a poem, paint a picture, compose a piece of music, was, to him, to show your mettle as a man. For example, Hartley, Williams remarked, in one of his pieces about his old friend who had had his own share of difficulties with that question, was just beginning to understand "what it means to be a painter—that is to say, a man." The artist was always a man for Williams, no matter how much he himself might have been influenced at one point by strong women poets such as Mina Loy and Marianne Moore. Had he ever been questioned on that point he would most likely have answered, like Weininger, that it was the "male" element in these women which had made them into poets, and that their influence on him had therefore been a "male" influence after all.

In "Midas," Williams indeed remarked that in America males

had so far taken over women's habits as to have lost their "revolutionary character." Going further he implied that all this had made American men effeminate, and had been "productive also of a matrix of undifferentiated thought, inimical to complete contacts as a general thing—with a throwback of female elements in the arts and in affairs: anti-revolutionary, complacent, quilted." Woman could be the subject of art, as in the paintings of Paul Delvaux, but "a female cast of thought in the arts and affairs," as he formulated it in an initial, handwritten note for "Midas," could only have a destructive effect. Caught early, like many of his generation, in an uncritical fascination with Weininger's rabidly anti-feminist, anti-woman, pseudoscientific psychologism, Williams never managed to shake the sexist dualism conveniently formulated for him in *Sex and Character*, which made the male into a progressive, intellectual being, ever striving for transcendent, spiritual excellence, only to be dragged back into the realms of worldly sexuality by woman, who, lazy, lying, and undifferentiated, would try to lure him into the mental and physical enslavement of erotic abandon. Eternally inimical to individualism, woman was forever scheming to prevent man from progressing to that realm of individualist consciousness which would allow him to transcend the material limitations of the woman's world.

When, in "The Poet in Time of Confusion," Williams listed as a question the artist—like the economist—must answer: "are women in public life the source of degeneration and homosexuality the source of genius?" he was formulating a question which preoccupied Weininger, and which the latter in fact answered affirmatively—just so long as, in the case of homosexuality, it was a matter among males, who might thereby reinforce their spiritual and artistic genius.

Weininger, to whom Williams refers, not frequently, to be sure, but with telling regularity throughout his career as a writer, may also have been the one to give focus to another of the destructive traits Williams shared with the majority of his generation, his unembarrassed anti-Semitism—even in the face of the Nazi atrocities of World War II. Anti-Semitic remarks crop up casually in many of his works, as they do in several of the essays included in this collection, and among the still unpublished manuscripts of the

poet there are several poems with a blatantly anti-Semitic focus.
When, in 1941, Williams came to attack Pound for taking the side
of the Fascists, in his already cited "Ezra 'Lackwit' Pound: Lord
GaGa," his criticisms were all directed toward his friend's literary
and intellectual judgment, not toward his anti-Semitism, which
entered only to be listed in passing. And when, in "The Poet in
Time of Confusion," he mentioned as another of the questions to
be resolved by the artist, "Will Germany be better for driving
Jewish blood from the veins of the race?" he betrayed his own
prejudice not so much in the diffidence of his response, as in his
very readiness to consider this a matter worthy of "serious
reflection" rather than angry dismissal.

It is of course tempting to proceed as if these negative aspects of
Williams's personality did not exist, but to do so would lead us to
falsify some of the central facets of his intellectual history. Williams
was a man of his time—he was the first to emphasize that: to be so
was the main purpose of his work as an artist—and, unfortunately,
his time was unabashedly racist. Stereotypes which are at last no
longer openly tolerated were still unquestioned as he grew up and
these consequently became an integral part of the structure of his
perceptions. By the time such stereotypes began to fall apart—at
least partially as a result of the world's horrified confrontation with
the monstrous effects of the exploitation of anti-Semitic feeling by
the Nazis—Williams was too old and settled in his opinions to adapt
to a changing focus. Thus, when, after Alfred Stieglitz's death in
1946, Dorothy Norman requested that he participate in a projected
volume of tributes to this crucial figure in the development of
twentieth-century American art, Williams responded less than
admirably. He was irritated by the fact that Stieglitz had always
been surrounded by a group of followers and acolytes who
regarded him with a reverence sometimes bordering on religious
fanaticism, while Williams, personally, after thirty-seven years of
publishing still felt neglected and was even, it seemed to him,
having to struggle to get his work into print. Consequently he
determined to demystify the public image of the photographer who
had been such an important influence on him, and whom he had
counted among his friends for more than three decades.

The result was "What of Alfred Stieglitz?" Clearly conscious

that his remarks were likely to rankle ("he who would excommunicate me, I excommunicate him"), he proceeded to "set the record
straight" about Stieglitz. Some of what he had to say serves indeed
as a useful antidote to the "crimson and orchidaceous surfaces" with
which the photographer had permitted others to surround him. But
Williams, in his eagerness to debunk the myths which had been
built up around Stieglitz, allowed himself to indulge in some
patently false statements. The most obvious of these was that
"Marsden Hartley got kicked out early" (from among the painters
under Stieglitz's protection). That there were stormy moments in
Hartley's relationship with Stieglitz is undeniable. But Hartley was
one of the first painters whose work Stieglitz exhibited (he gave
him a one man show as early as 1909), and he was one of the last:
Hartley had a show at "An American Place" as late as May 1937,
less than five years before the painter's death. During the twenty-
eight years in between, Stieglitz mounted numerous exhibitions of
Hartley's work. It is indeed, judging from the available evidence,
not Stieglitz who "dropped" Hartley, but Williams himself. More
than a month after Hartley's 1937 show at "An American Place"
had closed, Williams, in a letter to Stieglitz, in which he was
primarily concerned with other matters, still took time out to
criticize that exhibition harshly. He remarked that Hartley's work
"taxed the good will of the spectator pretty hard because of the
monotonous tone of the pictures." Some of the paintings, he added,
"seemed not to have come off at all, they looked flat and lifeless.
Others were so full of mannerisms that the good of them seemed
buried, completely buried."[24] Hartley's recent work failed,
Williams concluded, because the painter seemed to have "himself
too much at heart."

Just as Williams frequently appropriated the opinions of others
without a great deal of critical scrutiny, so he seems to have had a
disconcerting habit of attributing those of his own opinions, which
for one reason or another he associated with someone else, to that
other person when he, himself, had begun to change his mind.
Hartley was, in Williams's eyes, one of Stieglitz's painters, and it
had been at Stieglitz's gallery that Williams had first encountered
his work. Thus when, decades later, Williams criticized the work
of his old acquaintance, he ended up by transferring this opinion,

which he apparently came to see as disloyal, to Stieglitz who, after all, had been responsible for bringing Hartley to his attention. Something similar had taken place a few years earlier in Williams's attack upon Pound. For when he derided Pound for championing Gaudier-Brzeska, Remy de Gourmont, and Francis Picabia, he conveniently forgot his own "Vortex," written in response to that of the sculptor, his equation of the importance of Picasso and de Gourmont for Americans in *Contact,* and his letter of high praise to the editors of *The Little Review* for their special Picabia issue. In a curious way it is a special testimony to the strength of the influence of such personalities as Stieglitz and Pound (and, for that matter, Weininger as well) on Williams's patterns of thought, that he ultimately came to blame them for opinions of his own which, correctly or incorrectly, he strongly associated with them.

In the case of Stieglitz, what seems to have been the most likely reason for Williams's ultimate irritation is that he had been frustrated by the fact that the work of the American artists to whom he felt the closest affinity, that of Marin, Demuth, and Hartley as well, had, as their fame grew, come to be priced, as he remarked in his "Beginnings: Marsden Hartley," too high for his pocketbook. It appears that Williams, sometime during the early Forties, had tried to convince Stieglitz to let him have a work by John Marin for considerably less than Stieglitz thought it to be worth. As Williams should have known, Stieglitz's motivation in this matter could hardly have been "mercenary" in nature, since, as far as can be ascertained, Stieglitz did not take commissions for the work of his protégés sold in his gallery. He had an adequate personal income, and his first concern was to make sure that the painters whose work he admired could continue their work as little burdened by financial concerns as possible. Yet, tense and overwrought by the details of his personal life and his neglect by the American public, Williams now saw Stieglitz's refusal to make a special deal with him as evidence of the photographer's "love for the big money." Anyone who has seen the studies, by other photographers, of Stieglitz as an old man, huddled on a bunk bed in a corner of his "American Place," among spare furnishings and white walls, will find it hard to give credence to Williams's claim.

What seems to have happened is that, in the midst of frustration,

Williams found solace in one of the oldest and most pernicious syllogisms of racism: Jews were supposed to be money-hungry, and, as he emphasized in his article, Stieglitz was a Jew. However, if this were the only focus of Williams's piece on Stieglitz there would be little point in dragging the article into the light at this late date. Williams himself apparently did want to see it published, for he sent the manuscript to Dorothy Norman for inclusion in the book of tributes she was preparing. But Norman, quite appropriately, refused to accept it. My reason for including it here is that, while it sheds some light on an unpleasant side of Williams's character, there is, at the same time, much in it which illuminates Williams the artist. More than any other piece in this collection it presents us with a statement of the reckless, no-nonsense, outrageously opinionated, intellectualized anti-intellectualism which forms the "American" core of Williams's work as a poet. What is more, the article is a vivid testimony to the importance of Williams's indebtedness to Stieglitz, for, notwithstanding Williams's irritation with the photographer, it reads very much like the grudging last tribute of a rebellious son to a father who, he knows, has shaped his values far more extensively than he would like to admit.

Toward the close of the article, Williams even negates his own prejudicial judgment of Stieglitz as a "money-loving Jew" by eulogizing him as a "profound prophet of real values as opposed to the murderous falsity of cash over everything else." Intense, unreasoning subjectivity and straightforward common sense had a tendency to alternate rapidly in Williams's perceptions. Certainly "What of Alfred Stieglitz?" makes it clear that the racist component in Williams's consciousness was a good deal more elusive and complexly qualified than it was in many of his equally illustrious contemporaries.

The same must be said about the sexist aspects of Williams's observations about women, which are featured very prominently in his "Woman as Operator." This article was inspired by Romare Bearden's painting *Women with an Oracle,* and was written in conjuction with an exhibition of paintings of "Women" organized by Samuel Kootz. As an afterthought Kootz had requested a number of writers, ranging from Jean-Paul Sartre and Benjamin Péret to Paul Goodman and Williams, to note down their impressions of one or another of the works included in the show. Williams responded with "Woman as Operator."

In this article, Otto Weininger's enduring influence on Williams's conceptions about women is particularly striking. Mike Weaver has noted "the correlation in ideas, and very occasionally, in verbal expression between [Weininger's] book and Williams's early letters."[25] But Weininger's influence did not stop there. He was a strong and explicit factor in the sexual theory of *Rome,* a noticeable, and acknowledged presence in the notebooks of 1928–1930, and the authority on whose views concerning the nature of woman Williams relied in his article on Brancusi, written as late as 1955. Weininger, too, was the unacknowledged source of the theories underlying Williams's discussion of the portrayal of women in art in "Woman as Operator."

The poet's statement that contrary to the male, woman, in painting, "doesn't need to be so particularized," can only be understood within the context of Weininger's claim that men are "monads," but that women are undifferentiated. Hence Williams's assertion that when you paint "man" you must paint *a* man, while, if you paint a woman, you cannot avoid painting "Woman." Williams's portrayal of woman as a primarily sensuous entity and man as given to abstraction and the pursuit of ideals, was straight out of Weininger, who saw this as the basic reason for what Williams equally categorically designated as "the impossibility of a meeting between the sexes." The details and motivation for Williams's identification of "female men" and "male women" in ads and travel pictures can also be found in Weininger, who had devised a complicated system of classifying specific "male" and "female" character traits. Even Williams's statement "imagine showing a prostitute at her trade, naked, in any position you like, French postcards: it could be any wife, in a painting, unless you labeled it," echoes Weininger's assertion that woman's disposition for and inclination to prostitution was as organic as her capacity for motherhood. In fact, the connections between Williams's "Woman as Operator" and *Sex and Character* are so immediate that it would not be surprising to discover that Williams had reread Weininger in order to write this article.[26]

However, it must be said that, sexist philosophy and all, what is perhaps most distinctive about "Woman as Operator" is its extraordinary insight into the expressive significance of the painting on which the article is based. For all that Williams said accurately reflects the sentiments which underlie Bearden's painting, and, while one might have wished to see more critical distance, and a good deal less enthusiastic empathy on Williams's part, his essay remains one of the shrewdest pieces of interpretation in the collection of articles inspired by the paintings in Kootz's exhibition.

It may very well be Williams's nearly unfailing insight into the artistic strengths and weaknesses of the work of individual painters and sculptors which, together with the important materials providing the student of Williams's poetry with details about the nature of his artistic intentions, will prove to be the most enduring feature of this collection of the poet's writings. His articles on Tchelitchew, Sheeler, Walker Evans, Hartley, and Brancusi are full of extraordinary perceptions about the formal motivation of their procedures, as well as their success and failure in attempting to translate their intentions into art. His review of the exhibition of American primitive paintings from the Garbisch collection at the National Gallery of Art is a remarkable sequence of subtle perceptions concerning the visual values of the works on display. In the writing of these articles as in "Woman as Operator," he was obviously helped immeasurably by the special affinity of his own point of view to that of the artists he was writing about: in his thumbnail sketches of their subject matter, in Sheeler's "contours of farm building," his industrial plants, "lucid and geometric," his image of "a yacht's sails bellying in the wind," in Hartley's "two birches broken off leaning together in the woods," his flower still lifes, "particularly his lily pieces," or his "boulder standing alone, a split boulder, the halves eternally separated," we recognize instantly some of the central items from the subject inventory of Williams's own poetry.

As I have already emphasized, and as should become readily apparent from this collection, it is the work of these painters, and that of Marin, Demuth, and Stieglitz which meant most to him—

theirs, and the work of the French. For Williams, American art was still largely in a "fallow" period, and, while in the work of the Stieglitz group, and later, that of Robert Motherwell and the Abstract Expressionists he saw evidence of "that time-drift which has brought our culture pattern, what we call America, to the fore," it was "French painting since 1820" which remained, throughout his life, his first and foremost source of inspiration. First and last there was Cézanne—then Picasso and the Cubists, then the Dadaists, and finally, in the Thirties and Forties, the Surrealists—a steady stream of sylistic innovation which caused Williams to cry out in *View:* "Oh we do not realize what France means to the world!"[27] In fact, in the face of what he saw as France's continued hegemony in the field of the visual arts, Williams even modified, somewhat, his ground rules for a truly "local" art. When we turn to Williams's comments on Surrealism, we discover that, while he was still using pretty much the same arguments as in his discussions of the uses of Dada for Americans, when dealing with the question of the interaction between the "local impulse" and foreign influences, he had now come to believe that it was perhaps not always entirely necessary for movements which had originated in Paris, to remain in Paris to retain their legitimacy, or to be completely transformed to fit within the American perceptual configurations: "Concepts originating in one milieu may, when the base is the same, unite with those of another," he remarked in "Midas." This could be true, however, only when "the basic problem is conceived as the same"—when, for example, a "common ground" for the Surrealist impulse was discovered in America, allowing the European artists in exile to interact with American artists.

For Surrealism Williams indeed saw such a common ground in America, and, ironically, he saw it in what he conceived of as the resistance of Surrealism to political co-optation—ignoring André Breton's belligerent assertions concerning the political function of Surrealism, or, perhaps understanding better than he that in its ultimate conceptualization of the fluctuating structures of personal reality, Surrealism did not really fulfill the revolutionary function Breton envisaged for it. Williams, in any case, declared that in its resistance to "political urgencies," Surrealism found its common ground with American art: a search for that "alchemy of the mind" which would turn perception into the "gold" of art—for "the mind is not a political animal, even though man may be." The remark once again illustrates Williams's narrow conception of what was "political." He saw the term as referring only to the overt manifestations of doctrine and consistently failed to consider the incursions of the dominant ideology into the structures of desire, the patterns of perception and expectation which populate the human mind in all its stages of development. He continued to see the "gold" of artistic creation as untainted by any ideological influences, and, in a characteristic paradox, insisted that this was precisely why it was "revolutionary" in its implications.

Williams's enthusiasm for all things French went so far as to make him contend that American English had a special affinity to French, not shared by British English or other languages:

> When I myself attempted to translate something that René Char had written in French into English, I had to warn myself, as I always do under such circumstances, that I was using not English at all for my work, but the American idiom. That gave me a certain stylistic advantage; rhythmical! I could approach the French much more confidently than if, we'll say, I were an Oxford don or even an Evelyn Waugh. But could my language be recognized for what it was even by my own countrymen? The French should come over into my language more readily than into German or Russian. Its subtle variations of poetic accent are, I feel, much more congenial to a modern American turn of phrase than, at least, to formal English.[28]

One of the most important, and earliest stylistic considerations Williams had learned from the French, from Duchamp, Picasso, and Cubism in general, was that in modern life reality consisted of a gathering of incomplete observations, of "broken" images, not of the false coherence lesser painters always seemed so tempted to give to their work. It was on the basis of that understanding, for example, that Williams, be it in an unusually tactful manner, criticized, and finally dismissed, E. E. Cummings's paintings as the "nice tries" of a poet out of his true medium. Paintings, Williams argued, should be paint, color, design—that was their meaning.

What a painter literally *said* in his image, was indeed speech, was literary, and was likely to be of no importance to the visual value of his work. Paintings should be of the eye, and when a painting bypassed the eye it failed. Paintings which tried to deceive the eye, which were *trompe l'oeil* in structure, bypassed that great synthesizing organ of the imagination: bypass the eye, Williams felt, and you bypass the mind.

But by breaking the sequence of normal experience, by even breaking the image itself when necessary, the artist could come to a genuine recognition of the structures which constitute the objects of our perception. The force of deconstruction was that it was ultimately the structuring agent toward a new and more accurate mode of vision. In a grade school notebook belonging to one of his sons, Williams once, in a rapid scrawl, gave a very felicitous delineation of what he meant:

> Some intimation of the character of this force may be discovered, I think, in the much greater interest felt in the snatches of pictures, shown at the movies between the regular films, to advertise pictures coming the following week—than the regular features themselves. The experience is of something much more vivid and much more sensual than the entire film will be. It is because the banality of the sequence has been removed.
>
> The bits exceed the whole in interest—or to be correct let us not say in interest—since interest is too variable a quantity—but in vividness, in sensual reality—an intimation of the very good reason for the brokenness of some modern compositions. The force is in it—perhaps.
>
> This is the principle we can utilize to our profit in estimating the quality of any piece of writing: by reading it backward, paragraph by paragraph, from somewhere near the end back to the beginning and then finishing. I find my own sensual pleasure greatly increased by so doing—I am much better able to judge of the force of the work in this way.
>
> Only after careful consideration can a work be fully appreciated when read glibly from start to finish—unless it be made expressly for no other purpose—to avoid closer scrutiny.[29]

Much later, when Williams's body had itself, in the aftermath of several strokes, become fragmentary in its responses to his demands for movement, his mind, struggling through the chaos of disorientation, began to put renewed emphasis on this aspect of his theory. Broken by illness, he focused on the fragmented world of Emanuel Romano's canvases, or returned, as in his piece on Henry Niese and his commentary on the photographs chosen to accompany a selection of Whitman's *Leaves of Grass,* to the significance of the broken imagery of movie previews, or the stilling of motion in photographs. It is a moving testimony to Williams's indomitable creative spirit, that, wracked by illness, he rose up to reassert the dicta of his youth, as if to prove to himself and to the world that broken images were the essence of good art, and that therefore, more than ever, he had what it took to be an artist—that life was still worth living.

It is fitting that Williams's last major essay should have been a tribute to Brancusi, the Rumanian shepherd from whose spare forms and fragmentary moldings Williams had first learned how to eliminate the inessential in his work, more than forty years earlier. Brancusi's sculptures had hovered in the back of his mind ever since, helping to give form to some of the finest poems ever written by an American—an American who had insisted on searching among the rubble of an industrial environment which was becoming ever more brutalized, for images of spare and unassuming, but, he was convinced, "lifesaving" simplicity comparable to the fragments of ancient statues he imagined Brancusi as having spent his time gathering from the fields of his native land.

As Williams's long life began to draw to a close, he became more and more preoccupied with the works of the grand old masters of Western art, with Brueghel, Rembrandt, El Greco, Michelangelo. Undoubtedly this was at least partially due to his concern about the place his own poetry was to take in the world after his death. He felt that he still had it in him, hampered as his body might be by infirmities, to write things that would have a true "ability to last," and it is clear that when he remarked that "the finest work of Rembrandt, of Titian, was painted when they were old," he was in effect speaking words of self-encouragement, to gain from that "fulness of the senses" which he saw as coming with old age, the ripeness of a poetry in which he would live on. For he believed, as he wrote in his article on Calas's exploration of the mind of Bosch, that "men do not die if their attack is kept alive by their works, hence the masters secreted their meanings in their paintings, to have them live, if chance favored them, forever."

All indications are that he did not have serious reason to worry. Taught meticulously and durably by the painters whose work he loved, to see, and *how* to see, he may not always have understood what he saw, but in his bright joy for the shape of things, and in his fiery determination to lift the small beauties of our everyday environment to the center of our vision, he has indeed given the world a most valuable legacy: the gift of accurate observation. In the best of his poems he has, like Bosch, Brueghel, or Cézanne, like the master painters he most admired, secreted his meaning: the shrewd and durable sight of his extraordinary eye.

B. D.

Footnotes

[1]"Poetry," The Columbia Review, XIX, 1 (November 1937), 3.

[2]The Little Review (May 1929), 87.

[3]Unpublished ms. C–94, Williams Collection, Lockwood Memorial Library, State University of New York, Buffalo.

[4]Untitled lecture, Williams Collection, Beinecke Rare Book and Manuscript Library, Yale University.

[5]See, for example, my The Hieroglyphics of a New Speech: Cubism, Stieglitz, and the Early Poetry of William Carlos Williams (Princeton 1969), and "Wallace Stevens and William Carlos Williams: Poetry, Painting and the Function of Reality," in Encounters: Essays on Literature and the Visual Arts, ed. John Dixon Hunt (London: Studio Vista, 1971), 156–72. Valuable information regarding Williams's connections with the visual arts can also be found in James Guimond, The Art of William Carlos Williams: A Discovery and Possession of America (Urbana: University of Illinois Press, 1968); Mike Weaver, William Carlos Williams: The American Background (New York: Cambridge University Press, 1971); Jerome Mazzaro, William Carlos Williams, The Later Poems (Ithaca: Cornell University Press, 1973); Rod Townley, The Early Poetry of William Carlos Williams (Ithaca: Cornell University Press, 1975); and Dickran Tashjian, Skyscraper Primitives: Dada and the American Avant-Garde, 1910–1925 (Middletown: Wesleyan University Press, 1975).

[6]"The Poet in his World," unpublished ms. C–109, Buffalo.

[7]See Williams's unpublished correspondence with Edmund Brown, especially his letter of May 14, 1921, at Yale.

[8]"Museum Reading, 3/28/50," unpublished ms., Yale (Za Williams 174).

[9]Walter Sutton, "A Visit with William Carlos Williams," The Minnesota Review, I, 3 (April 1961), 309–324. Reprinted in Interviews with William Carlos Williams: Speaking Straight Ahead, ed. Linda Welshimer Wagner (New York: New Directions, 1976).

[10]Ibid.

[11]Charles Norman, The Magic Maker: E. E. Cummings (New York: Macmillan Co., 1958), 272. The title of Moore's poem is "Nevertheless"; see The Complete Poems of Marianne Moore (New York: Macmillan, 1967), p. 125.

[12]Unpublished ms. C–106, Buffalo.

[13]"Comment," Contact, I, 3 (1932), 109.

[14]Unpublished letter to Edgar Williams, October 21, 1908, ms. F–1118, Buffalo.

[15]Unpublished letter to Edgar Williams, April 6, 1909, Thirlwall transcription, Yale.

[16]Harold Stearns, "Illusions of the Sophisticated," *The Freeman*, II (December 15, 1920), pp. 320–322.

[17]Ibid.

[18]*Rome,* unpublished ms. B-104, Buffalo.

[19]I am quoting from Buffalo ms. C-57, "Ezra 'Lackwit' Pound: Lord GaGa!" A slightly more temperate version of this essay can be found in *Decision*, II, 3 (September 1941), 16–24. For Pound's views on art, see *Ezra Pound and the Visual Arts,* ed. Harriet Zinnes, forthcoming from New Directions.

[20]See *Rome.*

[21]Reed Whittemore, *William Carlos Williams, Poet from Jersey* (Boston: Houghton Mifflin Co., 1975), 260; Weaver, *American Background,* 103–105.

[22]See *Rome.*

[23]William Carlos Williams, *In the American Grain* (New York: New Directions, 1956), 189.

[24]William Carlos Williams, *Selected Letters,* ed. John C. Thirlwall (New York: McDowell, Obolensky, 1957), 168.

[25]Weaver, *American Background,* 18.

[26]Both Mike Weaver and Jerome Mazzaro, the only critics who have as yet bothered to explore the connection between Weininger and Williams at all, underestimate Weininger's influence and overstress Williams's apparent disagreement with the young Viennese philosopher concerning the functions of man and woman. In his second rebuttal to Dora Marsden's "Lingual Philosophy," Williams had said: "Man is the vague generalizer, woman the concrete thinker, and not the reverse as he [Weininger] imagined." Weaver and Mazzaro take Williams's claim that Weininger thought "the reverse" at face value. But the poet had set up a false disagreement with Weininger, possibly in an attempt to lend credence to his independence as a thinker. In fact, the central argument of both of his pieces on "The Great Sex Spiral" in the *Egoist* (April and August 1917), follows Weininger very closely. When Williams described the realm of the male as being that of the intellect, of "pure knowledge," and his movement "not toward the earth, but away from it," he was simply repeating what Weininger had already contended, and the same is true of his designation of woman as "factual" and "characterized by a trend not away from, but toward the earth, toward concreteness." When Weininger described man as a "monad," and woman as only capable of thinking in terms of "henids," he was essentially arguing that the male was capable of individuation, and hence capable of transcending the material world, while woman, in her earthbound sexuality, remained undifferentiated at all times. Williams, in switching Weininger's terms around, did indeed no more than just that: he made an essentially insignificant switch in terminology. Very insignificant, in fact, for there is no indication at all—witness what he said in "Woman as Operator"—that he at any time wanted to attribute a capacity for individuation to woman and make her into a "monad." Williams's contention that the poles of male and female psychology could never be conjoined, that "the completely opposed sense-experience of the male on the one hand and the female on the other cannot enter the other's consciousness" was also taken directly from Weininger, as he indeed acknowledged himself. But Weininger did not, as Williams seemed to claim, "seek to discover a third gender," or champion a form of androgyny. His contention that there were "female" elements in most males and some "male" elements in most women, was simply

meant to explain why some women seemed capable of thinking in patterns which he had designated as "male," and why most men were incapable of attaining the conceptions of the Ideal, the Platonic types, which he saw as their existential goal. For this transcendence to take place, the male would ultimately have to get rid of the woman in him, and, ideally, stop associating with women altogether, Weininger argued. Williams's association of woman with the earth, with the experience of the concrete particularity of existence, in effect equated her with the other "raw materials," the "local objects" out of which he wanted to form the transendent universal communication of his art. With Weininger he denied that woman had the capacity for genius, although she could be the means through which (male) genius could express itself. But only the male was capable of creating great art. As Weininger had put it, having no moral capacity of her own, woman served as a receptacle for the moral projections of the male, and since, by herself she had no capacity to do either good or evil, she neither resisted nor resented the imposition by the male of ideal structures on her personality. From this Williams extrapolated that since she was part of the raw materials of art, and was inherently empathetic with the objects of the concrete world, the earth, "nature," which were to be shaped into art by the universalizing genius of the male, the part of the male which was capable of apprehending the artistic significance of material objects—or of women—was part of what Weininger had designated as the "female" component of the self. But it was only the male component, artistic genius, which could turn these perceptions into art. And it was essential that these male and female elements of thought and perception remain separated: "As long as there is vigorous life in the realm of thought it is essential that both poles be firmly established," Williams emphasized. It is therefore not accurate to designate Weininger's concept of genius, and Williams's transposition of that concept to the realm of poetic creation, as "androgynetic," as Mazzaro does. The concept of androgyny represents the *fusion* of male and female. Both Weininger and Williams emphasized the *polarity* of male and female, even in the same person.

27Review of André Breton's *Young Cherry Trees Secured Against Hares, View,* VII, 1 (Fall 1946).

28"A Poet Who Cannot Pause," *The New Republic,* CXXXV, 12 (September 17, 1956), 18.

29"What is the Use of Poetry?" unpublished ms. C–150, Buffalo.

A Note on the Text

IN SELECTING items for inclusion in this collection of William Carlos Williams's writings on art and artists, I have, as part of an effort to establish thematic unity, let myself be guided by the poet's own clear-cut preference for the visual arts. Williams wrote voluminously, and among his writings, both published and still in manuscript, there are many passages devoted to the arts. To try to include all of these would have led to an aphoristic miscellany of enormous proportions. Instead I have chosen to limit inclusion to work in the following categories: In the first place, complete or apparently complete articles entirely or predominantly concerned with the role of the artist in the world, whenever it was clear that Williams was using the term "artist" not simply as a synonym for "poet." Secondly, articles or notes about specific painters, sculptors, or photographers. Not included are a few complete pieces dealing with music or dance, whose focus tends to be slightly different from the work included here, and whose tentative nature reflects the poet's diffidence concerning his understanding of their function in his visually oriented world. ("Music doesn't mean much to me," he remarked to Walter Sutton.)

Within the context of these limitations I have attempted to make this collection a virtually complete record of Williams's organized writings on the visual arts and their relationship to his own work. In a few instances this has meant I have found it necessary to include articles which are already available in other collections of Williams's writings. In only one instance, however—that of the note on French painting taken from Ron Loewinsohn's edition of *The Embodiment of Knowledge*—have I reprinted such an item exactly as available in these other editions. In the other cases, all involving articles also to be found in the *Selected Essays,* I have gone back to Williams's original manuscripts to reconstruct their initial format, which usually, and for a variety of reasons, turned out to be considerably different from the published version. In some cases I have reinserted material omitted from the published articles, in others I have removed stylistic emendations and alterations of meaning imposed on the essays before publication by persons other than Williams.

These changes have resulted in the augmentation of such articles as "Midas," or the 1939 article on Sheeler, to nearly twice their original length. On the other hand, changes in such an article as "An Afternoon with Tchelitchew" have been limited to the restoration of a few important words and phrases to their original form.

There are good reasons for this procedure. In the case of the Tchelitchew article, for instance, someone whose insight into the peculiarities of Williams's style of writing was decidedly dim, made some handwritten changes in Williams's typescript before it went to the printers. The least important of these changes was the unnecessary and infelicitous emendation of Williams's term "sheer facility" to "deftness," one of those "elegant" literary terms which Williams had deliberately excluded from his vocabulary. More directly obstructive were changes in the structure of some sentences which drastically altered their meaning, as well as impairing their coherence. When the article was reprinted by John C. Thirlwall in the *Selected Essays,* the emendations included in the first publication of the piece in the British magazine *Life and Letters Today* were simply perpetuated.

As demonstrated in the case of the Tchelitchew article, the significance of Williams's insistence on writing in an *American* idiom was not always understood by those who edited his prose for publication. Williams had little patience with the conventional rules of written English. He spurned nicely balanced and sub-divided sentences in favor of a sometimes clearly ungrammatical directness, and he was unconcerned about repeating the same word several times in a single short paragraph, or about running a number of non-parallel sentence fragments together, often without so much as a comma to separate them. Consequently it was not uncommon for his editors to try to straighten out his prose. The formalist sensibilities of a *New Republic* editor, for example, were sufficiently disturbed by Williams's peculiarities of style, to make him step in and "normalize" the text of Williams's review of Walker Evans's *American Photographs.* The result was a printed text in which dependent clauses and word order had been subtly, and on the whole, intelligently, regularized—but at the expense of the loose fit and ease of Williams's habitual prose. In addition, and less acceptably, the editor in question saw fit to drop several complete sentences from Williams's original text, probably because he (inaccurately) considered them repetitious. The text of the Evans article printed here uses Williams's own final draft rather than the printed version, content to stay with the poet's quirks of language.

A similar kind of editorial interference can be detected in Williams's article on the Garbisch collection of American primitives. At the time that he wrote this article, Williams was suffering from the aftereffects of a stroke. He was able to type, but his handwriting was erratic. He therefore permitted someone else—judging from the handwriting, John C. Thirlwall—to prepare the text for publication. Thirlwall, in doing so, made a considerable number of emendations of rather dubious merit. For variety's sake, one assumes, he at one point changed Williams's habitual word for painting, "picture," to "view." Elsewhere he changed "trees" to "vegetation," "place" to "gallery," "thing" to "portrait." Even "to draw" became "to depict." In short, the simple vigor of the poet's prose was tampered with to fit someone else's very subjective sense of stylistic orthodoxy.

In cases such as this, I have consistently gone back to Williams's original texts, allowing them to stand, even where an editor's changes might have seemed to be justified, or even, as was also occasionally the case, felicitous. I have done so because, in the first place, Williams's prose has a particular kind of internal cohesion, which, it has become clear to me, can only be impaired by editorial interference, and which, even if it is not always graceful and easy to read, nonetheless represents a serious and consistent attempt on the poet's part to speak in characteristically American cadences. As he once remarked, "the thing has been with me to work the language in order to find what new may be done with it."[1] Secondly, it is a very difficult matter to try to second-guess a writer such as Williams, since even his apparent errors have a certain inherent logic of their own. In the manuscript of his essay on the American primitive painters, for example, Williams remarked at one point, in reference to a specific painting: "both my wife and eye were amazed." Thirlwall (if he was the editor in question) changed "eye" to "I"—a perfectly logical and reasonable emendation, but one which does not take into consideration Williams's lifelong pleasure in using the word "eye" as an equivalent for the creative capacity of the artist. Therefore, even if Williams, as is very possible, meant to use "I" in this context, his unconscious misspelling remains a variation with its own inherent justification.

It has therefore been my policy not to with the integrity of Williams's language and style, except in a very few cases where an obvious mistyping on Williams's part would otherwise have led to unnecessary confusion for the reader. In all cases where there could have been even the slightest doubt about the accuracy of a textual interpretation I might have been tempted to make, or wherever it was not entirely clear that a textual peculiarity was a spelling error or a case of "poetic license," I have chosen to let Williams's own versions stand. I have silently corrected only those obvious errors in orthography or spelling which seemed immediately obtrusive.

In writing his articles, Williams had an intriguing habit of first jotting down quick notes, then typing and retyping the article on which he was working, dropping or adding sentences and paragraphs here and there as he went along. Usually an article would start as a relatively short compilation of more-or-less self-contained paragraphs forming a number of fairly loosely interrelated observations. Later versions would expand these initial observations, while the final version—if there was one—was likely to be similar to the expanded versions in content, except for the ruthless excision of

[1]"Why he Selected Some Flower Studies," in *America's 93 Greatest Living Authors Present This is My Best*, ed. Whit Burnett and Burton C. Hoffman (New York, World Publishing Co., 1942), 641.

numerous paragraphs, to bring the article "down to size." Often Williams's reasons for cutting out one paragraph and retaining another seem altogether capricious. What was cut was usually as interesting, if not more so, than what was retained. One reasonable explanation is that Williams, being an impulsive man, tended to follow his moods of the moment. For example, the only reason why Williams deleted the important formulation of the procedure by which the artist could attain significant form, from the later drafts of his article on "Credit Monopoly," would seem to have been that when he decided to "depersonalize" his remarks, he simply removed this passage with the rest of the section, without giving the matter a second thought.

Williams was also very susceptible to criticisms of his work by friends and acquaintances. Often he followed the path of least resistance by simply cutting out entire sections if there was anything in them that was being questioned. An excellent case in point is what happened to the "Midas" article after Williams received Nicolas Calas's criticisms of an early draft he had sent him. Calas objected to Williams's use of the terms "anti-political, anti-terrorist," which he considered redundant, good art being, in his opinion, always anti-political. Williams responded by promptly deleting the offending passage, thereby making his agreement with Calas's position considerably less clear to his readers, who, after all, could not be expected to be privy to the nature of the correspondence on the matter between the two men. Similarly, when Calas indicated that he objected to Williams's intriguing statement that he came "of a criminal generation," Williams simply removed that statement, as well as nearly a page of related autobiographical material. Calas's observation that Williams was putting too much emphasis on the painter Delvaux in his article led to the disappearance of several telling references to the Belgian Surrealist.

Sometimes, however, Williams's deletions, as he moved from version to version, were more deliberate. One of the reasons why interviews such as that by Walter Sutton are an especially fruitful source of information about Williams's beliefs and theories is that, as a result of his impulsive nature, his first utterances tended to be unguarded, spontaneous reflections. The early versions of his essays were often of a similar spontaneity, which not infrequently disappeared as the articles moved toward their final state. It is, for example, characteristic of Williams's continuing uncertainty about the public's willingness to recognize his originality as an artist and the importance of his own contribution to the world of ideas, that there is a consistent pattern in his writing, in which time and again, in early drafts, he would generously announce the artistic or intellectual sources for certain of his opinions, only to delete all such references in the final versions.

Therefore, whatever the reasons may have been which caused Williams to delete various passages from his articles at one point or another, there can be no doubt that the sections which he deleted were in almost all cases at least as significant to an understanding of his ideas as those he decided to retain. Williams was himself clearly quite aware of this aspect of his writing procedure and took care to preserve all, or most, of the various fragments and versions of the essays he wrote. Taking my cue from the fact that he allowed these various versions to be deposited in the manuscript collections of two of our major universities, thereby showing himself unwilling to disown their contents, I decided to reconstruct the most complete version possible of each essay for which a number of early drafts have been preserved. I did so by reinserting those passages from earlier drafts which Williams had deleted at one point or another. This was no minor undertaking. In the case of some of the essays a dozen or more early drafts have been preserved. In writing the introduction to the Museum of Modern Art's Sheeler exhibition of 1939, Williams in fact accumulated a dossier of no less than twenty-nine different versions and fragments!

However, while constructing a "master version" on the basis of all available drafts was an arduous task, it was a labor considerably reduced in its complexity by the fact that Williams's writing tends to be aphoristic. Because of his predilection for categoric statements, his paragraphs are as a rule remarkably self-contained. This made it easy for him to take, as indeed he frequently did, a specific paragraph, or group of paragraphs, and simply transpose it or them from one part of the article he was writing, to another—or even, as also happened, from one essay to another. Thus my reinsertion of excised material rarely threatened to interfere with the readability of the essays in question.

As a consequence this collection of Williams's writings on art and artists can claim to contain *all* the poet's observations and considerations to be found in any of the available manuscript versions of the articles included. The reader interested in Williams's opinions about the visual arts therefore can rest assured that he is getting a complete record of the relevant contents of the works included in this collection.

In order to keep this compilation as enjoyable to read and as uncluttered as possible, I have designated the following procedure in recording the insertion of passages from other versions into the main text: In the section called "Sources," at the end of this book, I have given a complete record of the provenance of each of the articles, including a designation of all available manuscript versions which have come under my scrutiny. In each case I indicate which of the available versions I have used as my basic text. Insertions into this basic text of material from other manuscript versions are indicated as follows:

1. A passage in parentheses followed by an asterisk represents a passage deleted by Williams in the main text.

2. A passage in parentheses followed by a lower case letter designates a passage taken from another version of the manuscript, classified with that letter in the "Sources."

3. A passage in parentheses followed by a lower case letter and an asterisk designates a passage taken from another version of the manuscript, and classified with that letter in the "Sources," but having been deleted by Williams in that other version.

4. Passages in double parentheses interpolated into passages in parentheses represent material found in earlier versions of the main insertion not to be found in the primary passage inserted into the main text.

5. Square brackets represent editorial additions on my part, necessary to supply coherent transitions not supplied by Williams himself.

This system has the merit of remaining relatively unobtrusive while keeping the reader informed at all times about the insertion of material belonging to versions other than the basic text used. In a few cases where a secondary draft of a specific article, usually a later, but less complete, version, included a felicitous change of a single word within a phrase otherwise also included in the basic text used for publication in this collection, I have substituted in the text the more appropriate wording of the secondary version without further indicating such a substitution, in order to avoid burdening the text with too cumbersome an editorial apparatus.

I would like to thank James Laughlin for providing me with the impetus to undertake the compilation of this collection—even though the task proved to be a good deal more intricate and time consuming than I had expected it to be at the outset. Had I not been able to make extensive use of Emily Mitchell Wallace's excellent bibliography of Williams's writings, my task would have been all but impossible. Williams scholars must always owe a special debt of gratitude to her for her work. The bibliography of the Williams manuscripts at the Lockwood Memorial Library of SUNY Buffalo, compiled by Neil Baldwin and Steven Meyers, has also been of substantial help to me. I am furthermore grateful to Karl Gay and Beverly Ruth van der Kooy, of the Lockwood Library, and to Donald Gallup and his staff at the Beinecke Library at Yale, for their cooperation in providing me with the necessary copies of Williams's unpublished manuscripts.

B. D.

Prologue

Still Lifes

All poems can be represented by
still lifes not to say
water-colors, the violence of
the *Iliad* lends itself to an arrangement
of narcissi in a jar.
The slaughter of Hector by Achilles
can well be shown by them
casually assembled yellow upon white
radiantly making a circle
sword strokes violently given
in more or less haphazard disarray.

Vortex

Not previously published, 1915

I AFFIRM my existence by accepting other forces to be in juxtaposition to my own either in agreement or disagreement.[1]

Thus (in undertaking the composition of phrases to express my content)[b] I have no compunction in borrowing phrases from Brzeska's "Vortex," on the contrary I accept his show of force as an affirmation of my own, (and insofar as I take his phrases our forces are in agreement)[b].

Furthermore (by this acceptance)[b] I deny—(affirm my independence from)[b]—the accident of time and place[2] that brought the particular phrases to me, in that, now as always, I express my freedom from necessity and from accident by using whatever I find in my view without effort (to avoid or)[b] to find. Thus I am free to take whatever appearance fits my purpose.

I meet in agreement the force that will express its emotional content by an arrangement of appearances (, of planes)[c], for by appearances I know my emotion.

(I amplify "planes" to include sounds, smells, colors, touch used as planes in the geometric sense, *i.e.*, without limits except as intersected by other planes.)[3] (Substance is not considered, for

[1]Above a variation of this first statement, on typescript draft (b), there is the following handwritten note by Williams: "By the quality of the contacts I affirm its [*i.e.*, presumably "my existence's"] quality." If these—and other—handwritten additions by Williams were made contemporaneously to the composition of this manifesto, this would probably represent the first appearance of the term "contact" in Williams's work. There are, however, certain modulations in the handwriting which suggest that Williams may have added this note to the typescript at a later date, possibly in the early 1920's.

[2]In draft (b) Williams wrote "space" instead of "place."

[3]This passage is crossed out in the typescript, but here again the deletion—as in the matter of the handwritten additions noted earlier—seems to be the result of a passing attempt by Williams, at a later date, to reorganize his manifesto.

apart from transparency which shows nothing, it does not exist aside from surface or plane. [By means of] plane [surface] exists in apposition to substance. Plane is the appearance.

I affirm my existence and perceive its quality by apposition of planes.)[d]

(I am in agreement with Brzeska that the line has no existence being merely the meeting place of planes.)[c]

I will not stop at planes but go on to content.

Thus also by accepting the opportunity that has best satisfied my desire to express my emotions in the environment in which I have happened to be, I have defied my environment and denied its power to control me or [the power] of any accident that has made me write instead of cut stone.

By taking whatever character my environment has presented and turning it to my purpose, I have expressed my independence of it.

Thus in using words instead of stone I accept "plane" to be the affirmation of existence, the meeting of substances, whether it be stone meeting light or perfume striking mountain air or a sound of certain quality against one of another or against silence.

The affirmation of existence and freedom in the quality of the sound or the perfume or the stone.

The story, literal drawing is the line that has no existence.

I will express my emotions in the appearances: surfaces, sounds, smells, touch of the place in which I happen to be.

I will not make an effort to leave that place for I deny that I am dependent on any place.

I will not write differently now or at a hundred except as I am different and I will not value one part of my life more than another; therefore I shall not judge myself by a single standard that is not varied by time.

I seek my emotions for the reasons given above: to put them beside others by which I affirm and recognize both my existence and that of others which again react confirming mine.

And thus in the same way by expressing whatever emotion may occur, taking it without choice and putting it surface against surface, I affirm my independence of all emotions and my denial in time and place of the accident of their appearance.

I do not seek to change from writing to sculpture or painting or music—nor would I hesitate to change if I saw an advantage—for by refusing to attempt a new technique which I am too old to master or unsuited to master for some other reason—I affirm my independence from any one technique and so from all technique, and at the same time I deny that accident that gave me to write—or to carve or to paint.

Some Observations on Artists and Critics

I. More Swill

The Little Review, 1919

WHEN A LADY says a certain aria of Puccini's is "lovely" and that a certain other composition by Claudel is "ugly" she means something definite. She is using words accurately and for this reason her statement is not a mere matter of opinion but assumes the quality of being a definite point of illumination—for better or worse. She puts two separate things in apposition and distinctly chooses one: Puccini's aria will continue to remain "lovely" and Claudel's composition will continue to be "ugly"—one feels that sharply—no matter how she may subsequently alter her opinion. Her statement signalizes a fixed point of separation: one theme has escaped her understanding and one satisfies it.

The failure of loveliness is that it is possessed at large before it is composed and so can never be created. And the hell of creative work is that it is never possessed until after it has been set down and after the artist has lost his taste for it and then of course possessed only by one or two.

Americans are cursed with a desire to be understood. Everything must be "beautiful" or it must show this or that well-understood perfection, but it never occurs to an American, to an American critic in this case, to discover first whether he is dealing with a live thing or with the symmetries of a corpse.

It never occurs to an American critic to question whether or not a work shows evidences of creative thought, or at least this is not the first thing that occurs to him. Is it beautiful!? Yes but "beautiful" means something that tickles him, something that he can understand, and that thing must inevitably be to an artist *the ugly*. But all thought is ugly to the American critic—especially if it come from the left. And since in a work of art the form of the composition bespeaks the thought, then all new forms are inevitably anathema and this is not alone true of America.

So let us take off our undershirts, my friends, and scratch our backs in good company. At least we will not be praised because of our loveliness.

But of course that last paragraph is no more than a familiar halloo, a hoi-yo-to-hoi! The thing is that the difficulty between the critic and the artist has never been rightly understood. I do not make the same mistake as my predecessors; I have merely up to this point designated two objects of different nature, one of which, full of thought, concerns the artist and one of which, full of loveliness, concerns the critic. There is no transition between them. They remain forever separate, one forever to concern the artist and one forever to concern the critic.

But I differ from some of my companions in that I do not disdain to attack the critic. I do not disdain to soil my hands with death. I find a certain exhilaration in taking the heavy corpse in my arms and fox-trotting with it as far as I am able. It is not easy to dance with a dead thing in the arms.

And this is the eternal and until now slighted nature of the engagement between artist and critic. It is a dance! No man can be forced to dance. But I see no particular gain in mixing only with those of my own inherited cast of thought and feeling. I can of course appreciate the Chinese philosopher who lived alone by a waterfall, but aside from that perfection I see no reason for avoiding the arms of a critic. It teaches me to dance.

That there is no transition between critic and artist I will maintain as well as I am able. A man may be one, then the other, but never one within the other. It is a common impossibility. Witness alone the silence of the returned soldier among whom are men well able to express themselves: Phillip Gibbs has it, "Non-combatants do not understand and never will, not from now until the ending of the world. 'Cut it out about the brave boys in the trenches!' So it is difficult to describe them, or to give any idea of what goes on in their minds, for they belong to another world than the world of peace that we knew, and there is no code which can decipher their secret, nor any means of self-expression on their lips."

To a soldier war, to an artist his art, to a critic his criticism, to them all the dance!

II. What Every Artist Knows

A Letter to the Editors of The Freeman, *1920*
Sirs: The article by Mr. Harold Stearns, "Illusions of the Sophisticated," in *The Freeman,* 15 December, 1920, discloses two things which merit comment: 1. a sensitive intelligence well adapted to make artistic divisions; 2. the habitual error which occurs when art is discussed from the intellectual platform. Since the artist, in poverty-stricken America, should find his best friends among just such men as Mr. Stearns, an immediate effort should be made to combat the point of view he expresses in his article.

Mr. Stearns well points out that art is "a happy marriage between instinct and instinct's object," that it has no relation except to reality, no relation whatever to "impassioned recollection" or "rosy hopefulness in the future." Then, turning about, he speaks of art as existing in certain periods, spasmodically, between which, as at present, men must live without it. He directly implies that art is a spontaneous creation, a by-product of happy conjugations between emotions, instincts and their environment *which only great periods afford.*

This is the illusion which intellectuals like Mr. Stearns habitually accept; it is art from the outside, an effect "important as a fact only when it is unconscious," a half accidental effervescence of something else. Whereas the thing may have been working within itself for many generations. Mr. Stearns sees art only as a social phenomenon. There appear to him only isolated patches on the screen, related to nothing but the politico-social events to which they happen to be adherent.

Art lives when men of a certain sort are in contact with their environment and then only. This may occur at any time. Art becomes a social phenomenon in great periods only accidentally when external circumstances approach its constant requirements.

But the intellectual gives himself entirely away when, for instance, he tells us that to talk about art is, in effect, a social crime. Art, so he says, is a fact of importance only as such; to talk about it is futile. But Mr. Stearns neglects to make the important distinction that he refers only to philosophico-social discussion. He neglects to note that art can be talked about profitably at any time—but by artists.

It is his social, extraneous viewpoint, the constant attempt to "solve" art that the intellectual always makes, and attempts to make art dependent upon something else, to deny it its true, self-related, if disturbing, existence.

The thing which every artist sees without the necessity of demonstration because it is part of his own body, the thing which the philosopher writing about art never can see, is that art is the product of a certain sort of living contact that can be made to live, even for discussion, in no other way; that the so-called fallow periods are no less possessed in this passionate satisfaction than any other. In fact, that in regard to it all periods are the same.

The one thing that an intellectual writing about art can properly emphasize is that he, the intellectual, is not among those who are enjoying life in a certain way. So that in spite of himself, as far as art goes, being lean, he is forced to indulge in the very things he despises, on the one hand, recollections, and on the other, hopefulness about the future.

Yet he persists in discussing art. What he says is usually worth reading, when there is nothing better, because in his confusions he is seen to be struggling to get into contact with reality.

After all, this is perhaps the true province of intellectualism—to bridge over the secret periods. But the thing that is needed is not less discussion about art but more and more—but always by artists. America is especially in need of just such talk today, talk that tends more than anything to quicken the artists themselves into those public demonstrations of their instincts which we are starving for. In a poverty-stricken country such as ours is today, attempts to brand as unimportant even the smallest phenomenon of spiritual contact with life, which art is, are nothing more than vicious.

Comment on Contact

I.

Contact I, 1920

Contact is issued in the conviction that art which attains is indigenous of experience and relations, and that the artist works to express perceptions rather than to attain standards of achievement: however much information and past art may have served to clarify his perceptions and sophisticate his comprehensions, they will be no standard by which his work shall be adjudged. For if there are standards in reality and in existence, if there are values and relations which are absolute, they will apply to art. Otherwise any standard of criticism is a mere mental exercise, and past art signifies nothing.

We are here because of our faith in the existence of native artists who are capable of having, comprehending and recording extraordinary experience; who possess intellect sufficient to carry over the force of their emotional vigor; who do not weaken their work with humanitarianism; who deal with our situations, realizing that it is the degree of understanding about, and not situations themselves, which is of prime importance, and who receive meagre recognition.

Attainment is meaningless unless there be some basis of measurement. Wishing to be open-minded toward all experiment—ourselves feeling that many literary forms, the novel, the short story, and metrical verse, are mannered, copied and pretentious technique—we still do not intend becoming spokesman for any movement, group or theory, and as thoroughly dislike a modern traditionalism as any manner of perceiving the arts. That artists are sophisticated beings who utilize their own contacts in art creation, and erudition incidentally as it has been assimilated,[1] is an assumption of ours. They will be scientific insofar as medium is concerned, but their substance is no more scientific than is that of existence.

[1]The mimeographed typescript of the first issue of *Contact* reads "assimulated," an amusing, and perhaps appropriate misspelling, but probably not an intentional one.

We will be American, because we are of America; racial or international as the contactual realizations of those whose work we publish have been these. Particularly we will adopt no aggressive or inferior attitude toward "imported thought" or art.

Our only insistences are upon standards which reality as the artist senses it creates, in contradistinction to standards of social, moral or scholastic value—hangovers from past generations no better equipped to ascertain value than are we. Assuming sufficient insight and intellect to convey feelings valuably, we are interested in the writings of such individuals as are capable of putting a sense of contact, and of definite personal realization into their work.

II. Further Announcement

IN THE course of the next few months we will set down fully in these pages what we are proposing as a magazine. It wuld be idle to attempt to do so now when we have nothing to show but a beginning.

For native work in verse, fiction, criticism or whatever is written we mean to maintain a place, insisting on that which we have not found insisted upon before, the essential contact between words and the locality that breeds them, in this case America.

It is our object to discover, if possible, the terms in which good taste can be stated here. We find that whatever "good taste" is exhibited now in the one or two decent magazines we have is as a matter of fact extremely poor taste being provincial in the worst sense because wholly derivative and dependent upon nothing that could possibly give it authenticity. We call attention, at the same time, and acknowledge our debt to all importation of excellence from abroad.

We would limit our effort not only to give it force but to give it universality, that which cannot be bought by smearing a lick of borrowed culture over so many pages.

There is no money with which to pay for mss. We want no work that can be sold to other magazines unless the artist sees an advantage in appearing upon these pages that would outweigh all other considerations. I suppose I had better add that no one need expect us to publish his things simply because they happen to have been written in the United States.

What more? We intend no course in literature. Nor do we aim to make ourselves the objects of posthumous praise. We wish above all things to speak for the present.

Why not in that case have devoted ourselves to Dadaism, that latest development of the French soul, which we are about to see extensively exploited in New York this winter without there being—we venture to say—any sense whatever of its significance, and fulfil Rodker's prediction?

Here one might go into the nature of faith which we take to be no more than knowledge of the earth which in certain ages decomposes and leaves the intellect to itself, barren. And we might go on to the effect that the conventional, Tolstoian, mystical concept of faith has never been more than a superficial decoration permissible in ages of great knowledge of the earth and its uses.

Well America is a bastard country where decomposition is the prevalent spectacle but the contour is not particularly dadaesque and that's the gist of it.

We should be able to profit by this French orchid but only on condition that we have the local terms. As it is we should know what is before us, what it is and why. Or at least we should know our own part in the matter: which amounts to the same thing. Not that Dadaism is particularly important but—there it is. And where are we?

We do not seek to "transfer the center of the universe" here. We seek only contact with the local conditions which confront us. We believe that in the perfection of that contact is the beginning not only of the concept of art among us but the key to the technique also.

III. Sample Critical Statement

Contact IV, 1921

Contact has never in the least intimated that the American artist in preparing his position "should forget all about Europe." On the contrary the assertion has been that he should acquaint himself with everything pertaining to his wish that he can gather from European sources. He will in fact go about where he pleases and take or leave whatever necessity guides him to decide upon.

In exploiting his position in America the artist, aware of the universal physical laws of his craft, will however take off only from the sensual accidents of his immediate contacts. This achievement of a *locus, Contact* has maintained, is the one thing which will put his work on a comparable basis with the best work created abroad. Before the approach to anything of a serious character there must be this separate implantation of the sperm in each case.

Nothing will be forwarded, as it is persistently coughed at us for our children to believe, by a conscious regard for traditions which have arrived at their perfection by force of the stimuli of special circumstance foreign to us, the same which gave them birth and dynamize them today. Paris for painting, if you will, but it is the genius of the locality; the painting which centers in Paris is French painting, no matter by whom produced, Spaniard or Greek, French painting, long implanted and constantly held to the living circumstance by men of genius. Though no painting today can compare with it and though all must study it who will paint, it must be understood as French, the product of a locality, before it can be fully comprehended, a thing which, by every conceivable impulse of life converging immediately upon it from the French environment, has been brought into flower. It is living evidence of the essential nature of the local contact in art.

To attempt to live and to paint in New York by force of the same impulses which animate Paris is the occupation of adulatory provincials, to speak of "art" under these circumstances is the mark of our shallowness. The profit from French work begins when the student realizes that it is a special, a foreign, a peculiar growth, in its best examples every part discoverably related to some local turn of color or contour and so alone addressed to reality, able to be what it is, a living thing.

It is not art but French art that one goes to Paris to study, and one returns to Tokyo or New York to practice, not art, nor French art but—to adore the gods of the locality as the French have taught one to adore them. It is this alone that could produce work of any use to Paris. African wood carving.

All that I have to say is after all just that the artist might profit largely by an American experience—if he exists. If Americans are to be blessed with important work it will be through intelligent, informed contact with the locality which alone can infuse it with reality.

American periodic literature, magazines which represent no position taken but which offer at best certain snippets in juxtaposition, implying that when one piece is like the other both are good, this is the worst in the local environment carried to the logical conclusion. The worst of the anthology method in magazine making is that, in taking no definite regard to position, innocent of local effects upon itself, it cannot possibly present foreign work in anything but a blurred light, on a constantly wavering screen. Work like Benda's, once forcibly removed from its very special and sensitive local field of action and pushed into unlocated pages, becomes nearly completely unintelligible, like a severed hand.

To bring to America the work of Picasso or de Gourmont, the first thing to do is to establish our own position by thorough knowledge of our own locality, thus giving the foreign work a place to which to arrive. This is the opportunity of the creative artist.

French Painting

(Its Importance, a Definition, and the Influence Upon Modern Writing Traceable to It)

The Embodiment of Knowledge, 1928

THERE IS a progressive excellence moving through the periods marked each by an ism in the last hundred years of French painting. It is technical and its influence is traceable there as well as in the other arts. It is a longer phase than the generational modalities of it which attract periodic attention.

It is, in paint, an effect of this plain problem: How shall the multiplicity of a natural object, impossible to detail or completely encircle, be presented by pigment on canvas. Plainly it is not to trace it as it stands for that intelligence is impossible, repetitious and uncalled for. (It is, in effect, an analysis, first, of the scene, followed by technical virtuosity.) It is to represent some phase of this object that the schools point. Each pose caught being a success.

Realizing this, the exhilarating resourcefulness and fertility of the French is shown, but being part of a general problem, there is (beyond that) a liberalizing implication to it which releases from the particular train—train of the French thing of the moment, which seduces artisans in the same craft elsewhere.

It is a fundamental technical problem. It is faced when a tree is to be put on canvas. (Shall it be one etched leaf in the foreground? a contour of massed branches, a color—or what?)

Facing it, realizing that it is pigment on a surface, French painting went as far as Braque, it became a surface of paint and that is what it represented. It went to this extreme to free itself of misconceptions as to its function, after that and before that, what? for that was its simplest and most extreme, most sanitary phase. (It remains the pivot for an appraisal of its continued activity.)

For this is the flat of it: all painting is representation and cannot be anything else. This must be stated in order to clear the looseness of some thought concerning it and to understand it properly. It was

69

a mistake to say, as it was said twenty years ago, that the object of modern painting was to escape representation. Not so. (It was to escape triteness, the stupidity of a loose verisimilitude—to trace a scene and thus to confuse paint values with natural objects.)

It *is* to represent nature. The only problem being: what shall we represent and how? In that choice lies the whole of the artist's realm. It is evidence of the exercise of this choice that is to be judged, finally, as excellent. It is a technique along with a stress of experience (the understanding, intelligence) that shall not at least be false thought, stale emotion and lying pretense (of delineation).

Invention (creation) being basically the mark of intelligence, selecting and rejecting its material—as it would be in an engineer that turns to the time for his opportunity.

French painting from this viewpoint escaping the cliché of the predominant ism of the moment can be highly instructive to the writer—and has been to me—being as I believe it to have been for a hundred years one of the cleanest, most alert and fecund avenues of human endeavor, a positive point of intelligent insistence from which work may depart in any direction.

The writer is to describe, to represent just as the painter must do—but what? and how?

It is the same question of words and technique in their arrangement—Stein has stressed, as Braque did paint, words. So the significance of her personal motto: A rose is a rose—which printed in a circle means two things: A rose is, to be sure, a rose. But on the other hand the words: A rose is—are words which stand for all words and are very definitely not roses—but are nevertheless subject to arrangement for effect—as are roses—and shall be, for themselves, as meaningless-or as the arrangement which is jointed upon them shall please. In this case the words are put there to represent words, the rose spoken of being left to be a rose.

Let it be noted that these two phases, writing and painting, occurred synchronously. The basis is, presumably, a common one. As thought underlies.

1. The artist "idea" is not to limit, not to constrict, but not to fly off into "universals," into vapors, either. That is what it is to be an artist with his material before him. It is to be a kind of laborer—a

workman—a maker in a very plain sense—nothing vague or transcendental about it: that is the artist—at base.

2. The basis being—that one can come up through to excellence in the arts—as to an intelligent use of his life—anywhere—at any time—tho' with variations—and this is a liberal understanding of the world and an American one.

3. (last bit) It is because we confuse the narrow sense of parochialism in its limiting implication, that we fail to see the complement of the same: that the local in a full sense *is* the freeing agency to all thought, in that it is everywhere accessible to all: not in the temple, of a class, but for every place where men have eyes, brains, vigor and the desire to partake with others of that same variant in other *places* which unites us all—if we are able.

4. And how do the French do this: Strictly by following a local tradition. Their painting is a consecutive series of modulations on a craft. It has two collateral phases (1) taking from Japanese, Italian, Spanish—any craft, and being able to do so because the local permits it and (2) attracting other craftsmen in a great manner whose genius to use for themselves: Picasso, Gris—Cosmopolis be damned. Cosmopolis is where I happen to be. The virtue of Paris is not that it is a world capital of art. Facile nonsense. It is that Paris is a French city, dominated by French ideas—attracting the good to that, to that positive. None more local than the French: its vigor. It is the local that is the focus of work—everywhere available. It *is* (the local—with myself present in it) cosmopolis, a theoretical universal which is constricting—a self-apparent denial of the universality of the very fact of art itself.

1. The painters have paid too much attention to the ism and not enough to the painting. I'm for the painting where it is, in America or elsewhere, but I'm not for morons—vigor, worth, fervor—wherever it is and don't be seduced by it save for the pleasure and the impregnating point of it—which isn't an ism—or of the moment.

2. Someone by the name of Stearns has kicked against the pricks of French painting, saying that it has seduced American painters as it has, save for a few. All right. If the rest are not witty enough to circumvent, even use, that influence—to hell with them.

French painting has been, is a living, vigorous thing. There are not enough such in thought and act in the world on that plane. As a writer I enjoyed and profited. Here's the solution.

3. As to the laying on of the pigment, of course, I know nothing—save from common observation: that there are many ways—in work that is excellent from Van Dyke through Rembrandt to Cézanne.

4. What shall be seen then in America? Nothing French surely. What is there to see? A tree—it's been painted a myriad times from the Renaissance background down to Derain.

Well, what does one see? to paint? Why the tree, of course, is the facile answer. Not at all. The tree as a tree does not exist literally, figuratively or any way you please—for the appraising eye of the artist—or any man—the tree does not exist. What does exist, and in heightened intensity for the artist is the impression created by the shape and color of an object before him in his sensual being—his whole body (not his eyes) his body, his mind, his memory, his place: himself—that is what he sees—And in America—escape it he cannot—it is an American tree.

Render that in pigment and he asserts his own existence and that of men about him—he becomes prophet and seer—in so far as he is wholly worthy to be so.

That is the significance, the penetration, the wit and power of a picture. If he can record that with (and it is always a technical problem of) mastery and material, he will be presenting a tree. To do less, to ape a French manner is to put out his eye—then surely he has not seen the tree at all. She is the appendage of someone else who has subjugated him.

Notes on Art

Not previously published, 1928
ART BEING a mode by which anything may be said, is amoral in its conceptions. It is wrong to say, though, that art is amoral since, as it penetrates morality, among other things, it is penetrated too by moral conceptions. So it must have a moral aspect. But this is not its concern.

Being without concern for morality art cannot usurp to itself moral prerogatives without weakening itself. For this reason satire is a secondary form of art.

By shocking, a work of art acknowledges its own inadequacy of form. It must find its own mode which morality cannot attack without weakening itself, in its turn. But a vague sense of morality outraged is at the back of all popular objection to new art forms. The list is interminable: The *form* has made a *statement* beyond present conceptions, but strictly in the realm of art, that is pure form. This statement is unrelated to morality. But a moral conception of like nature is correlated. The vague perception of this subtle fact inspires fear in everyone, fear or the exhilaration of new life discovered, as one is not, or is, awake to the values of art.

In art, though, distinct from morality, the humane and so perfect principle is this, that not only is a full statement permissible, whereas in morality it is always partial and imperfect, but in art a complete statement is compulsory.

I thrive in a matrix of confusion (balance).

Do not talk of Parisian pose. It is the Ph.D. of stupidity to do so, puritanical and cross-eyed. If you wish to, you may speak of the influence of Berlin or Paris or the Riviera, on the maimed New

Englander; an amputated thing, when it hits sunlight is grotesquely exaggerated—but true. It is Paris, it is Berlin, it is the Riviera that has made it show true. Paris is a way to an understanding of the truth, *i.e.* Hartley. But it is not amiss but important to observe the points of Parisian achievement, especially in the art of painting—since it is the cap of the world—to understand as parcel of your own statement. What you see is not a pose but an elucidation, as the woman on the corner with an umbrella, an elucidation of mood at least, sometimes of structure, that should be grasped. Good God but to compare the principles of composition as related in Picasso and El Greco, THAT is waste of time. Of course there is identity. But tell me wherein they *differ* in spite of an identity of composition. Here especially, in painting, lies the truth of Duchamp, Picasso.

In England, in Europe, they have a sense of being part of a historical movement of no great permanence—it has happened more or less the same before—like the great white-collar army of the present day. But we Americans are too near our beginnings to know our real detachment from permanence, we still believe we are solid, unfolding—and not folding up also.

Art and Politics: The Editorship of BLAST

Not previously published, 1933

I ACCEPT the editorship of *BLAST* on these conditions:

1. that I have no work to do in connection with it,

2. that it be understood to be and remain a magazine devoted to writing (first and last) though in the service of the proletariat, and

3. that it adhere reasonably closely to the following program—(I will write exclusively, consciously and with a purpose to be understood by—and to instruct in the objectives of my craft—those avowed Communists who need what I can give. [I will be of service] insofar as the best in writing which such a determination does not negate can be of service, and will devote myself exclusively to helping your purpose by every means known to me as a writer—known to the art of writing.)[a]

This is a statement of what appears to be the way writers (and other artists) must face their responsibilities toward the world revolution: to clarify [it] by examples—more effective writing. A dilemma has been broached when the artist has been conscripted and forced to subordinate his training and skill to party necessity for a purpose. What is he to do? Has he no choice? Must he practice sabotage on his art? No. This magazine holds that in order to serve the cause of the proletariat he must not under any circumstances debase his art to any purpose, but, if he will subordinate *himself* to the party, he would rather allow himself to be eliminated entirely, humbly, than commit the offence against his party of doing less than he is capable of as an artist. This is fundamental. Bad writing never helped anybody. Much proletarian writing is ineffective since it is bad. It is the business of the artist to make this more effective *in the cause* by applying the perfected principles of his art to it. And by doing so, we believe, he must benefit his art also.

The worst fault in writing and the one of which proletarian

writing by accomplished artists of another regime [has been most guilty] has been to try to write down to an audience. This, however, is characteristic of bad writing at all times and not only of bad proletarian writing.

(Red Front: Such work being second-rate art will always have an air of being good enough for the proletariat—which is an impossible condition. There is no alternative: it must be, first, good art. And this is possible—rather, it is inevitable.)[a]

On what principle shall a writer, who has perfected a complicated method or methods, bring himself to men willing to listen to what they can understand but who have no knowledge of the complexities of a difficult technique? We do not ask how it is to be done, we ask how, within himself, shall the writer get to the task without first compromising his intelligence?

The answer lies in the known resurgence, wilting and decline of art itself in the past—as in the present day.

With these principles in view I will limit myself to an attempt to bring the excellences of writing to the understanding and service of men whose illumination by the principles of Communism makes them capable of rewarding the effort the artist would make by secrets he could not arrive at otherwise.

Writing along with all other living things tends to die out at the top at a point of approximate excellence. This is true either of the wood duck or Greek poetry. We may react to it as we please. We may look around from our ruined tower at a waste land or join the decadents and the art for art sakers—and not without justice on our side. In fact distinction often lies that way.

But there is another way in which the situation may be faced. The clue to this lies in the approximate nature of all excellence. There is no absolute in art and no absolute end toward which art is directed. In the end the objective escapes and a purgation occurs. Art itself has been purged away. There remains a nostalgic shell whose image fills us with regrets and infinite longings, with bitterness and despair. This is the ancient balefulness in all beauty. About this fact religion has embroidered a hundred creeds and tenets, a thousand precepts—the gist of them all being the spirit of good which is beyond art.

But all this lies in a speculative field which does not concern the artist. He is a practical man, an artisan working with materials (which he knows from the first)[1] and can have no time for gossip. (It is not his concern to what end he is working: his concern is to work and to work well . . .).[1] His problem is extremely simple. When he no longer knows why he is putting one stone on top of another, one word next to another, one color next to another, he'd better stop work until he finds out. And it isn't just a matter of stresses so that the structure won't fall down or apart. But why is he, why is *he,* the man, engaged on the job, doing it?

It's at about that time that the art, so-called, has disappeared. Why is he modeling a cat, Adam and Eve, the legs of a woman; why rhyming up a sonnet? Why?

Thus we come to the end of physics, chemistry, the sonata form, sex morality, philosophical dicta, the religious dogmas—and it ends—as art does from time to time, and as birds and animals—in why? The thing has escaped—the means have become fragile, brittle—Why?

Communism poses such a question to art. All very well for Romain Rolland to say that all writing which does not lead to action is so much garbage—but why? There are several steps in the approach to such a fiat which must be answered first.

The place most of us have stuck is this: Shall we give up the essential individualism of artists to serve a proletarian state—no matter how temporarily or for what urgent reasons—or shall we cling to the drastic compulsions of the artists even at the cost of having the new state excommunicate us? To me there is only one answer possible: We are first, last and always artists and can never be compelled by the state. Otherwise we are just liars. Everything begins from the spark of one man, in the Communist state as in any other, whether it be a unification under a holy apostolic see or

[1]The phrases in parentheses here are from a paragraph preceding this one on the same page, of which the content is nearly identical to the one reprinted here, but which Williams abandoned in mid-sentence.

otherwise. It is too readily forgotten that the thirteenth century, like every other, and in spite of an approximate excellence, decayed like any other. There is no more holiness in "holiness" than in any sensual life we can know.

But the artist makes a mistake if he believes that there is no way to serve the new mode implied in a present-day Communism—which is intellectually inescapable—save by jettisoning his personal integrity as an artist. It may be demanded of him—he must deny the demand. His only answer must be, No.

However, there is no point in taking the opposite stand: that Communism as such is opposed to him and that he must dash himself to death against it.

And he must watch carefully the heresy that it, Communism, gives him his opportunity. Wait a minute. His opportunity lies in art, not Communism. That he is left working in a vacuum and that now he will be reinvigorated: yes, that is true—but again, not by anything but rediscoveries in *art*, not Communism. The category is inflexible—that it may be of service.

The thing he, as an artist, faces is a revision of the code. This he can accept, in fact this he must accept, it is essential to him to do so and this is the opportunity Communism presents to him, an opportunity to regain an understanding—Why?

He remains an artist, this must be said over and over again. He is useless unless he remains an artist. But since his art has reached an impasse, since it can go no further for the very reason that it has reached an excellence, he goes back, he must go back, with full and reasonable compulsion to a sounder basis.

As where all impasses are discovered it is a signal seldom to go forward—and if so never far—but nearly always to go back.

If the intellectual tends to die out and to become mixed, so that less differentiated types take his place, it is because the means have been faulty—a bad use of materials—and the elimination of the result [therefore represents] a salutary sloughing.[1] It is sad to see the

[1]Williams abandoned the second part of this sentence in mid-phrase, probably intending to return to it later. In the ms. this part reads as follows: " . . . it is because the means has been faulty and the—a bad use of materials and the elimination of the result a salutary sloughing."

highly differentiated types vanish. But one cannot say therefore that to look back is to retrograde.

Order itself is subversive when all the claws, spurs, and other irregular protuberances have been clipped off to achieve it.

There is no communistic writing. There is only writing—which goes forward or back at will, in order to remain in reasonable contact with [the] organization of its materials, [or to respond] to a continually revalued estimate of the nature of its materials.[1] Now it must go back according to the new stress which Communism places on words and their uses. Communism has cut away whole bales of misconceptions in form—art then quite naturally retreats to organize its position. It must retreat. It isn't flattered to do so. It doesn't set out to serve the proletariat. It remains art, but it retreats. Takes up its place not where it will but where it can. Absorbs some of the warmth, perhaps, in doing so. Retains its integrity. And for *this* must be valued. By its integrity.

For as to the artist his art is his measuring rod. To all others (who don't give a damn about art for itself) the artist is valuable because of the common virtues he presents—his integrity, in short.

It doesn't matter to the others that this is not to *them* but to his materials. To them it is integrity. Why look further? Proust is tremendously read by Communists—perhaps because he depicts the decay of a bourgeoisie—but more than that because he *does* depict them, decadent though many phases of his consciousness, of his whole activity, may be. There in his art, he is a whole man—the only place where he is whole.

Aragon's poem is not read. It is "old stuff" in the dress of Communism. It is poor art. Do we think the Communists themselves are such fools that they do not know integrity? That they do not smell out good art? Invention? It is propaganda. It has some good lines. But it is not good writing and *for that reason* it is of little use to Communism itself.

So today a question is posed which has to be answered: What is

---

[1]In the ms. this sentence reads: "There is only writing—which goes forward or back at will in order to remain in reasonable contact with—organization of its materials.—according to a continually revalued estimate of the nature of its

the place of writing in a communistic state? My answer is: The same it has always been, only—since there is no remaining objective left to the writer in the forms which have decayed away under his fingers—he must go back for his clue, realistically look for new forms in a more simple organization of social materials.[1]

Once he has found it, he becomes as always an enemy to society attacking it at every quarter. Only for the briefest moment can he chime with the others.

A magazine which accepts (1) the idea that most Communist writing is bad and that it should be better—as writing. That (2) there is no reason why it should not be written to be understood. That (3) because it is plain does not necessarily involve writing down to a willing, if uncultured, man; (4) that it is possible for writing to gain in integrity with its materials by observation of a similar process in society; (5) that the decay at the top is due to materials (forms) which have lost meaning and become insensitive by careless use; and that (6) there is a gain to writing by a retreat to essentials, an opportunity which can be intelligently taken.

Having been burned as editor, half-editor, quarter-editor, I am willing to have those interested use my name, for whatever it may stand for, as editor, provided I will not have to do any of the pressing physical work connected with the venture or hold myself responsible for everything that is said in it. My name to remain so long as the magazine deals with writing which is attempting to discover in the communistic onslaught materials which are essential to it—to which its life is jointly dedicated along with theirs—as the history and suffering for the art of writing amply testifies. No Communist should care for the color of the skins of his comrades.

The artist is a man with a skin the color of the rainbow—with black added.

---

materials." In this case, too, Williams probably intended originally to go back over the text at some future date and select the formulation he preferred, or construct the type of conjunction I present here.

[1]Again, in the ms. the last part of this sentence has a fragmented, tentative form: " . . . he must realistically look for new forms in the—he must go back—in a more simple organization of social materials—for his clue."

Good writing is a matter of integrity to the materials—with whatever we find it in our hearts to build with them.

Then call me the editor—call me anything you please.

The Neglected Artist

Not previously published, 1936

(BEING A physician, one of those who get the brunt of human misfortune day in day out all their lives, and being a man of fifty and more, I came recently under the observation of a curious individual. We met at the house of a friend one night at a party. He saw something in me which interested him and wanted to do a portrait study. He was an artist.

I invited him to come to my office some afternoon the following week.

When he arrived a few days later and had set up his easel and board, he began to talk.)[f]* Not, he said, because I want to speak of myself or to air my opinions but because I find it easier to talk than to listen when I am concentrating on the work before me. I answered him from time to time in moments of relaxation such as he allowed. But in general he talked away rather steadily by himself for most of the two hours I posed for him.

(I found what he had to say very interesting; ((it opened up a world unfamiliar to me. I studied the man))[b] as he scowled, pinched up his lips, smiled and beamed triumphantly working to seize the something he wanted in what he called the "map of my face." It was a hunt as well, apparently, as a construction that was going on.

The man himself was a dark, undersized fellow with bushy hair, keen black eyes, and a somewhat Slavic cast of face—though he might have denied having Slavic blood in him. A typical "foreigner," I should have said, to most Americans; just what you might expect the American conception of an artist to be. His voice was gentle and pitched rather high. But he expressed himself with the greatest firmness and clarity when he was able to reach the difficult points he was making.)[c]

It is my purpose to give a somewhat full report of his conversation.

Such and such a man is a fool, he began. He is a fool because he thinks he is doing one thing and is really doing something else. That is a fool. And it is a pity, too, because he is full of genius. But he has forgotten what a painter is for. That is, to paint. He has let himself be led astray into politics and that has ruined him. In the time of Michelangelo they used to bend two trees together and tie a man's limbs to them. Then they would let go so that the trees tore him apart. But the artist did not turn aside for such cruelty. He had only to paint, to approach the world indirectly through his art.

The whole Renaissance was a rule of so many tyrants. It was they who hired the masters to work for them. The great artists of the time did not stop to attack such men. They were their friends. Instead they made masterpieces. And in their work lies a depth of understanding which must ultimately do away with all tyrants and cruelty, all violence of which art is the antithesis.

Look at Beethoven. He did not directly attack the political absurdities of his day, except in the strict concepts of his art, which were in themselves a world to him. And those liberations which he then set in motion have lasted until today and will last perhaps forever still breathing their power.

Please notice, he added, that when I use the word "forever" I say something definite, something human, something with a meaning that can be understood. It is not an abstraction, so used.

I am a painter, so I speak of painting, but what I say applies to all the arts. It is a world very little understood today, even by the artists. One must approach a painting always from that world, always from the outside. Yes, I know, an artist deals only in the materials of his art. He is a mechanic. He must objectify everything. But he must *see* something first. He must know *what* he sees and what he wants to do with it. He must not turn it round the other way.

(He must be trained too. What do you think of Van Gogh? He knew nothing about painting. He is only good when he is unconscious; when his enthusiasm makes him *see*, like a child. But when he tries to do according to what he thinks he should do he is very bad. His *Potato Eaters* for instance is very bad. Peasants are happy people. They are not that way. That is perverse, empty.)[b]

When I paint it is because I see something, something beyond the mere materials to be used. (That is what I am painting. Then I look to discover in the materials what it is that reveals that thing to me.)* And as I look I am at work. I do not know what my hand is doing—though it is well trained to follow me. I see and my hand automatically follows my perception. I am not drawing a face. I am looking to discover what it is that I saw and to describe it. There is no other approach to good art.

(They say that Cézanne is as great a painter as Leonardo. That is ridiculous. What did he see?)[f*]

That is the trouble with most moderns. Picasso too. They have approached painting from the wrong direction, from the material side of it, (and that is the wrong way.)[f*] Of course, it is paint. It is a two dimensional convention in which certain symbols are used to produce an effect of three dimensions, of light, of objects surrounded by space. That is true. But there is sometimes also a fourth dimension. And that is genius. (The genius which they lack.)[f*] It is this that makes a work immortal, that is, extending indefinitely through time. That is the fourth dimension. And that too, in painting is a convention. But how?

Art is all of human beings, they forget that. What else can it be? Without that there is only nature, the (unconscious)[c] birds (and animals)[c] and the stones. But man is conscious, he is conscious of the passage of time. And it is this consciousness of a man in a work of art that makes it live. Most of us[1] have not been able to rise from consideration of the materials to that state of the soul which must inspire us if we are to succeed.

The soul? I said. Do you believe in the immortality (or even the existence)[b] of the soul?

The immortality is of no importance. But the existence, yes, of

---

[1] In draft (c) and several other early drafts, the text reads: "Picasso has not been able to rise from a consideration of his materials," etc.

course. We are speaking of art, we are speaking of practical things. It is the soul alone that makes life possible to thought. It is the integrity of the artist's soul in us that gives the only reason for existence—the only reason, I say, that we know. (That is not just another philosophical conception, it is so because we have experienced it, we have found it within ourselves.)ᶜ*

Do not mistake me, he went on, your moderns have done a useful piece of work. And they have done it well. They have destroyed Ruskin, they have destroyed the pseudo-artists (, the fakers, those who served to block a comprehensive knowledge of the world in their day.)ᵇ At the same time they have been (too material,)ᵇtoo bound to science, too limited to the mechanics of their craft, too self-conscious. (They have forgotten from which world they must approach what they have to do. Even Rousseau, *le Douanier,* was self-conscious, don't you think? He was not a true primitive. Just a little self-conscious.)ᶠ*

(In cubism and all the really important technical work of the schools that came after there is too much that is self-conscious. They have been dealing too much with the means of art, and not enough with the meaning.

Has art a meaning?

It is a world. Shall we ask of it more meaning than we ask of the other worlds of our thought which we take seriously?)ᶜ I once asked John Dewey at a banquet, Do you believe there is anything self-conscious in art? Please do not answer me offhand, I cautioned him, but give me your considered opinion. And he said, In great art, no, there is nothing self-conscious.

But, I interposed, has it not been the virtue of the French School that they are *not* self-conscious? They go on wherever their inclination leads them, without restraint, to the end. It is, in my own opinion, a great virtue. (We cannot go back to the primitive as Rivera has tried to do. We must go on to further discovery and comprehension.)ᶜ

Yes. But without a necessary control that can be mere abandon. There must be a check—

Ah ha!

And that is humanity. They have forgotten that.

(But they do recognize humanity. They are extremely human in their belief that complete abandon will bring them to the truth.)[c]

No, he insisted. It is with them only another theory. (You can see it in their work. No really human beings as subjects from which to discover their art, only human beings as objects wholly external—not from the inside.)[b]* And the proof is that humanity has turned against them, does not recognize what they do. It even finds them antagonistic (and such an instinct is correct. The fourth dimension is missing.)

The fault is, perhaps, not their own but lies embedded in the age. Of what are we most proud in the world today? Our science. Is it not true? I recognize, he continued, that we do not find today in art that solidity which science represents. But that was precisely the strength of Leonardo, to which, as an artist, he added a fourth dimension, the concept of man.

(Goethe says, if a man understand something he reads he makes it his own. It is his to do with and to use. This is the free world of the intelligence and of the artist. From this world he paints everything.

In art the freedom of the soul of man is established. We need in this the solidity which today we find only in the sciences. In great art this is enlarged to include with the three-dimensional world the concept of man.)[b] Has not science, which we thought so solid, itself reached a crisis today? An end to its resources? We hear of the division of the atom into smaller and smaller parts. To what effect? The release of greater and greater energy, conceivable at last in terms only of infinity. The process runs off inevitably into metaphysics. Impossible to tell which is energy, which matter.

(But this is a real world, not a relative one. The concept of a Euclidian geometry represents a real condition. There are not a number of geometries of which that of Euclid is one, as the mathematicians say. There is only the one geometry, which Euclid was able to discover in the conditions of three-dimensional space with which he found himself actually surrounded.)[c] In the practical world of the artist this impasse was known long since and the knowledge put to superb use—by Michelangelo. In what do they think his power lies? Not surely in (the tortured bulk of his work,)[f] in the colossal size of his masterpieces. Many have been deceived by that. No. The secret of his power lies in the subtlety of his modeling, by the fineness of the divisions of it rendering up the power.

All this time my artist had been looking, measuring, drawing. Then his face lighted up. Now we are getting something, he said. Something important. He turned the board around. There lightly sketched I saw my head, the "map of my face" as he had called it, from which, sharply, in full detail, appeared one eye, my right, startlingly alive. He looked at me to see if I were pleased.

Man is the theme, his solitary existence in time, the point where, in a three-dimensional world, time and its creature, man, give a fourth dimension. In art it can be worked out. In that sphere, today when no other way is offered, the great tradition lives.

Man's dignity and importance in the world and his responsibility: the great tradition. Yes, I thought, in a sad state today.

America, he began again.

America. Yes, I said. What about America?

(It is here the opportunity for the artist is greatest.)ᶠ* There never was a people so starved for what the world of art has to give as this country.¹ (Through the arts only lies our way toward an adult conception of the world—without vulgarity. It is possible. But there is no way but through the discipline of art.)ᶜ Americans, with their history of divorce from the hereditary cultures of Europe, of denial and spiritual bereavement, are infantile and crass in judgments relating to their deeper needs. They suffer without knowing why (, the prey to foolish isms and empty cults. This is still the proselytizing ground for all the follies of Christendom and some

¹In early drafts, of which (c) is the most complete, only a single paragraph separates Williams's question: "What about America," from the departure of the artist. In those drafts most of the material subsequent to Williams's question included in the version printed here, up to the paragraph beginning "As the light failed," actually belonged to Williams's record of his own reflections after the artist's departure—a fact which clearly presents the reader with an excellent reason to take Williams's assertion: "I think he was right in his estimate of the American view of [the world of the artist]" very seriously.

The original paragraph—separating Williams's question and the artist's departure—in draft (c) reads as follows: "There never was a people so starved for the arts others, concoctions of the dull-witted and the unscrupulous.)[c]

It may seem straining the point but[1] there is nothing new in the idea, really, that America has the crime, the violence which superficially characterize it, because it wants rapine, arson, violence of all sorts. We seek it as relief from the intolerable state of our minds that in a general way know no other satisfaction. And when the culprit is taken, in answer to our righteous demands, we immediately shower him with sympathy. Why, do you suppose? Because he is ourselves. We are sorry for him. (It is terrfying but true.

In the world of the artists lies the answer to this paradox also.)[c] We are starved, we are thirsty for that which we cannot attain. We know money is not the thing, we have been told so until we want to puke at mention of it again. But what else have we to strive for? So we still defraud and murder, to say nothing of slaving our hearts out in the name of "holy" work—for money!—thinking it may yet buy us what we want.

(But we do very little to supply by other means the things money cannot buy. In the world of the artist lies the answer.)[c] Do you blame the artist, then, if he is arrogant—in the manner of Rembrandt? It is because he knows. He is the feeder, the supplier. The rich like the rest of us need what he has to offer. We must have it or we shall die. Do you believe that? He should have special inducements to his art. He must have special care, special remunerations. He should be given a lavish tolerance. (Not wealth, of necessity,

as this country. But at the same time they drive the artist away—to despair, to the supernatural—there is a strong cult of the supernatural in American literature. They drive the artist to despair. Yet you cannot blame them. They are right. They have been cheated, none more so. They are wary. As a group they have had all the abortions of the fakers and pseudo-artists forced on them, in their want, more than any other peoples—and for generations. They should very properly beware. Because it is a matter of the greatest importance to them. It is a healthy sign that they despise 'art.' They are perfectly right in this. But the lack remains."

[1]In draft (c), where, as indicated above, this passage still belonged to the author's reflections subsequent to the artist's departure, Williams remarked at this point: "but to a physician there is nothing strange in the idea that America . . ." etc. It is clear that Williams's attempts at disguising his own voice in these passages were not always successful—or, for that matter, undertaken with much care—for where in draft (c) Williams's artist was careful to designate "the Americans" as "they," thereby revealing his own "foreign origins," Williams frequently continues to use "we" in these paragraphs borrowed from his own later observations.

but opportunity to be heard, to be seen, to be read, without let, in proper American style.)ᶜ No use fighting with the artist, he has beaten us before we start. He can live on soda biscuit and water and still make fools of us. But that is not the way.

I do not think Americans really wish to drive the artist from them. In fact they have not done so, entirely. But there is a fear, a niggardliness in their dealings with him that is quite unlovely. So that, as a matter of fact, they do drive him away, to despair, to unfruitful isolation—to the supernatural. There is a strong cult of the supernatural, you know, in American literature. Where else shall a man turn when he is cast off from his fellows?

You cannot blame Americans, really. The people are right. They act from experience. They have been too often cheated to believe anything any more. As a group they have had the abortions of all the fakers and pseudo-artists forced on them, in their want, more than any other peoples on earth—and for generations. They must very properly beware, for it is of vital importance to them. It is a healthy sign that they despise "art." They are perfectly right in this. But the terrible lack remains.

As the light failed my friend put away his drawing, folded his easel, packed all his things together and, after a few further words, left, to return and continue his work another time.

I remained behind, thinking.

What sort of individual was this? (A strange creature. Should one say a Sir Thomas More or a potential bedlamite?)ᶜ A little cracked perhaps, with his Quattrocento obsession (, his fourth dimension. Henry Adams or just another of the brutalized and the defeated, seeking—what? Escape in fantasy?)ᶜ Another of the envious millions who make up a democracy, the theorists, the dreamers of impossible dreams which they try to foist on a world already overburdened. Yet I found myself impressed with what he had been saying. (Apart from his opinions, with which here and there one might differ, [his remarks struck] me as serious evidence of a world full of potentialities for America today. And I think he was right in his estimate of the American view of it.)ᵈ

(What he had had to say set me thinking of the neglect an artist suffers in America and the consequences of it. And it made me think also that there were a good many flesh and blood inhabitants of that region of existence of whom we think very little, generally, but who might have a valuable quota to contribute to our moves toward betterment of our existence: the world of the artist.)ᶜ*

As a matter of course most of us think of the world of the artist as something strange—exotic is the word commonly used to describe it. But if we should stop to think, that world remains still, as he said, no more, no less, that of the great tradition. (What is the great tradition which we have today so largely forgotten, what if not the dignity and importance of man in the universe and his actual responsibility here? It is this, he thinks, the arts alone continue.)ᶜ

Properly put is it not we who are the exotic, living in a fanciful creation of the unreal if not the misshapen and the grotesque? It is frightening to think what shadows we may well be. (And we do live in fear, every day, for lack of that which he, the artist, if we would, might transmit to us)* (: that assurance which, we believe, one day filled the world. The great masterworks of art are its record.)ᶜ What do we believe?

The distortion of our minds does really need no more than its daily reflection in the newspapers for verification. (We, and that means the people we know about us, hate, we satisfy ourselves in licentiousness of a sort—and, rather pitifully, we drive from us, out of a semiconscious sense of inferiority, the very world we most need for our enlightenment, the same of which I have been speaking.

We do not really desire to drive the artist from us. How does it come about? By our niggardliness toward him we in some measure make a bastard amends for the neglect we dole him. By it we do really assert his importance. We dare not quite ignore him but must keep him from our sight—because we desire so very much to know what he is doing and thinking and are so afraid of being cheated.

Yet we *must* know. Or we shall come to disaster. There can be no other pattern for existence in the world but his. But the limit of this article is to point out that in our distraught world today, there is a kernel, a world where trial may go on without disaster and that as Americans we should recognize and guard it zealously—much more than we have done heretofore.)ᶜ

We are truly disfigured as compared with that tradition whose excellence appeared from century to century in the work of the masters. *That* is the real world where the great concepts of living meet and cast themselves into time, today a world of almost total neglect. Such were my thoughts.

All we know is that from this world come from time to time, pictures, books, plays, sculpture—with considerable difficulty very often. They seem to strike against the world of daily affairs and are hard put to it to gain entrance. They startle or they are neglected. But almost never do we think of them as evidence, *evidence of a world* which they represent, a world of final importance to us, it may well be a world which this man, regardless of his minor opinions, represents.

It was in this spirit that I found myself eager to accept, at least tentatively, what this man had been saying. I would accept him as evidence of a world unknown or at least unfrequented by minds, like my own, subject to the usual contacts of the day to the exclusion of nearly all else, those perhaps who have put us where we are and can no longer tell the way out. Might it not be wise to look further? (The fourth dimension, Time, that is to say Man. The world of the artist.)[c]

No doubt about it, politics is at a crossroads, science is at the end of its rope as an interpretation of life, religion is in heavy need of rehabilitation; practical affairs, public morality, finances are torn apart. May it not be that the world of art does offer an asylum, a working place for the reestablishment of order? There must be order, there must be discipline—without destruction of the variables which often hold the new direction among them.

We should begin by seeing the arts in the large as a world which may be a haven for us—not just a picture or two, a concert or two, but a great, continuous tradition, a contemporary world from which we may draw power and enlightenment in a very practical manner today.

We do not see it large enough. It is a world. It is a world which may be entered freely. We must broaden the concept of its usefulness to the man of intelligence and emotion in the other constricted spheres of cosmopolitan life. Give it greater leeway as a reservoir of intelligent interest. Turn to it more alertly to discover its potentialities as exercise to the mind. We are too narrow in our view of it. We think it is a piece of sculpture, a picture, a book. But those are only so many ambassadors from its world. It is the world itself that should be entered—and supported—not from a sense of charity!

It is a battleground, not a bland Elysium, but at the same time we will realize that the battle is taking place within a world that can and does contain it. It is a battleground where differences of emotional and intellectual opinion may be engaged to the enhancement of the soul. It is a battleground where men contend to enlarge their vision and to refresh and engage their minds and emotions. From which, or by virtue of whose works, the man of affairs, if he give them the play they merit, may draw refreshment and power.

But if the arts run off at the beck and call of every other fancy, no matter how temporarily useful it may seem, they have missed their cue completely.

We need the world of the artists to remain intact, that to it we may *go,* as the monks and Popes of the Quattrocento went for confirmation and the verification of their faiths which only great art affords. And America, having the wealth, should find better ways of giving the arts sustenance. It must cultivate the habit of looking toward the world of art for direction. In the arts only will the mode for our conduct toward life be discovered. . . .[1]

[That is why] we can starve [the artist] and chortle over it and still come out the losers. We've got to get over the irritation we feel at his peccadilloes and find him to be what he is and reward him for it.)c

It may be said that America has already done enough for the arts. "We are doing our share" is the usual way of putting it. I decided to

[1]In draft (c) there follow at this point most of the remarks Williams later decided to have his artist make in response to his question "What about America?" (See footnote 1, p. 87.) Furthermore, Williams transposed the passage beginning with "But if the arts run off at the beck and call . . ." and ending with "the verification of their faiths which only great art affords," to an earlier section, to be spoken by the artist: in draft (g) this passage was therefore inserted near the beginning of the article as a separate paragraph, between the paragraphs beginning "The whole Renaissance . . ." and "Look at Beethoven."

draw up a random list in this respect covering a part of the subject to see where it would take me:

Begin with writing. There are the libraries and the books on the stands. But if these books are put there solely to sell at a profit or because they have been accepted in the past, we have already stultified or killed all major interest in writing from the start. It wouldn't go with a surgeon or a chemist. Then why with a writer? Mass publication won't help us. A means must be found to publish books of better quality, if less general appeal than the ordinary, on some other than a purely commercial basis. New thought, not at once acceptable, and new work must be encouraged and rewarded, not munificently perhaps but with understanding.

The literary fellowships to be offered by the Book-of-the-Month Club this year for "good volumes of poor sale" are a step in the right direction.

There should be more, many more, smaller editions of cheaper books, much more widely broadcast than is the case today. "Put them where they can lay their hands on them cheap and they will pick them up." There is an audience for them if it can be reached. But we have no organized network of small, alert stores where poetry, essays, and the better books generally can be obtained. Can there be anything more ridiculous than to know what book is wanted, to have the money ready for it and not to be able to find it— while it is lying on the shelf of some publisher, unsold? This occurs every day with the smaller editions.

Naturally such books will not all be good but they will be read if distributed and a taste for better reading stimulated. But when reputable publishing houses say they are not interested in anything that hasn't a sales possibility for the movies—the result to writing cannot be anything but disastrous.

We especially need a more alive and better informed criticism, by critics who have at least made an effort to read what is written in their day. (Something which does not exist at the present time.)ᶜ The Sunday Supplements do a small business among the various categories but they little more than follow the turnover of the presses. (There's nothing there but a guarded reference to work issued, together with the exposure of certain unlovely habits of mind among certain elderly gentlemen who should be living in the country on pensions.)[d]

There is no critical journal of writing in America worthy of the name, none with any scope to carry it past stodgy boundaries. And none with sufficient space, space is what we want! to permit it to be inclusive. None especially with a critic behind it whose knowledge and range, to say nothing of genius, can be respected. (The unfortunate names in criticism are more the limitations of the imagination than the free wind back of talent or genius which they should be.)[c]

In Portland, Oregon, there isn't a theater for the legitimate stage, only the auditorium with seats along both sides. In Los Angeles the Art Museum has little else in it than Gainsboroughs.

In music it is the same. A few big orchestras, presided over by reputations whose chief attainments are beautiful readings of old scores. Everything, naturally, is founded on that. But it is inadequate. It becomes finally an arrest of the mind.

Such great institutions as those few orchestras and opera companies constitute occupy the same relation to music that the New York Public Library and a professor of English here and there at one or another of the universities bear to letters. Where, anywhere, does a feeling for a world of music growing about one, in which new ideas are perhaps maturing, find an adequate backing in America? I mean a backing commensurate with our means. The struggle to be *heard* is altogether too killing for anything but the toughest, most hard pruned skeleton of a music to survive it and then only within the strictest limits of conventionality. It is not wise or useful for the conditions to be so forbidding. (It's rather stupid, in fact, where the need for liberality and encouragement is so great.)[d] A fragile, perhaps, but living if incomplete world of music is simply crushed out of existence in so bruising a struggle for survival. It calls to be heard as the music of the American composer Ives has been calling to be heard—through a gale of mediocrity—for two generations past with scarcely enough success to make him known as yet outside of New York City.

There are endowments of value, both public and private, but they are mostly for the young and the needlessly submissive. But take a man with a full orchestral work to be produced, a man whose talent, naturally, since it is new is divergent from the usual teaching in the schools. His opportunity to get a hearing takes often the best years of his life.

(As Americans we know too well our deficiencies,)ᶜ we are too humble, we lack confidence and the daring to go ahead. Such humility throws us back on the staid and the accepted. But it is folly to remain that way. It is against our talents and opportunities. We should change, try our own valuations on new work (—as Hollywood did on the dress designs for its women—)* make mistakes, but venture, learn, train ourselves to be the judge. To do this we must first gain access to the work. We must get *to* the books, *hear* the music, *see* the pictures and sculpture, attend the new plays, to ten times the degree now common to us. We can well afford it. (And win! A world of pertinences is languishing, in music alone, because we cannot get to it. We haven't the heart.

Sculpture, the same. Even in architecture we have not had sufficient confidence to dare, following the skyscraper epoch, now past.

We are too cramped, too restricted in our understanding of the arts in America. There must be more interest, more tolerance for them all and greater opportunities.)ᶜ

How is this to be done? I don't know. Nor is it my business here to say. If cost be the answer then we should at least realize what the cost is and balance cost with cost. If the answer is more leisure then again we must first realize what the lack of leisure costs us. My purpose is no more than to call attention to the lack.

Whether the responsibility for our awakening (with profit) is to be taken by the state, by private endowment or business foresight and enterprise is not entered into here. What I have tried to do is to emphasize the importance of the issue, the disastrous consequences of its neglect and that it is up to this country to go ahead with the work. (It will have to be done one way or the other if we are not to remain mentally and morally stalled in the present confusion.)ᵉ

(It's not that we want, each of us, ourselves to become artists. Nor do we want tea talks on the arts. It's far more than that and far less.)* We want to be able to turn easily toward excellence in the arts when we are in need of it, to look through such excellence to the world which it represents, a ground, perhaps the only one, on which, putting aside violence, we may rebuild a decent living in the world (, so that a code of freedom and broad tolerance—such as the arts only afford will spread and take root elsewhere in our harassed and sometimes needlessly brutalized existence).[c]

3. *Vincent Van Gogh, The Potato Eaters.* Oil on canvas, 82 cm. × 114 cm. Collection, National Museum Vincent Van Gogh, Amsterdam.

4. Rembrandt, *Nightwatch*. Oil. Collection, Rijksmuseum, Amsterdam.

(Revolutions Revalued:)ᵃ

The Attack on Credit Monopoly from a Cultural Viewpoint

A Speech given at the Institute of Public Affairs, Charlottesville, Virginia, on July 11, 1936, not previously published.

(WE HAVE BEEN invited here to discuss a general topic, the Economics of the Power Age. We have been invited in groups from various camps, each man speaking for himself with perfect freedom, that as wide a range of viewpoints as possible may be represented. This complexion of the conference as a whole I wish to adopt in particular as the takeoff for my own relatively minor part in it.)ᶜ

(Speaking as a writer interested in the principles of the Social Credit movement advocated by Major Douglas, and not as a technical expert, let me approach the subject from that camp, as an ordinary thinking, feeling human being—one who has read a few books carefully and who was born and lives in the United States. It makes a difference. A humane viewpoint. At its best the cultural viewpoint.)ᵇ*

This is the Power Age as contrasted with an age just preceding it when Labor was predominant. This is an age in which the productive capacity of one man has been increased, by machines, forty times over former standards, but during which, purchasing power, as represented by wages or their equivalent, though it should have been expanded forty times to meet this contingency, has remained relatively stationary. Credit of one sort or another must bridge this gap. Credit, which has displaced a defunct capitalism, has not been socialized to keep pace with present-day requirements. It remains in the hands of a few individuals and institutions. This constitutes a monopoly, to end which and to socialize credit the modern attack must be directed.

(It may be objected, from certain quarters, that there has been too much talk and too little action incident to the social distresses which have accompanied the Power Age and its economics. Bust everything up, start again. Right or wrong, my viewpoint disagrees with that.)ᶜ (Our final objective can be nothing but action, but action not from passion so much as an intelligent application of the truth to the situation as we find it.)* (So that if the truth find it possible to insinuate itself through any part of the discussion it is expected that it will be effective.)ᶜ

(Action there must be or a lingering disaster, not for the nation but for many in the nation, will ensue—therefore in fact the nation. For there are social distresses which need righting and they are most certainly associated, as effect and cause, with a very badly managed, because poorly understood economics. The attack must begin with the best thought, the clearest ideas of which we are capable.)*

Briefly, what's to become of us? Economically? Today? And why? And what are we to do about it?

Inevitably the discussion drifts to politics and government. For it is through government that all economics is brought to focus on the individual citizen through regulation or lack of regulation of its forces—drowning him in taxes, tariffs, costs, losses and loans—or supporting him in a life that will be at least tolerably secure.

As an American I live in a democracy, an old-fashioned democracy, based upon ideas of liberalism and representative government. This government is being rocked to its foundation by the conflicting economic forces of the moment. Back of all of this lies credit and its control, the gist of the economics of the Power Age.

To me, an American, living in the United States, there is but one serious question involved: shall we under economic pressure retain the long fought for principles of representative democratic government which we inherit from the past or relinquish them today? In other words, shall we extend our present form of government to include the credit situation, making it more and more democratic, or renounce it in favor of some other scheme economically more desirable? Perhaps to the right, perhaps to the left?

I'm narrowing my attack, you see, to a matter of government, with a mysterious hand of credit seeking to gain management over the controls. (My plan being to offer evidence and draw one or two conclusions at the end—a sort of detective story, you might say, a touch of truth and the whole plot falls apart.

I shall base my argument on a single point: the desirability of preserving individual freedom under the law intact, threatened as it is today from both the right and the left, as an important agency of government.)*

(Forget everything else. That is why I spoke of my part here as a minor one. I rest entirely on the validity or invalidity of that one point. I shall hammer on it throughout what I have to say, convinced that if it prove to have been well taken, then the force of its truth will topple the whole argument.

Not that this is to be a closely argued thesis, quite the opposite— but the evidence, random as it may seem, will be toward the objective, the necessity for individual freedom under the law. Meanwhile, though the purpose of the conference is of a certain sort, a secondary purpose is not to bore the hardpressed listener. In a sense we've got to entertain you also in order to hold you. We can't just say here it is, rather lumpy and bitter stuff, but swallow it, it will do you good. Swallow it!

Let's ramble awhile, bearing in mind that it's a trap of a genial sort in which I hope to catch you later.)c

Here's the simple setup of the thing: the United States is a political democracy in form but one thoroughly subverted by a rival economic structure which in fact negates much of the democratic intention—as secured by the Constitution. The situation is historic; Presidents Jackson and Van Buren fought the first great battles in the campaign.

As the *New Standard Encyclopedia* of Funk & Wagnalls phrases it: "Van Buren's four years of office were darkened by the gloom of financial panic; but what one man could he did to lighten it, by wringing from Congress its assent to a measure for a treasury independent of private banks."

This is the sort of history we lack and must have. Everything possible was done, as pointed out in recent years by Ezra Pound, to keep Van Buren's telltale autobiography from the eyes of the people.

For the situation today two cures are proposed: one, to drive out the whole concept of liberalism, the open hand, and set up a Dictatorship of Labor, the clenched fist, in its stead; and the other, to strengthen the grip of the existent dictatorship by the banks, driving out what original liberalism yet remains to us and, by thus officially recognizing Credit Monopoly with its familiar trends, place Fascism definitely in control.

To escape these two and retain our present form of government, defective though it has proven in practice, and make it fully effective, I shall show that some such provision for the economic phase of it as Social Credit proposes is inescapable.

(Don't be fooled by the fiasco in Alberta, Canada. That had nothing to do with the ideas of Social Credit.)*

Let us avoid every thought for the moment of social this and social that, of land versus industry, of capital versus labor, of factory tyranny, mine brutalization, inadequate wages, the open shop, strikes, starvation, foul sweatshops, long hours, farm failures, squalor, despair, mental retardation, tuberculosis, syphilis, insanity—all the misery bred largely of our present condition. Put it aside if you can. "There are thousands hacking at the branches of Evil to one who is striking at the root," today as in the time of Confucius. The argument has been reduced to the simplest terms possible, to what in revolutionary times was called "freedom versus tyranny." I shall try to keep it there as I proceed. (My own part is taken from the experience of the artist.)[a]

Let me acknowledge, and it is an important point, that the original conception of a revolutionary America, in the minds of such agitators as Samuel Adams, Freneau and some others, was not very different from the objective of those advocating a classless society today! This was furthermore a direct inheritance from the America conceived as a commonwealth on board the Mayflower in Provincetown harbor when articles were drawn up and signed before the arrival at Plymouth. No attempt should be made to avoid such facts. These things were large in the minds of the founders.

At the same time, and this is equally important with the first part, there were some things which those men, the founders, would not do, a determination *not* recognized in the present-day advocacy of a classless society. They vowed to live in equality but to live and let live in such a way as to respect the freedom of others. And this was just as strong a principle with them as the first. The thrust toward America itself, like the lesser thrust of Roger Williams away from the Massachusetts Bay Colony toward Rhode Island, presupposes a respect for personal liberty which is basic. So from the history we have side by side: equality and liberty.

That was America in the conceit of the founders; it has been America and is still America in the imagination of Americans. It relies on the individual. And this reliance on the individual was inevitable and extremely useful in a pioneer society resting as it must have done on direct effort against primitive conditions. It produced much—both for itself and the world at large.

But in the belief of some, it went too far. This is without question true. By what shall we measure?

There is but the one test. At first and for a long time unrestricted individualism was a social asset of the first order, it was pro-social. If it has gone too far it is because now it has become anti-social. There is no other test and that is final—whether it be applied to the avowed criminal or the monopolist who deprives society of a necessity except at exorbitant cost for private gain.

Without question unrestricted individualism has proven really defective in our practice and not just alone today. Our history proves it. We started crooked, as a nation—under heavy stress, the weakness of the Confederation, the disorder of the currency after the Revolution, the danger of new foreign wars giving Hamilton his chance. The democratic prinicple in economic affairs fought hard to preserve itself useful and intact but succumbed in the end to Hamilton's successful drive for an industrial autocracy and consequent economic centralization under narrow control. From that time on economic freedom of the individual was a lost cause.

Freedom of the individual, however, at least in theory, remained the essential basis of traditional Americanism. (The danger of the present is that general liberty shall be taken away in the attempt to curb the unrestricted play of individualism—as if there were no other cure.)ᶜ Kill the goose—for the good of the barnyard. Very well. But it will be unfortunate if in sacrificing the individual unduly to society as a whole, we do ourselves a lasting injury by limiting that creative power upon which society may be wholly dependent. Might it not be wiser or even absolutely essential to our social effectiveness to preserve him and turn him again toward correct procedure—the basis for judgment being always the same, his social serviceability.[1]

(May not these failures of individuals, perhaps, be enumerated, studied, and provided against? Nail the faults, one by one, in order, if possible, to separate those characteristics of the individual which are reprehensible and to be discarded from others without which society cannot continue to exist.)ᵈ

We must find precisely where this creature went out of control, at the same time preserving, if possible, our traditional basis for social regenerative power in a free creative opportunity for him.

This would be a tremendous service in history but our history (has been bastardized,)ᶜ suppressed and badly taught. (Out of it is coming today that our means of distribution as a nation have been segregated from the start. The problem must be taken up again, piece by piece. A scheme must be found that aims directly at these defects. No other scheme will do.

History is the basis and should rightly be so. It stands to be built upon, not ignored—to be suffered again. A scheme must be found that will not subvert it, but answer its questions.)ᶜ

(The process of historical restudy will be a slow one and difficult but the results should not prove illusory. It may delay the millennium—but that will never be attained by sacrificing the foundations to expediency and taking the matter up later.)*
(Organization will whip disorganization—every time. The closed fist will beat the open hand—but the truth is the truth for all that, as Marianne Moore says. The wave may wash over it if it will—it is still there.

---

[1]Williams added the following, handwritten footnote to this statement in draft (f): "This is correct when we are thinking of the individual in the capacity of administrator. In the realm of policy, however, his supremacy and freedom are the essential basis."

It is still there in the arts. It is a basis of the arts. You can't use great art as propaganda—or any art. It will resist it.

You can't plow with a closed fist, or even feed yourself. You can't play anything but the drum with it. It is good for one thing only—to attack.)[a]

(It is not within the scope of this paper to initiate a study [of history]. The present purpose is rather a direct attack upon a certain class of individual, the artist, in his relation to society, to gather from this whatever I can of the individual in general and his social relationships.)[*]

(No one seems to have examined the qualities of this individual sufficiently whom it is planned to sacrifice for the benefit of the state—yet for whose benefit all the drastic measures of the state as a power are ultimately designed.)[c]

The very type of the rugged individual is who? Lenin, Mussolini—and my grandmother. Do we realize or distinguish properly what the discussion is about? Rugged individualism is not damnable because it is rugged or because of qualities inherent in the individual as an individual—but solely because, under certain circumstances, such qualities become anti-social in their effect. The very mergers of small businesses into great ones that constituted the formation of the first American trusts, the objective evidence of individual effort, and for which old-fashioned Capitalism was pilloried, had *up to a point* a well acknowledged and highly valued social function.

There is no conflict between the individual and society—unless the individual offend.[1] None but a fool contends that the function of society is to generate surpassing individuals, as it has been sneeringly said. That is antiquated reasoning. The truth is nearer and harder, merely that society, *to be served,* must generate individuals to serve it, and cannot do otherwise than to give such individuals full play—*until* or unless their activities prove anti-social.

---

[1]Williams used this paragraph, and selected subsequent ones, in his essay "The Basis of Faith in Art," where he appropriately placed them in quotation marks, remarking that he was citing from material he had written "for another purpose." See *Selected Essays,* pp. 193–195.

And if the demand is for bread. He too needs bread.

Society must and will and has always helped its servants to retire at the proper moment—whether it be the defeated general, the discredited statesman, the woman who has lost her beauty or the diseased mind. Heartlessly society discards them, and rightly so—but heaven help the society that fails to discard the heel, the sycophant liar who serves it only to flatter command—and yet does away with the useful dissenter.

But that function of society, to discard the anti-social individual, must be strengthened and enlarged to include also the more recent forms of anti-social power. That's where the overwhelmingly destructive arm of society should deal its blow, not against the individual because he is an individual and insists on remaining so.

(Society and the individual. I am trying to define this individual in the face of society, trying to defend his essential freedom as a social asset of the highest sort without which society itself will perish—and trying to put the problem of what is to be done with this individual on a sound basis.

This individual might be a poet—or an artist of some sort. Why not? They burn books and turn poets into propagandists if they can. So I have chosen to examine one of these for the wanted evidence— an individual of the genus Individual: one man.

I chose him, an artist, a writer, because he is strong, the type of subject wanted. He only can do what he does. But also because his life and doings come within my personal experience.

Let me begin by asserting that individual genius is the basis of all social excellence whether as inventor, organizer, or governor.)[c] And in defense of the artist as my specimen I say at once that the conception of him as a foam thrown off at the crest of a laboring society is thoroughly false and thoroughly orthodox.

That a wealthy and corrupt society indulges, conceivably, in the purchase of costly art works at the expense of the starving poor has no relation, I think we must agree, to the aspirations, accomplishments or the importance of the artist himself.

No matter what happens to his works, the artist is the truthfullest scribe of society that is found when he is left free. And if his works are purchased by corrupt or tyrannical fools or institutions, nevertheless, in those very works of art are likely to lie the disruptive seeds which will destory the very hosts who have taken them in—and preserved them for society even against their will.

(The artist is thus misled when he abandons his work as a freely thinking and acting individual, to fight a battle in which he is a tyro while neglecting a fight in which he is an expert. It is poor economy and poor social philosophy for him to do so.)ᶜ

The artist's success as an individual is to be judged in the end not by the purchasers of his work but inexorably *by society*—by society as a whole, the great being great only as society accepts and enthrones them. For what are men to do with themselves once they have been fed? The artist must be their preceptor.

(Thus I offer the poet's life as evidence against conscription by society and governmental dictation.)ᶜ It is essential to good government that the poet, as an individual, remain at liberty to possess his talent, answerable to no one *before the act* but to his own truth.

On the other hand he *is* answerable to society for his survival and he knows it, has no other returns for what he does and is goverend thus not indirectly by a political agency before the act but *directly* by society itself after the act. In this men differ from bees and ants since with man society must wait upon the individual and not the other way around. Therefore, Man.

(Society seldom recognizes this essential relationship between itself and the individual typified in the artist whose works, at their best, have always been strong social forces, one way or the other.)ᶜ

To the point is the case of the young Russian physicist, a brilliant man, who, working at Cambridge, England, among the equipment he needed and which was to be found there only, had pushed forward an important salient of scientific work with which he was concerned. Returning to Russia for a visit he found himself, much to his sorrow, detained there by the government for its own purposes. Naturally the advanced work he was doing in England came to an end forthwith. But the state needed him and took him.

Of course no one can say that it is not the privilege of society to attack such a man and to conscript his ability if it can. But it is unquestionably that man's duty, at the same time, to resist to the limit such a seizure—*on the grounds* that his work at Cambridge was more socially valuable, over a long reach, to Russia as to England, than that for which he was taken, and that no one is fitted to determine this so well as he.

Poe is not to be made to write pro- or anti-slavery doggerel. Society would lose largely were this so. His significance lies in his power to fix, recordize, reassert in cryptographic form (only vaguely sensed at the moment as greatness—but full of accurate meaning for all that) to make a cryptogram of his time, in form and content—with the passionate *regenerative force* of the artist underlying it.

Not seeking to compete with the great formulators of ideas, (the Cushing journals, the voluminous Veblen's and others) of his day he, the poet, at his best will see and enclose in the hard nut of the fruit, in the invention of his forms, the whole contemporary history.

Who shall tell him how or what he must write? His very function as a servant of society presupposes his ability to see clearly beyond the formulations of his day and to crystalize his findings in a durable form for social confirmation, that society may be built more praiseworthily.

He will be the critic of government whether the party in power like it or not.

(Shall I not eat because the government or the times do not like me? Or be compelled to write what I am told to do—after a rigid scheme of musts and don'ts like the contributors to the *Saturday Evening Post*— instead of what I do at my best? I mention the particular agent since such agencies, of which that is an example, are reflections, very definitely, of the type of government at any moment.)[d]*

What can society, as an organism, know of the compunctions, exigencies or incentives involved in composition? All it can know is what it can use or wishes to use at the moment. If it does not care for what is produced, it can do nothing but destroy it. It does not even know what it is destroying. That which it destroys may well be the seed of its own possible regeneration. Only the individual can know these things. To save itself, day in, day out, it must find a way to let the unappraisable creation of the individual survive its own destructive powers until reasonably brought to trial. It must preserve the liberty of the individual even if it involve the destruction of the very form of society extant at the time in order to do so. (This only the philosophy of Social Credit envisions and provides for.)ᵃ

(Dictatorship has learned recently by hard lessons to respect the imperatives of the machine, rigid to the last decimal. So with the individual provided only that his activities be not anti-social in their effect.)ᶜ

The government, if it be a government, should, socially conscious, serve *me*, protect me by guaranteeing me liberty to exist because, as a writer, I do not write books like those in the Drug Store Circulating Library at the corner—or the equivalent under some other governmental setup than ours. A rebel in a Jeffersonian sense, the individual must always be—like Galileo, even like Henry Ford, if society is to advance to its goal of the greatest good for the greatest number.

And the process is ancient and dynamic—that is to say, constantly operative under all conditions. All the best has been maintained in spite of government *as a limiting power*. Not *against* government, *not* against government but against usurpation of government by a class, a group, a set of any sort, king, bureaucracy or *sansculotte*—which would subvert the freedom of the individual for some temporary need.

(It is necessary now in the development of my thesis to speak of myself[1] : as an artist writing under the regime under which I have grown up.

For the past thirty years I have never been able to get one first-rate poem published in a commercial magazine. I have never been

---

[1]Williams refers directly to himself only in draft (a); later he went over this section and changed all references to himself to "he" and "an artist." In draft (c) he presents the account as a "specific case history." All references are in the third person. In later drafts this section is omitted entirely. Since Williams is in fact very clearly referring to his own case I have considered it appropriate to follow the practice of the uncorrected first draft.

able to get a single book of poems, no matter how small, published except by paying or partly paying for it myself or having it published by a friend or a group of friends. I say nothing as to the excellence or lack of it in the poems themselves other than this, that they are different in character from the volumes upon volumes of verse commercially published in that time and that the intention has been to make them accurate to the day, in form as well as content, to the full of my ability regardless of their commercial availability.

They did not sell, they were not bought, because the market for them did not exist. It showed the business acumen of the publishers. But it also revealed a situation offensive to my good sense as a man and repulsive to my hard won craftsmanship as an artist. And it is always so under the compulsion of a government based upon false values. ((To this, then, I am opposed, therefore I am opposed to that which has enforced this intellectual and moral code on my day and locality, the defective government, which permits, unopposed, such a state of affairs to exist. I maintain that the quality of individual effort as well as taste is to a large extent the reflection of the government that exists at the time.))c The sole criterion today as to a book's value is this, "Will it sell and pay a dividend?" No, mine would not. That makes them neither good nor bad. It merely indicates that even to get printed they must meet a false standard— one for which they were never intended.

Very well, it may be said that I have succeeded in spite of such a publishing setup. I have. But my success damns ((the conditions I have had to face. Shall I run from them to Oxford? But that is beside the point.))c

What I want to show is that an artist, as the type of a person who is creative, who has something to give to society, suffers necessarily under a present system of government, seen or unseen, ((enforcing an exaggerated, and almost exclusive, emphasis on the getting of money—perhaps a stimulus to the shrewd and the hardy—but as a method brutal and wasteful to real social benefit))c: as he must suffer under a dictatorship by any power or government which takes an *a priori* rule over him, forcing him to add or create by code to social betterment through a rigid limiting of his incentives— either by not publishing him or by driving him out, even burning his books.

When the technical flaws in the present economic system were demonstrated—and in the face of the petty tyranny already forced on me by those advocating a dictatorship by a mass group of the labor forces—the conceptions of the Social Credit outlook seemed to offer me an opportunity to live: an understandable, reasonable and present-day basis for continuation of my life as an artist—fastening upon the tradition of all art upon which I have trained myself to continue to build.

[The artist] has first to speak the truth. Second to share the truth in such a form that the form itself will be an image of what is said. So that not the least stroke will be amiss or redundant. Third, that the truth, as Ibsen said, becomes a lie every twenty years, and must be reborn in a new form every generation: significant form.

It is an image of the times then, in relation to other times, that the artist is attempting. And a continual, agelong criticism of past times to suit the necessities, the discoveries, the total knowledge, the greater release of the human spirit that each age seeks to add to the last. He begins in rebellion against a material through which shines the genius of the past—today not to be captured. He works with his own faulty materials and tries to recreate, in his day, the same glories, and to increase them.

But it is, in fact, a poem, so many words inscribed on a piece of paper. Language, our own everyday speech. The speech analysed for its variance from a classic norm, all the colors, the "defects" which give it its character of today. Its variations from the pace, the meter, as American varies from English. Our way of speaking. This is part of its social imperative.)[a]

[The artist, then,] must admit all classes of subject to his attention, even though he hang for it. This is his *work*. Nothing poetic in the feudal, aristocratic sense but a breaking down, rather, of those imposed tyrannies over his verse forms. Technical matters, certainly, but most important to an understanding of the poet as a social regenerator. The facts are enclosed in his verses like a fly in amber.

(I want to show that this is an important consideration for government. I want to show that this will not be understood by government, perhaps, but that it is of the very essence of government itself—as art is the test, the beam of the scales, relative to any government under which it exists.)ᶜ It is nothing that can be compelled. It is difficult. Its realization requires all a man's energies. It requires his life—and it will not be popular. You can't eat it or sell it. There is nothing a man can do but make it—slowly, piecemeal; go on perfecting it to the glory of society at large as long as he lives. If he can keep living.

(This attitude toward the arts, the most humane attitude possible, no philosophy of government at present operative in the world respects. It is not respected, in effect, by the monopolistic set-up of present-day America—whose symbol in writing has been mentioned. And it is not respected by the dictatorships of the various types operative elsewhere in the world.

This is a single, perhaps somewhat special example, of the subversive effects of government on the individual, but it is valid for all that. All governments, nowadays, assert that they are ultimately for the benefit of society. I say that in this instance their effect is quite the opposite from the claim. And I do not believe their final objective will be obtained by subverting that same objective at the beginning in order to attain it. A retreat is sometimes necessary but it should be acknowledged to be a retreat. It is a Jesuitical fallacy to believe that an end can be obtained by first denying it—as Spain is proving to us today, and Mexico also.

Be careful, suspicious, of temporary measures which subvert the published intent, [which advocate] the suppression of liberty in order to obtain it. It is impossible to gain a liberty by a tyranny. The ultimate purpose being peace, violence is believed to let it in. A war to end war is newspaper stuff.

Rather one should follow the attitude of Rembrandt, who went to live in the ghetto of Amsterdam rather than submit to coercion, and who, when he was commissioned to paint the Fusiliers painted a *picture,* not an agglomerate portrait of the members of the company themselves, recognizable by their wives and cousins. A picture. And for it had his masterpiece nearly rejected, hung in a dark hallway—for posterity.)ᶜ

(The artist is the type, his philosophy that [which] accepts only those who write well, paint well—who accepts Japanese, Singhalese, Jew, Russian on the only possible footing—that he is an artist: that is the only possible intelligent philosophy. And it can only live under a rule that recognizes the same philosophy.

Now that I am older, will the new gangs publish me? No—unless I specifically mention a piece of propaganda which, in the structure of the work, in essence (a poet's business) has been refined, purified—made into a poem.

Blocked coming and going. But not by the philosophy in back of Social Credit, which recognizes the pertinence of contemporary excellence.

It is the only peaceful [philosophy], insuring peace, the only thoroughly intelligent solution to our difficulties, the only modern, scientific solution using all the agencies of the best thought and effort of today, the only solution that does not depend upon brute force, medieval division of class against class—the best that can be done. As it is the only solution consistent with the history of the artist's world, since it only respects individual liberty as the basis of the state.

Society as a mass initiates nothing, it merely consumes.)ᵃ And by that seems to produce wealth, opportunity. But all initiative remains still with the individual. Society can have only one function relative to him, that it terminate his efforts when they become antagonistic to the group, anti-social; nothing more.

(Therefore it behooves society to preserve, as its very life, the individual which it must milk as it milks a cow to eat and to drink. All its best collective efforts must be given to *serve* that man,)ᶜ (to liberating that individual from other burdens and freeing him to do his exclusive originating. We are not bees born only to lay eggs or fertilize them or collect honey. It is the one outstanding human trait that we are unpredictable, variable.

It is ridiculous for me to pronounce such ex cathedra statements *except* as results of observation from experience, whether as a poet or a physician—as ridiculous as it is for an individual to propound a theory and to drive it through or have someone else drive it through, regardless of the past. The past is older and not to be dislodged. I can only say that to me this has been true. Therefore I offer it as evidence—for the judgment of society. As I offer in passing, that when society shall prejudge how a physician shall

behave relative to his patient and prescribes a code, it will succeed
only in making an official of him and not a better doctor. It must
judge *after* the act—it can do no more than remove him, as it did
kings, when he is useless or offensive to them as a body.)[a]

Except for the individual, society is a body without a head. But it
is the head that is of chiefest value. To regulate by decree what the
individual must do reduces that initiative, upon which society relies
for its continual readaptation to circumstances, to its least effective
potency.

Society as an organism is on a far lower biologic plane than one
man. In fact, unless appended to the individual, it has a mere
vegetative function. It takes no responsibility relative to either the
individual or itself—and can take none. (Responsibility is a purely
individual attribute.

But, if, as we might say, society takes the full responsibility
before the act—though it is never society as such that does so—it
reduces the man to some extent to the mentality of the servant if not
the slave, which, look at it how you please, is not his highest
condition. It reduces a man's responsibility to his own acts. It makes
him a soldier.

But society, like the army, takes no responsibility for any one
man—it merely places responsibility in him under certain conditions.)[c] (Someone is always responsible. Curious how in etymology
certain truths will lie embedded. Some *one* bears the responsibility—not society at large—a dictator, a general. It should be rather a
great number of individuals in a free community.)*

Always the individual, society always under his hand. But
responsibility vested in one man, or a few men, reverses the
pyramid and attempts to balance it on its point. Whereas responsibility vested in many free men puts society on its proper solid basis
for survival.

That's the answer. It cannot be predicted how society itself will
or shall go in the future, any more than it can be told, before the act,
how any useful activity in the world is likely to turn. But in any case
the individual must be conserved at his fullest potency—a free man.

All the great additions to knowledge, all great acts, have
originated in the head of one man or one woman. If at such a time

society has made up its mind in advance as to what is good and what is bad, according to some accepted code, it will persecute and seek to destroy that man as an imposter. As it would have destroyed Galileo or Lenin, whose dynamic determination, at all costs, to achieve that personal liberty of belief upon which society must always fall back for its regeneration, triumphed nevertheless.

(What is the heresy that shall *save*, not destroy the good in any setup? Certainly we may be sure it lies there in Marxism as in the present Credit Monopoly of the world that dominates other governments.

That heresy rests with one man, it is his sense of responsibility that brings it out and makes him fight and die for it. It is a wise society that does not make him die for it. It is a better society that provides for such heresies in the freedom of the individual, who constitutes its head, not his domination by code as [a controlled society] would by making poets write propaganda or doctors work under political domination.)[a]

(It is characteristic of today that there must be a blanket reform of everything. You must not think. You must do, with a sweep—knocking everything down for the one thing. Our forms are antiquated—this poetry also teaches—but to smash everything is to learn nothing. Life is and must be continuous—for if it disappears we have no way of recreating it. So that we must always build upon the past, replacing the obsolete with the new. If we lose that basis which lies embedded in history we must remake it—or degenerate—a task which might prove impossible once the continuity had been lost.

A great virtue of the Social Credit philosophy is that it provokes thought, not limits it, buttresses the individual by insuring his economic competence so long as the state lasts—relieves him of being subject to the whims of either right or left: so long as he serve the state by bringing his powers to the full.)[c]

Responsibility is the key word. (As it recedes from the individual to be concentrated—perhaps under stress—to narrower bounds, you endanger more and more the social structure upon which the state rests most secure.)[c] You cannot take responsibility away from the individual without vitiating him in some way. It is to kindle that, as his highest attribute, to make it socially effective that the individual must be free, above all else, to go his unpredictable way. Even savagely against the setup of society as it exists in his time if must be.

It is one of the most admirable characteristics of the French that they permit differences to exist side by side among them, not peaceably, to be sure, but with the greatest native tolerance. And it may well be the French who will show us, as Jules Romains said on his recent arrival here, that with the dominance of the Left in the Chamber of Deputies it may be possible to bring over and adopt for France many of the socially advantageous achievements of Communism in Russia—without the misfortune of a stupid and bloody revolution and subsequent dictatorship by one group or another.

Should they do so, however it come about, the socialization of credit must be their first move (, the currency reform so intelligently invented and advocated by Major Douglas, to which Communism and Marxism—as at present set up—have not the ability otherwise to attain)[a].

To sum up—having spoken of the individual in his relation to society at large and the necessity for preserving his freedom, I have shown him beset, as at present in the United States, from the right by a virtual dictatorship through economic forces centered in Credit Monopoly, which blocks every move to socialize the means of exchange, subsidizes bad writing, and places the cultural stress on false values. And on the left by a threat from a diminishingly numerous group of labor threatening a dictatorship from that side. In either case, the freedom of the individual would at once disappear under the success of either at winning overt power.

Between—very much threatened and harassed—stands the traditional American policy of individual freedom—if it exists at all today. By that, government must be seized again, taken back into responsible hands—which means in this case the control of our credit—in the sense of Jackson who said—when he was defending the national treasury against the First Bank of the U.S.—that the safest place for a man's money was in his pants pocket.

To regain democratic control over our credit—unlawfully seized and held by the banks today—a definite means has been found in the proposals designated Social Credit.

(There's nothing miraculous or demagogic or easy about it—any more than there is in the recipe for the making of good beer or keeping a business solvent. It takes work, attention to detail, clean vats, and accurate books carefully attended to gain those ends. That is its difficulty and its soundness.)ᶜ

And though the most apparent feature of the Social Credit philosophy may make it appear little more than a currency measure, that is merely the pricking point in an economic-social attack of far more extensive and significant proportions.

(It is the effect, the visible effect and advance point of a social attack—the bayonet into the bowels of the problem, a matter of control of the means of exchange, the equable distribution of the collective products of society. As a philosophy it stands on the firm, if endangered, ground between ((fascism—in this country only definable as Credit Monopoly, in the hands of a select group, seeking control of government—))ᵃ on one side and dictatorship by labor— ((a Proletarian Revolution seeking to win government by force of arms if necessary for a classless society limiting freedom—))ᵃ on the other, from both of which the abolition of personal liberty must be immediately expected once they succeed in their purposes.)ᶜ

No use to wink the danger. (There are powerful forces involved.)ᶜ

A labor revolution by a society seeking to be in fact classless is both great and traditionally American in its appeal. Its strength lies today in a continued need for the bare necessities of life by tens of millions of the inhabitants of this wealthy nation as well as the emotional appeal of brute action to all degrees of intelligence which might be involved. To violently effect, by a brave stroke, the ejection of an inhuman and anti-social domination by those who have an effective control over the means of our common livelihood for their private gain—would appeal to the American character if once put into motion.

But this narrowing of the attack to a fanatical and static fixation on a class war—that permits no thought but one (:Are you for or against the Revolution)ᶜ—has a palpable and glaring defect: the immediate intention to suppress all liberty of thought so characteristically American, once power should be assumed.

It would ignore also, this projected Revolution, the nature of the battle which when one speaks of "the Revolution" is left undefined and has perhaps, in recent years, gone somewhat stale in a changing world. (I have been blamed for calling the whole modern revolutionary project static. Definitely this is so, since thought concerning it seems to have stopped long since. Under the fixation toward direct action the character of whatever revolution is possible has altered greatly since the Manifesto of 1848[1]—though not in the minds of those who seem most to advocate it. It has altered with the change of labor conditions in the world from a simple intent to seize capital to a far more complex fight for control of power—very shifty and hard to trace to its lair.)[c]

After all, a revolution, like any other mechanism or exercise of power, has a gist, a basis, a rationale—must have an accuracy and finely aimed direction to *win*. And this has changed with time, as knowledge has increased and power has taken the place of labor and credit the place of capital.

This gist *is* the control of power by credit—in all states alike, whether affected or unaffected by revolution, past, present or future. The force of the Social Credit philosophy is a clear-sighted envisioning of this gist of a perhaps necessary revolution which some of the ardent fighters for it seem to have lost sight of.

Is a man for or against the Revolution? The answer is, first, What revolution? And after that has been defined, then, certainly *not* for violence, bloodshed and a resultant tyranny if by the exercise of courage and acute intelligence the end can be obtained otherwise.

(And who is so unmodern as to say that with the proper *knowledge* this is impossible?)[c]

Or if it be true that only by bloody combat can great changes in the governments of the world take place—that doesn't mean that by carnage they *will* take place. But even so, if the philosophy of Social Credit, at its worst, lacks the appeal, the basic emotional instinctive

---

[1] In draft (a) Williams refers to "the Manifesto of 1880," and in draft (c), the text used here, to "the Manifesto of 1884." Since there can be no doubt that Williams means Marx's and Engels's *Communist Manifesto* of 1848, I have changed the date accordingly.

and summative power of a clenched fist, it yet remains the heart of any real advance which by bloody fights or less drastic realization must come about.

Certainly no American by his history but would try first to come to some sort of agreement with the subversive social forces affecting him—as he tried first to do with England before the Revolution of 1775. But failing that, he will, reluctantly, turn to force rather than submit to subservience and domination by subtle mortgagors.

And certainly, as between a stroke for freedom by labor and fascism through Credit Monopoly, what American would not throw in his lot with labor, taking a chance on the result? But his reason for doing so, you may bet on it, would be solely his estimate of the chances for preserving his personal freedom thereby.

It is not easy to see the way through to national social regeneration. Nothing worthwhile is ever attained against odds except after violent struggle. But there were battles fought about the figure of George Washington more important to our condition today than Yorktown or Monmouth. The memorable engagement centering about the new Cosntitution, when Hamilton and Jefferson split the Cabinet of the first President, lost us the real fruits of the win from the resort to arms.

It may be the same again. But if the basis could have been grasped then—if the social demands Jackson later realized and fought for— the avenues that had been left open permitting the Biddle group to get hold of the public moneys under the guise of the First Bank of the United States—if such ways toward subtle tyranny by Credit Monopoly could have been foreseen and forestalled at the beginning by some such philosophy as Social Credit now proposes—the dearest fruits of the first Revolution could have been unending to this day.

Revolutions are not won by violence alone but by the accuracy of the thought back of them.

More has often been lost in a fight than gained. But the most is won when the grounds for it have been clarified to the utmost and only then fought for. Hence such a conference as this, here in old Virginia.

The philosophy of Social Credit is in many ways essentially a clarification of the whole situation affecting every phase of the modern social impasse—depending as it does on a liberation of the means of exchange. Its enemies are on two sides—each for his own reasons willing to gloss over the essential and inescapable facts.

It is the plain duty of the intelligence to insist on those facts.

An Afternoon with Tchelitchew

Life and Letters Today, 1937
A HOT JUNE afternoon, 1937. East 57th St., N.Y., studio apartment, 5th floor, rear. 5 P.M. The model about to leave, waiting,
before going home to her husband, to pour tea for us.

Any who would know and profit by his knowledge of the great
must lead a life of violent opposites. The deeper at moments of
penetration is his mastery of their work, the more vigorously at
other moments must he fling himself off from them to remain a man
himself. But if he himself would do great works also only by this
violence, this completeness of his wrenching free will he be able to
use that of which their greatness has consisted.

The failure to understand this condemns the perennial student
who has, in short, by a sort of sluggishness shown himself to have
succumbed to the effects of former greatness and not profited by it
to establish his own mastery. This is the banality of the academic,
maliciously called the cultivation of "tradition," maliciously because under it is implied an attack upon the "radical" who does not
submit himself to such respectable negation.

A man must know but he will not be told how he must know nor
submit to the terms of those who make knowledge no more very
often than self-denial in subservience to the academy, a series of
honorific symbols by which they seek to maintain dominance over
others who seek the substance at cost of the letter. But it is the man
who must be saved.

These convictions had come to life in the presence of
Tchelitchew's canvasses. Not a very "good" painter. He was
saying so himself, in deep respect for the sheer facility of the
Spanish and French moderns among his friends. He only wished he
might be able to handle his materials with their ease, their amazing
facility. He referred to the new sensations, to Dali especially.

They are my good friends, he said. Dali is a jeweler in paint. And he sees everything. He has eyes that stick out, like the eyes of a crab. And he eats the world of the eyes, like a crab. Numb, numb, numb, numb! And T. brought the fingers of both hands up before his mouth rapidly wiggling them toward his moving lips as if it was a crab or a lobster jiggling his mandibles and feeding. It is very beautiful, he said. But what are they doing? Sucking it in and passing it out again, their charming compositions. What do we care? They have eaten. We are very glad. There is nothing they do not eat, there is nothing they do not see. Such eyes! They make very fine compositions. That is the French influence.

Yesterday, he said, there was a woman here in the studio. A very rich old woman. Ooo! I did not dare offend her. She had on a hat with feathers and ribbons like—I can't describe it. Many many different colors. Like a parrot. And a dress! with a piece of lace, a piece of silk, a piece of blue, green—anything you can imagine. And she talked, cha, cha, cha, cha, cha, cha! all the time. Like a parrot. She was a parrot. Perfect.

It was amazing. It was bewildering. You would not believe there could be such a person. And she was interested. She wanted to see.

So I showed her the big canvas I am working on. This here. She looked and in her voice, like a parrot, she said, Oh Mr. Tchelitchew! you paint nothing but monsters!

The painting was before us. I looked at it for a long time. Nothing but human monsters of one sort or another. It was a canvas of perhaps eight by twelve feet. It wasn't finished, though most of it had been drawn in. Figures of all sorts filled it, of all sizes, spreading out upon a background of mountain, classical ruin, and Mexican adobe house, with sea and sky going off toward the top and back. Small in the center was the face of an old woman, a tormented, wrinkled face—as if under a lens; above that a sort of tennis court with naked figures on it under a glacier prospect made of ice-heads, infants packed in as though they were rounded ice cubes in a modern refrigerator—

To the left, the signature, a man with one enormous foot, the back of Diego Rivera it may be, painting the wall of a house. Siamese twins, women with six breasts, acephalic monsters, three-

5. Pavel Tchelitchew, *Phenomena* (1936–38). Oil on canvas, 79″ × 106½″. Collection, Tretyakoff State Gallery, Moscow.

6. Detail of the above.

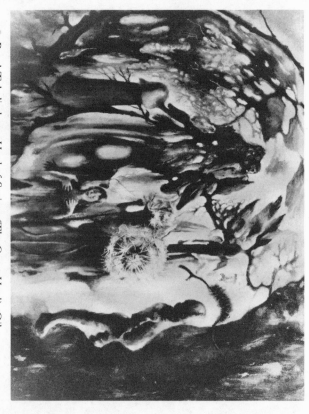

7. Pavel Tchelitchew, *Head of Spring (The Green Head)*. Oil on canvas, 20″ × 25″. Collection, Mrs. R. Kirk Askew, Jr., New York.

legged children, double-headed monsters, sexual freaks, dwarfs, giants, achondroplastic midgets, mongolian idiots and the starved, bloated, misshapen by idea and social accident—of all the walks of life.

In the foreground was a surf with a girl in a pink bathing suit. They ask me if it is surrealist! What do you think? he looked at me.

As a physician, no, I answered. And why not? Because these things are drawn from life, I said. You see that, you see that! he was delighted. Of course, you are a doctor. That is beautiful. He was delighted.

What is surrealism? Anybody can do that. What a lot of fooling nonsense.

As a fact every monster in the picture was authentic. It was actually what is found in life. He has taken things which do occur every day for his mirror. It is a mirror, he added, for them to see themselves.

Our life is horrible, he said. We are monsters. We hate each other and we try to destroy everything that is lovely. And we hide it. No. We *are* beasts—I beg pardon to the beasts. Even our language is distorted, we say we are like "beasts" who are lovely. But we are disgusting. And when I show them how disgusting they are they say, He only wants to paint monsters!

I don't want to paint monsters. Pretty soon I will be tired of monsters. I want to communicate with people. That is painting. The ancients knew what painting was. It is to say something. It is to communicate. It is to use beautiful colors because we love them. We enjoy what is lovely and we paint to speak of it. Because we want to tell somebody that we like this and they must see it because we like it.

That is why I want to paint everything soft. Because I love feathers and pearls and fluffy things that hold the light and split it into rainbows. I am a very poor painter. I cannot paint like those Spaniards. I work very hard but I go very slow. When I have filled these spaces—pointing to unfinished places on the picture—then I will work to get the texture I desire. I want to make it beautiful, everything the most delicate shading of the colors, light as a feather. That is why I have painted it as a double rainbow. Because the

rainbow is phenomenal. It is charming to me. I like it. I will paint it
that way.

Indeed all the figures in the picture, the monsters waiting to be
beautified of the softness and the colors were, as they occurred in
various parts of the picture, either green or red or purple or blue—
but the colors quite realistically modulated. As if they had been seen
toward evening here, at noon there, and at sunrise there, before a
storm, as it might be.

What do they mean by composition? There are half a dozen
compositions. Everybody knows them. What is that? They balance
here, there. What does it mean? Cézanne! Pooh. Yes, he could
paint a good composition. He knew how to paint colors. But what is
it? Another tree. Another orange. Another table with flowers.
What does it mean? Always the same. I am tired of that.

That is enough of that. He turned the big picture to the wall. Let
me show you some portraits.

Do you like this one? I paint my portraits all after I have made the
sketch, a year afterward perhaps. When I feel what I wish to see
and I know how to do it. This morning I painted this face of Edith
Sitwell all over. I could finish it today. What do you think?

It was a white-looking woman in a nun's habit. She was sitting as
if in a straightback medieval chair completely self-absorbed, ascetic,
rather severe. It was a shock to me after what I thought I had known
of the woman's verse.

She is like that, he said. A very beautiful woman. She is alone.
She is very positive and very emotional. She takes herself very
seriously and seems to be cold as ice. She is not so. I wanted to paint
her as I know her. What do you think?

I am glad to know her. I didn't know her. Never thought much of
her verse.

Oh, you don't know her then, he said. This will be your
introduction. You will see if I am not right. An amazing woman.

And these—this is Ford and his sister. He showed me the
portraits of the two young Americans. Their faces were made to
radiate the opalescent colors he loves. I looked back at the Sitwell
again. Her face I saw now was not white but all the colors of the

rainbow minutely blended, not *pointilliste*, but soft as feathers, as down.

You have seen enough painting, he said, for one afternoon. Next year you shall see the big one—when I have been able to finish it. You will see the difference. Every part of it must be done as I have done the face of Edith Sitwell—this morning. Delicate and soft, with all the colors of the rainbow. You will like it then.

Cache Cache

View, 1942

I IMAGINE the angels will have forgotten, by that time, whether they had been niggers, archbishops—or even the sex of their parents. Memory will not be their occupation, they will have escaped it or escaped all its less significant details. When they look at the new pictures of those who remain artists among them they will seek qualities more mineral than protoplasmic, to be graded as they repel, absorb, or transmit light.

But we—are full of memories and the best we can do is to seek in them for the luminous. As Tchelitchew says: Every picture has a heart of light, a mind and—remains a composition on a flat surface revealing too much. Cache cache! It is made of all that the painter should hide—of himself, of his times. It gives him away. It is shocking, disgraceful. It reveals him in his secret, perhaps, as very stupid. Not the details. These are beefsteak or something else quite as necessary. Nothing is shocking that you can see. It is what you cannot see that may be shocking. Or superb. The pure chemistry of insight, geometric, borrowed from a rotting memory, shall we say? revealed, crystalline, to the imagination. In words, a triviality. In a picture, an arresting possibility.

Raphael cannot be imitated unless we know and identify ourselves with the core of his secret. The secrets of Greek perfection, the concepts that made them as they were, are essential to the knowledge of one who would borrow from them. Raphael was a crystal sphere. His realizations are of the sphere, crystalline, transmitters of light. How can they be followed, even with every addition of contemporary paraphernalia, without that realization. Impossible! Each creator has as his base some such secret core. Unless we hit to the base of the underlying purity from which ALL a man's work emerges we produce—in trying to realize Raphael's purity and tranquility, his luminous quality of the sphere—the opacity and confusion of Ingres' scene in the harem.

A man, in America, surrounds himself with a forest, to be able to continue to desire to discover a means to exist. I gathered from looking about the penthouse studio—the seaweed, the stump, the muddy statue, the debris of all sorts from breaking and moss, that here was an indestructible something masquerading, for survival! under brokenness. Obscene as an eel. The Indians have cursed this country, he said. Sand and feathers. I am sure they have put a curse on it. Painting, deciphering, reassembling, clarifying, packing, packing, packing the sphere within the cube, the cube within the sphere. Tchelitchew does not treat lightly the tenets of magic and necromancy.

There is nothing recondite in this, nothing—What is the word used by the hemiplegics?—nothing esoteric! It is plain sense, like a tree. A seed is planted. Well, there it lies, in the ground. The ground is a man's life partaking of life as a whole. Tchelitchew saw a tree and made a sketch of it in England ten years ago. There it lies. Very childish, very naive. He says so himself. But it is a seed. Maybe it will grow, maybe it will die. In this case it grows. Five years later there is another sketch that has developed from the first. The seed did not rot. The tree is growing into a new area of the imagination. It was an old, gnarled tree to begin with. Now it is indulging in vagaries, it is getting new attributes that no other tree ever experienced. Children's faces, nine of them, are beginning to appear as outlines in the crotches between the trunk and the main branches. They have open mouths. The leaves, from the first red hands opening, through the extended full of the green maturity, to the mottled reds of winter approaching, assume their parts.

Tchelitchew would not let us see the picture. Cache cache! It is a large square canvas of a tree with a dandelion seed-head, a luminous sphere, growing under it. The picture is to be shown to no one until after he, Tchelitchew, has left the country. It speaks and he does not want to be present when it says what it has to say. By that time he will be in the tropics. He showed us only the sketches he had made over several years, sketches slowly evolving into the thing, the organization, the composition on a flat surface, the seed that has developed, the shocking discovery it holds, the fulfillment it signalizes, the confession, the sweeping out, the purification of memory it represents, the nostalgia, the skills, the contempt, the humor, the despair, the translucence—summarizing poetry, flattening out superficial differences and resemblances—overfelt details, details that catch the eye as the thorns on a blackberry bush catch the hand and the sleeve as we reach for the fruit.

The tree has become monstrous. Only in the monstrous do we approach the moon, the sun, and the stars! plant roots and the heart of a man. The imagination has horns and a tail, therefore we have created ourselves in that image. Tchelitchew has lifted the dry sphere of the dandelion seed-head also into the text of his picture. Monsters frequent the earth everywhere. Science is the accident and the accidental the true. Our very lives prove how we are bedevilled by the supernatural, we see it in everything especially in architecture. But if we run from these things we return to our childhood. Nobody can predetermine the secret of this tree, the tree of the artist's life or growing out of the upturned end of his left great toe, what difference? The world is monstrous, only the monstrous can be true of it. Or the world is not monstrous, only the monstrous can truly reveal that fatal error. The foot is for the shoe as the shoe is for the foot. Paint!

Either the picture portrays the core of a man or it is not a picture. Place your emphasis where you have the ability to place it. I speak out of my recollection of what Tchelitchew said. He has strong and substantial opinions concerning the relative merits of French and Italian painting. He laughs! If they knew *why* Giotto painted as he did! He saw first, then he painted what he saw. He saw nothing the way they wanted him to see it. He saw as little boys see who paint their thrilling anatomical concepts on the insides of water closet doors. Why did Giorgione . . . Why, why, why? You have to know those things. Seurat was completely unknown. He died at thirty-two and everything he attempted turned out to be a masterpiece. Why? He knew what he was doing. It remains a secret, a realization of the miraculous—on a flat surface, an effect of the light.

Some hands are silver, some of gold and a very few—very, very few! are like diamonds. But these are not of artists.

Good-bye Tchelitchew! be at home with your old friend to whom you can talk without the necessity of explanations. Walk barefoot in the sand to your heart's content. If you go broke, paper your walls with newspapers, upside down! V for victory. You are leaving us—this cold and damp New York that gives us stiff necks or dries the blood in summer with its baked concrete flame— forever! you say. You say you left Russia the same way, with nothing but a pocketful of pigments as your possessions. What you left there I don't know but you are leaving us, bespeaking your affection, this picture, a hidden treasure; so you mean it and so I accept it for the others. It is a great treasure to you and that is how you leave it. If no one wants to look at it, that's just too bad. It is your seed. You have signally honored our soil by wishing to plant it here.

This man is a monster, a very terrible monster. Cats have funny little faces, he says, but the faces of tigers are never funny. As soon as I have the opportunity I intend to look long and hard at the face of this, Tchelitchew's latest work. It is the labor of the last two years of his residence with us in New York. I know the monster revealed there will not be smiling. *Cache cache.* The gods are chasing the children along the edge of the sea below Positano, where the old priest in a gingham dress stands watching them from the cliff's edge.

Effie Deans

Not previously published, c. 1937

WHO THE DICKENS is Effie Dean? said Floss to me when I came in for lunch.

Got me, why?

The funniest thing happened this morning. I'll tell you about it. But who is Effie Dean?

Whyn't you look it up? As far as I know she must be—I don't know. I think it's some revolutionary heroine from the South, Georgia, something like that. What happened?

Oh it seems that you admired a picture years ago. A Mrs. Rumbold called up and wants to give it to you. Effie Dean. Let me look it up.

I've got to be more careful, I said. I'm always getting into trouble like that.

I love pictures. Nine times out of ten when I go into a house and have to wait a moment or two for whoever it is to appear, I begin looking around for pictures. And it's surprising how often I find interesting ones to look at, in the plainest households sometimes. This was I supposed another case of the sort. I hadn't any recollection of it whatever.

Don't you remember?

No.

Never shall I forget my embarrassment a month or two ago when I dropped in to see one of my best friends one evening with Floss and sat opposite a watercolor well-known to me and which I began at once to praise as I had often praised it formerly. It was a still life, red and green, straight up and down lines, two long bunches of pepper berries hanging among the foliage. It has always pleased me, that's all.

I always admire that picture, I said to my friend Stuart

128

Donaldson, whose grandfather had invented baking powder and once had an office on Maiden Lane.

Yes, said his wife. I know. That's yours. Stuart even has your name on it, across the back. We have no one to leave things to, so when we go we want you to have that picture. We always call it yours.

I could feel my face flush crimson, and swore on the spot never to audibly admire anything in a friend's house again.

As a matter of fact a physician often comes upon delightful *objets d'art* inauspiciously lighting the days and years of some obscure household in almost any suburban town—anywhere, everywhere on his rounds. All sorts of things which, if he is fortunate, he will share with his friends and acquaintances in praising. My own small town Rutherford is like any other in that.

So much is this so, that I have more than once amused myself making collections of rare and beautiful objects about the town, in my mind of course, that it is a pity so few can see to enjoy.

All are not prize pieces but what I see always has interest, sometimes charm and associational qualities of note and occasionally great beauty.

I mean not pictures alone but all sorts of things, furniture, fabrics, books, letters even, occasional pieces of jewelry such as my own mother's filigree earrings, all of greatest interest.

I know a woman who has ten of the most pleasing bed quilts her grandmother left her years ago. You just want to lift them and hold them in your hand they are so fine.

Why not, I have thought, why not, when some charitable object or project is to be financed, have a show! Have a show and gather together whatever we could dig up in a town such as ours. I'll bet you'd be surprised at the people that would come to see it. I began to enumerate.

It's too late now, they've moved away, but I remember a portrait of some member of the family Mrs. Morse had, painted by the great inventor. We could start there, a lovely thing, full-length. Floss and I have our own Demuths, the Sheeler still life, the New Mexico pastel of Hartley's, the Hiler—

The trouble would be the selection. What a battle! You'd have to have one person for that whose word would be law—to keep the junk out and make the necessary enemies. We could hold the show in the Woman's Club. Just the place, that big former millionaire's barn of brown stone. Partitions could be put up at small expense. Of course you'd have to insure everything, you'd have to engage a detective agency for protection . . . oh well.

But I think the interest would be keen. You could charge a quarter for admission. And it would be fun and funny as hell too. Run it for two or three weeks.

I've still got those two pictures in the attic painted by that little English woman, what was her name? wife of the dyer. Marvelous.

When I first saw those wildly efflorescent garden scenes I could not help but think of Rousseau Douanier. Mina Loy happened to be in Rutherford at the time and I took her to see them. You never saw such flowers! The canvas was made of nothing else. There was an arbor but it couldn't have been needed, the flowers were thick enough to stand by their own pressures. A wild imagination that made you want to laugh and cry in spite of yourself. We looked at it for a moment, then Mina broke the spell. She shook herself as if breaking a dream and said, What fools we are to stand here like this comparing them with Rousseau—

Certainly mother's portrait painted by Ludovic when she was in Paris in 1876, the Spanish headdress with a black mantilla, would have to be there.

But any number of girlish daubs, such as the waterfall dear old Mrs. Clanny had in her dining room, the water sliding sidewise off the rocks, have an interest. I always looked at it and always felt the same, an alarm, a feeling of uneasiness, waiting for the awful catastrophe from that unsupported river—

I think we could get a whole arsenal of Revolutionary firearms, muskets and pistols, swords and powder horns. Mrs. Kittredge alone could fill a whole room, her husband representing the first break in the family tradition of Dr. Kittredges, a line seven in a row from the first who was with the American forces at Bunker Hill. What a collection they have. Marvelous!

There's the low mahogany table, an unusual specimen because of

8. Charles Demuth, *Pink Lady Slippers.* Courtesy of the Estate of Florence
H. Williams.

9. Charles Demuth, *Flowers*. Courtesy of the Estate of Florence H. Williams.

10. Charles Demuth, *End of the Parade: Coatsville, Pa.* (1920). Tempera, 19½″ × 15½″. Courtesy of the Estate of Florence H. Williams.

11. Charles Sheeler, *Photos of an Old Dutch Farm*. Courtesy of the Estate of Florence H. Williams.

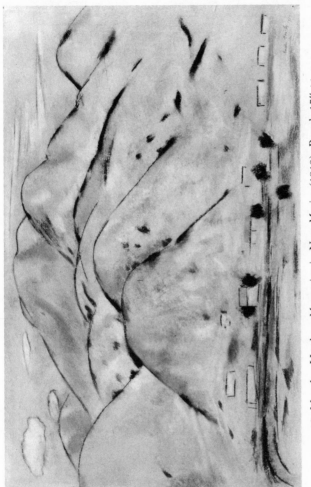

12. Marsden Hartley, *Mountains in New Mexico* (1919). Pastel, 17″ × 27¼″. Courtesy of the Estate of Florence H. Williams.

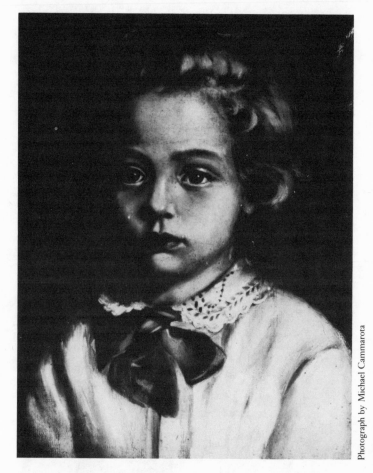

13. Hélène Williams, *Portrait of a Niece in Mayaquez.* Courtesy of the Estate of Florence H. Williams.

its height. The low sofa with the high back and the two cherubic young ladies with eyes that follow you about the room above it in their gold frame, pink cheeks and hair in clustering ringlets—deftly limned.

Mrs. Kittredge showed me a child's doll they would like to have at the Metropolitan Museum. And all sorts of small things, the candied glass paperweight, the watercolor drawing of the tombstone, weeping willows and names carved in the stone, which she keeps above the head of her bed.

And who has that other glass ball with something—some small metal object, an old British coin I think, pressed into the center of it when it was cooling. Who has that?

And Frances Fetterly's harmonium. Somebody else's old clock with its terrible ticking—Oh yes, Doris Hussey! of the Nantucket Husseys, and a bell on it that when it rings it's like a tenor in the opera!

And dear Mr. Ferry, the reformed gambler, and his things. What in the world has happened to his treasures? If only he had lived he would have given us the other pieces of that set of grey plush chairs and narrow sofa with the carved ornaments capping the backs, that come off in your hand when you try to lift the piece.

What things he had! The cracklewear, the sandwich glass—if I could remember half of them. Where are they now?

There's a beautiful spindle-backed colonial chair I sat in at the Buchanans' only yesterday. All pegged together and worn—I don't know what makes it look so satisfying and so different from today. The very pearwood cane that the old lady uses to knock on the floor with when she wants assistance, split all around where the grain has opened up with age, the brass ferule, the hart's horn handle, old as the nation.

We ought to get Elizabeth Heckman's two granduncles back again. I never passed them up—or their story, when I went there for a call. One was sour faced, in black, his mouth drawn down bitterly at the corners. He was the one who made the money. The other, his younger brother, in a blue coat, his cheeks suspiciously bright red, his head cocked back haughtily, his mouth curled upward with a smile. He it was who ate a ten dollar bill between two slices of his mother's bread to show his amusement and indifference. We'd have to have those.

Didn't Stockton write "The Lady and the Tiger" in Rutherford? Couldn't we have pictures of the Kipp house, the old stone house of the Kingslands, really delightful houses of the early Dutch and English settlers?

Oh and I remember the day I was crossing on the ferry. That was before they put the Hudson Tunnels through. I was parked toward the back of the boat. A middle-aged man came up to me, rather diffidently, and asked if I was going anywhere near Hackensack—where George Washington rested after the retreat from Fort Lee.

I said, Yes. Do you want a ride? Yes, he said and scrambled eagerly into the seat beside me.

I'm tired, he said. And broke. I've been walking the streets of New York all day. I'm a gilder by trade.

What?

A gilder. And he reached inside his overcoat and drew out a small object wrapped in cloth. Work like this, he said. It was a beautifully finished thing, a flower medallion finished in gold leaf flawlessly.

I used to do a good business, he said. I refinished the whole—some collection of paintings—at the Manhattan Storage House that had been there for years. A big job. I'm from Czechoslovakia. I make violins too. Refinish paintings. Could I do anything for you?

Well, I engaged him then and there to clean, varnish and regild the frame of a portrait my mother did of her little niece in Mayagüez in – the old days. He did a wonder job of it. Nothing better, and reasonable too, just ten dollars.

So Floss introduced him to an old friend of hers, Helen Van Buren, who has a number of old portraits black with age and in dull frames that need refurbishing. Among other things he discovered in Helen's house a pair of blackened bellows.

Let me fix these up for you, he begged. No. Let me just finish a corner of it, I'll charge you nothing. No. But they let him do a portrait. They were amazed at the result. Had no idea it was so lovely.

He pleaded for the bellows, a large broken pair, that had been lying there for years. I think not. I can't spend that much on such old things.

Let me try. So they let him have the bellows to clean up finally. They almost fell over in a faint when he brought them back again. They were a pair given by the French Ambassador to President Van Buren during his administration. A most beautifully painted and gilded work of art. We'd have to have that in our show.

Indian arrowheads and stone war clubs galore. The Sullivans have a bronze tomahawk, beautifully engraved, made I think in England but a very early piece of work. I've never seen anything to equal it. And we had a small piece of Aztec work in stone in the house somewhere for years. It seems to me it was of granite, very low, for pounding pigments on. I remember that as a child. I wonder where it is now.

And the marvelous double clay flute that Mr. Hooper showed me and the clay medallions, and figurines each wrapped in tissue paper, Maya work. Of course, they'd have to be skilfully exhibited. I'll bet you I could get Edith Halpert to do it for us, just for the interest of it. She's that kind.

That's right, the Early Americana—my Lord! Stuff they threw away. Glazed paper decorations in black frames. Pictures of fruit, the things the Yearances had here on the farm long even before Van Buren was a boy. They used to call them ugly and put them up in the attic when the golden oak craze came in. Priceless, or at any rate fascinating now. Crudely drawn bananas, grapes, peaches.

Stuart has a lifelike peach, I saw just two weeks ago, lying beside a small pool of water and reflected there. Amazingly real. All these things would get new life if they were cleaned—by such a man as my Czech—and the frames touched up. Like Drew Spence's portrait of his great-grandfather—who owned from 47th to 57th St. and 10th Ave. to the river—if he weren't so damned Scotch about it.

And fabrics! that sixteen-foot bedspread Mable Leeds gave us, bless her heart, all woven of white linen in flowers and fronds. They wanted to make two of it but she said she'd rather give it away than see it cut. That *would* make a display.

And Drew Spence's Paisley shawls. His great-grandfather on

the other side designed and printed them. He has all the careful pencil patterns too, still there. Marvelous detail work—with a letter of thanks from Catherine the Great for the one he sent her.

The late Dr. Minor's collection of minerals, superbly brilliant. That alone would fill a room. But the works of art would have to come first. Manuscripts, shells, butterflies. Our own very delightful Audubon which Ed Brown gave me once out of the kindness of his heart—

You're wrong, said Flossie. Do you know who Effie Deans was— it's Effie Deans, not Dean. Listen! She was the sister of Jeanie Deans, the heroine of Sir Walter Scott's tale, *The Heart of Midlothian.* She murdered her own child and was condemned to death but Jeanie went on foot to London and obtained a pardon for her from the queen. She later married her lover and became a lady of the court.

But what about it?

Well, said Flossie, it seems that once some years ago you admired the picture.

Yes.

You didn't know it but it was this Mrs. Rumbold's prize possession. She adored it and nobody else in her family ever cared for it at all. In fact they didn't want it around. So when you admired it, she was delighted.

It must have been lost sight of after that, for yesterday she went down in the cellar for something and without knowing it she stepped on Effie, lying frameless on the cellar floor. It nearly broke her heart.

She went to the phone at once and called you up. She was almost crying. She didn't want to blame anyone, she said, but she knew who had done it. Someone had taken Effie from her frame, she thought, to steal the frame and glass and Effie had been tossed on the floor without a thought.

Will Dr. Williams take her? she said. I want Effie to have a good home. I don't want to die and think that Effie is neglected. If he will take her and keep her I want him to have her. I'll never forget how he spoke of her years ago. It meant so much to me.

Can't you remember it? said Floss.

Can't for the life of me, I said. But there must be something good or unusual about it. Tell her I'll take care of Effie. Call her up and promise her that we'll do whatever she wishes. Dear old gal.

What a show we could make of it!

Of what? said Floss.

Oh I was just thinking.

Walker Evans: American Photographs

The New Republic, 1938
THIS IS an 8 × 9 book of 95 photographs on glazed paper taken in the eastern part of the U.S. during the past seven years by a man named Walker Evans, a record of what was in that place for Mr. Evans to see and what Mr. Evans saw there in that time.

(This is a good work, a pleasure to the eye and a satisfaction to the intelligence. I'm glad for us that the pictures are of America instead of being just good pictures, because being so particularly of that place makes them universal. Gives them currency.)ʸ (Permits us to some extent to deal with all places. Enhances the value of other places for us.)ʸ*

In a work of art (and I should say that these pictures are works of art)ʸ* place is everything.

Evans's photographs represent, as Lincoln Kirstein says in his notes to the book, a straight puritanical stare—though not entirely without humor. There is much in them strongly reminiscent of the early practitioners of the photographic art. The composition is of secondary importance in these clear statements. Their beauty permits little of that.

The book is in two parts about evenly divided between portraits and architecture, the products and remains of a life that is constantly in process of passing. The range is from *Parked Car, Small Town Main Street,* 1932, to *Tin Relic,* 1931 and from *Alabama Cotton Tenant Farmer's Wife,* 1936, to *Main Pump,* 1933. They particularize as Atget did for the Paris of his day. By this the eye and consequently the mind is induced to partake of the list that has been prepared—that we may know it.

The total effect is of a social upheaval, not a photographic picnic.

There is pointed reference in Mr. Kirstein's notes to the work of Brady during the War between the States. In Evans's pictures also

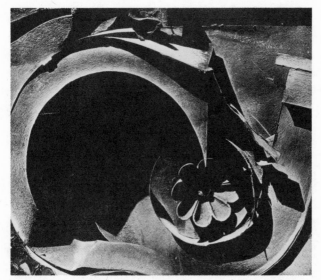

14. Walker Evans, *Tin Relic* (1930). From *American Photographs,* The Museum of Modern Art, 1938.

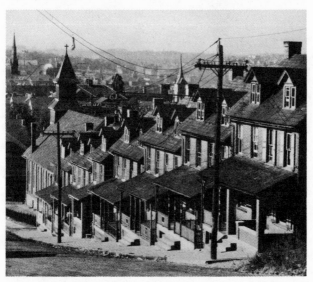

15. Walker Evans, *Two-family Houses in Bethlehem, Pennsylvania* (1936). From *American Photographs,* The Museum of Modern Art, 1938.

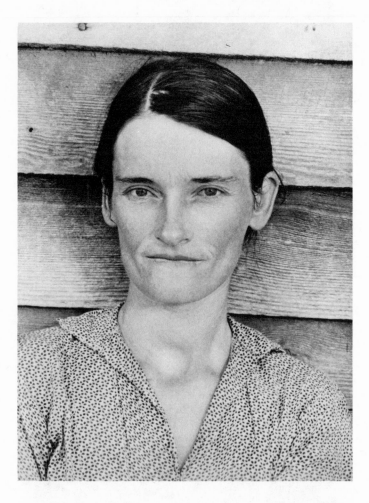

16. Walker Evans, *Alabama Cotton Tenant Farmer's Wife* (1936). From *American Photographs,* The Museum of Modern Art, 1938.

we are seeing fields of battle after the withdrawal of the forces engaged. The jumbled wreckage, human and material, is not always so grim in the present case but for all the detachment of the approach the effect is often no less poignant.

But that's not all. These are without question works of art having their own identity, their own flavor, their own breath by which they live for us—and without which we shouldn't look at them past Sunday afternoon. They're good and reward repeated examination.

I'm glad that Evans has promenaded his eyes about America in this case rather than France. (Not that, in the long run, it makes a damned bit of difference—Yes it does. It emphasizes the excellence of the French. Why, at best, brought into relief by our own perceptions they gain brilliancy for us. It was absolutely essential for someone to begin what Evans has done so well.

And we shall see our own country and its implications the better for Evans's work and come to realize that the realm of art is here quite as well as elsewhere.)^y We go about blind and deaf. We fight off convictions that could we possibly get ourselves into the right mind we should welcome for water in the desert (, convictions that are the very calcium and vitamins without which our bones melt under us)^y. The artist must save us. He's the only one who can. First we have to see. Or first we have to be taught to see. We have to be taught to see here, because here is everywhere, related to everywhere else, and if we don't see, hear, taste, smell and feel in this place—not only will we never know anything but the world of sense will be by that much diminished everywhere.

(Jealousies relative to the arts are unthinkable. In such pictures as those of Evans the insects of the arts have laid their eggs against a present winter to go on breeding and puncturing the hides of the dull witted forever.)^y

Evans saw what he saw here, in this place—this was his universal. In this place he saw what is universal. By his photographs he proves it. Atget would like that.

(One of my pet aversions is the belief that you have to go to special places to find excellence in the arts on the principle that you don't find whales in a mill pond. You don't. Neither do you find brains by drinking cheap wine in a bistro, or knowledge merely by eating tripe from a dish stamped with the coat of arms of Christ College.)[y]

Of only one thing, relative to a work of art, can we be sure: it was bred of a place. It comes from an application of the senses to that place, a music, and that place can be the middle of the African jungle, the Mexican plateau, a Parisian whorehouse, a room where Oxford chippies sip tea together or a downhill street in a Pennsylvania small town.

(Let the abstract artist go hang his coat back of the door where he sits down, the abstractions he thinks he is freeing are as definitely bound to a place as the work of the most representational artist that ever lived, the only difference being that one sees so much more than the other. And relates it so much more acutely to his purpose.

Not that training isn't necessary. But the real thing the runners-away are after, if they know it, is convenience. It's hard to get the best out of an undeveloped milieu. The word "milieu" shows what I mean. We don't use the American equivalent, place, readily enough, so we run to a French one. But it's nothing but convenience and a certain inability that makes the runner-away[1] at his worst. At his best he is the bringer-in of the means of intercommunication in the arts—though he often forgets that and believes himself exalted in direct proportion to his removal from his basis.)[y]

It is the particularization of the universal that is important. It is the unique field of the artist. Evans is an artist.

It is ourselves we see, ourselves lifted from a parochial setting. We see what we have not theretofore realized, ourselves made worthy in our anonymity. What the artist does applies to everything, every day, everywhere to quicken and elucidate, to fortify and enlarge the life about him and make it eloquent—to make it scream, as Evans does at times, gurgle, laugh and speak masterfully when the occasion offers. (By this, by the multiplicity of the approach, the aggregate of many artists in all possible locations,

---

[1]Williams here originally wrote "expatriate" but crossed it out and substituted "runner-away."

each, with his own materials making the same excellence—men are drawn closer and made to feel their separate greatness.

Evans is that. He belongs.)y

So here's a book of photographs about America. It's not the first, perhaps not even the best book of pictures of us, but it's an eloquent one, one of the most fluent I have come across and enjoyed. The pictures are for the most part mild, but in spite of this, though always exquisitely clear in reasoning and in visual quality, they pack a wicked punch. There's nothing oppressively "photographic" here, it isn't a long nose poking into dirty corners for propaganda and for scandal, there are no trick shots, the composition isn't a particular feature—but the pictures talk to us. And they say plenty.

Charles Sheeler

Introduction, MOMA Catalogue, 1939
HERE FOR the first time, I think, the paintings of Charles Sheeler have been assembled for a complete retrospective view giving him and others an opportunity to witness them as a whole. This is an important moment for contemporary painting. Apart from the enjoyment received, it provides a means for the study and evaluation of the work in all its phases as well as a cross-check on painting generally today.

The catalogue details elsewhere a chronological list of the exhibits. No comment on the individual pieces will be made nor does it seem appropriate to more than mention the biography so ably covered in previous publications. All that is intended is a bird's-eye view of the exhibit and a quick pencil sketch of some of its features and implications—as they appeal to one who is not a painter, a bad thing perhaps, writers incline to be gassy.

I think Sheeler is particularly valuable (for us in America)ᵛ because of the bewildering directness of his vision, without blur, through the fantastic overlay (of crazy impositions)ʷ with which our lives so vastly are concerned, "the real," as we say, contrasted with the artist's "fabrications," ([and] because of his sanity, seeing as he does directly, without hallucination, through the impost which occupies almost all of our attention, walls which close us in and which we do not surpass, ((to a barn or a leaf in a glass of water.))ʷ So he paints.)ᵛ

This is the traditional thin soup and cold room of the artist, to inhabit some chance "reality" whose every dish and spoon he knows as he knows the language that was taught him as a child. Meanwhile, a citizen of the arts, he must keep his eye without fault upon those things he values, to which officials constantly refuse to give the proper names.

(We are isolated from each other by many shades of difference. It is too easy, for conviviality, to try to weld the two worlds.)[s] (That is where the artist often slips. He paints what he sees before him, with his eyes, and is tempted to give it some trivial name or resemblance, incidental and unworthy, purely transient, so that those he lives with may recognize, as children may be led to recognize by association, what they should see.)[r] (And the disappointing thing is that in trying thus to present it, a completely simple thing, before it can be told, it gets the appearance of the complex by our trying to carry it over from the one world to the other.)[s]

The difficulty is to know the valuable from the impost and to paint that only. The rest of us live in confusion between these things, isolated from each other by the effects of it, a primitive and complex world without air conditioning. It is the measurable disproportion between what a man sees and knows that gives the artist his opportunity. He is the watcher and surveyor of that world where the past is always occurring contemporaneously and the present always dead, needing a miracle of resuscitation to revive it.

(That there should be artists, especially the most vivid of them, painters, in an age characterized by its unreality, and that there should be such a one as Charles Sheeler among them, may be all that saves some of us from comparative madness, a complete night. I say "comparative" because in this age no one would be so indiscreet as to allow himself to go completely mad, [just] as he would not dare to believe himself completely sane: no one that is but the artist, touching either the heights or the depths.)[v]

More and more alone as time goes on, shut off from each other in spite of facile means of communication we shrink within ourselves the more the others strike against our privacy. We cannot be forced to love and talk, the gangsters are right (in their code of silence)[v]—I should say they are the mirrors. Nor can it be told by looking into a man's face what he is thinking or in what hovel-sized confinement he exists. But the monasteries of our thoughts have walls like any others for paintings to carry us beyond them to reality. Lucky the man who can dispel them with a Sheeler.

And let it be strictly noted, the arresting thing is that this world of the artist (often maligned, is not of gauze but honest wood and steel and plaster. You can't write on emptiness. ((You don't paint on the idea of walls but upon walls.))ᵖ It is the world in which men meet and work with pick and shovel, talk and write long-winded books. It is the same world we go to war in. God knows no one can say the bombs on Guernica were not real, even to the place of manufacture stamped on them.)ᵛ Pictures are made with paint and a brush on canvas.

(So that if a man is to paint unless we know what he's painting unless we know what structure he's seeking to enliven we cannot understand his painting.)ᵛ

Any picture worth hanging, is of this world—under our noses often—which amazes us, into which we can walk upon real grass. It's no "fabrication," we realize that at once, but what we have always sought against that shrunken pulp (from which everyone is running faster nowadays than ever) called, monstrously, "the real."

Charles Sheeler gives us such a world, of elements we can believe in, things for our associations long familiar or which we have always thought familiar. (Without embarrassment, rather with complete unconstraint, intensity and variety of resource, he uses what he sees and what we see for what he has to say. By that we speak of him as an American painter and know what we're talking about.)ᵏ (He sees the universal in our midst, with his eyes, and makes it up for us in detail from those things we know, with paint on a piece of stretched cloth.)ᶠ (To cipher his widest reaches of understanding he has used characters of intensely local bearing. And the wider his understanding, the more intense have become his perceptions of the local.)ʰ

Driving down for illumination into the local, Sheeler has had his Welsh blood to set him on. There is a Sheelerville, Pa., up in the old mining district (—a blood hard upon locality for its good as a barnacle upon a rock. There are dangers there but there are virtues also.)ˡ The Shakers express the same feeling in maple, pine and birch, pieces which Sheeler out of admiration for what they could do with those materials keeps about him.

But the world is always seeking meanings! breaking down everything to its "component parts," not always without loss. The arts have not escaped this tendency, nor did Sheeler whose early work leaned toward abstraction, in the drawing and composition, the familiar ironing out of planes. Something of it still lingers in his color.

Later Sheeler turned, where his growth was to lie, to a subtler particularization, the abstract if you will but left by the artist integral with its native detail.

(The artist's world can never be anything but a world of the senses. Essences, the abstract and its abstraction, have major facets in philosophy and science:)[1] The tree grows and makes leaves which fall and lie in the swamp-water. The ages change, as the imagination changes, and of the resultant coal we draw off an electric fluid. But for the artist, for Sheeler as an artist, it is in the shape of the thing that the essence lies.

To be an artist, as to be a good artisan, a man must know his materials. But in addition he must possess that really glandular perception of their uniqueness which realizes in them an end in itself, each piece irreplaceable by a substitute, not to be broken down to other meaning. Not to pull out, transubstantiate, boil, unglue, hammer, melt, digest, and psychoanalyze, not even to distill but to see and keep what the understanding touches intact—as grapes are round and come in bunches.

(Add again a balance of mind sufficient to prevent bemusement before traditional habits of choice out of which the vigor has gone. And a sense for the color of events, the color itself and what cannot be seen behind what can be seen.)[k]

It is this eye for the thing that most distinguishes Charles Sheeler—and along with it to know that every hair on every body, now or then, in its minute distinctiveness is the same hair, on every body anywhere, at any time, changed as it may be to feather, quill, or scale.

(It is the real world, the world of things with which the artist has to do, this cannot ever be too strongly emphasized. In this emphasis Sheeler's work has a special place. The artist must be a veritable animal the way he has to smell his way most of the time through the difficulties.)[x]

The local is the universal (, or there could be no painting.)[l] It was a banana to Cézanne.

(The purpose of art is to make the world big again, to lift what is about our feet to the level of the imagination where alone it gains a quality fitting it for the uses of exchange: a fluidity—keeping its character—that is the release of the local into the universal, but not, for the arts, at the expense of detail, by staring past which to grow purblind.)[k]

Look! that's where painting begins. A bird, up above, flying, may be the essence of it—but a dead canary, with glazed eye, has no less an eye for that, well seen becomes sight and song itself. (The common is dignified into the uncommon. . . . The place where the eye impinges is everywhere—unless we are hypnotized by it. I have to laugh at the abstractionists.)[g] (The facile deception—not without a use—that in an abstraction is caught the essence of a thing is the mark: fatal. The essence lies in the thing, and shapes it, variously, but the sensual particularization is the proof, the connection which proves that the senses see a reality. It is the artist's incentive. In the particularization the artist gains his authority.)[g] It is in things that for the artist the power lies, not beyond them. Only where the eye hits does sight occur. (The moment sight ceases art ceases. The moment sight dims, the essence, in the arts, is fissured. The senses atrophy from lack of use. Look cross-eyed for a few years and see what happens to one of your eyes. You can't see two things at the same time so one eye ceases to function. Stop looking intensely at a chair, or a cat, or a flower in a pot, or a factory and—sooner or later you won't be able to see either those things or anything.)[g] Take a cross-eyed child at birth. For him to see at all one of the eyes must go blind, he cannot focus it. But let him look past the object to "abstraction" long enough and soon the other eye will follow.

(Sheeler has devoted himself mainly to still lifes, landscapes with little direct reference to humanity. This does not in the least make him inhuman, since when man becomes insignificant in his attributes and swollen to fill the horizon the representation of the human face is not enlightening.)[x] (Inhuman is a word commonly used to describe the efficiency of the modern industrial setup, as in some minds coldness is often associated with Sheeler's work—incorrectly. Sheeler chose as he did from temperament doubtless but also from thought and a clear vision of the contemporary dilemma.)[x]

The exhibits date back approximately a quarter of a century, but their quality is singularly uniform, lucid, and geometric from the first. It was an early perception of general changes taking place, a passage over from heated surfaces and vaguely differentiated detail to the cool and thorough organizations today about us, familiar in industry, which Sheeler has come more and more to celebrate.

Sheeler had especially not to be afraid to use the photographic camera in making up a picture. It could perform a function unduplicatable by other means. Sheeler took it that by its powers his subject should be intensified, carved out, illuminated—for anyone (I don't know that he said this to himself) whose eyes might be blurred by the general fog that he might, if he cared to, see again. (The best pictures take us most wholly into another world.)[o] (When we were children we were told that if we dug down deep enough we'd come to China. I once did find an old piece of broken crockery.)[d]

It is ourselves we seek to see upon the canvas, as no one ever saw us, before we lost our courage and our love. So that, to a Chinaman, Sheeler at his best should be a heartfelt recognition, as Sheeler, looking at some ancient Chinese painted screen, would hope fervently to see himself again. A picture at its best is pure exchange, men flow in and out of it, it doesn't matter how. I think Sheeler at his best is that, a way of painting powerfully articulate. But after all, so is all good painting.

Charles Sheeler—Postscript

Art in America, 1954

WHEN A painter faces his canvas he has, with every new work, problems to solve which are as old as the art of painting itself. If he has a style for which he is known, even famous, the problem is only intensified. Is he going to make a change in his style or go on developing it as before? As a man grows older we ask of him not so much the new but how he has served the gift he originally possessed. Does he see to it that he paints always better pictures?

How is one painting better than another? By sticking to his style a man establishes himself. He strives to prove the innerness of his primary vision, to make it more clearly apparent to the beholder, to slough aside all extraneous matter, that his meaning may always be clearer. The better his picture the more that meaning stands out.

Charles Sheeler has lived in a mechanical age. To deny that was to lose your life. That, the artist early recognized. In the world which immediately surrounded him it was more apparent than anywhere else on earth. What was he to do about it? He accepted it as the source of materials for his compositions.

Sheeler made a clean sweep of it. The man found himself impressed by the contours of the machine; he was not impressed by the romantic aspects of what the machine represents but the machine itself. The machine as just another "flower" or "fish," just another "arrangement" to fill the spaces on his paintings has not interested him. Sheeler was too hardheaded for that. Therefore his interest in photography.

By faking the psychologic appearance of the machine, making perhaps a "woman" of it, so that it appears to be what it is not is no gain to painting. Neither is the ignoring of the machine's contours until it entirely disappears from our consciousness. To take the

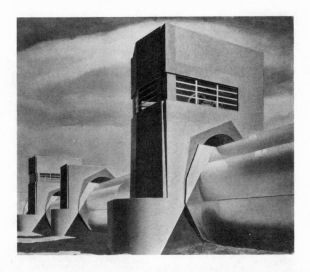

17. Charles Sheeler, *Water*. Oil on canvas, 24" × 29⅛". Collection, The Metropolitan Museum of Art, New York (Arthur H. Hearn Fund, 1949).

18. Charles Sheeler, *Bucks County Barn* (1923). Tempera and crayon, 19½" × 25½". Collection, The Whitney Museum of American Art, New York.

19. Charles Sheeler, *Pertaining to Yachts and Yachting* (1922). Collection, Philadelphia Museum of Art (Bequest of Margaretta S. Hinchman).

20. Charles Sheeler, *Classic Landscape* (1931). Courtesy of the Estate of Mrs. Edsel B. Ford.

machine and make its contours acceptable to our eye by using it in our compositions is admirable in a modern artist.

His industrial plants and barns, the elementary shapes he has chosen to work with, force a recognition on us very often which makes them sing. I don't know what more we can ask of a man. Sheeler's paintings are often spoken of as cold, but when a man is mastered, as he is, by an overwhelming reticence, his paintings are possessed by an emotional power hard to put your fingers on. It is always so with masterwork and the best of the paintings of Charles Sheeler are just that.

It is interesting to witness how Sheeler has progressed to his present stand. We can see how in his early years he was influenced by the French school but the adored Cézanne had already passed into history. An element from the outside seems to be disturbing the balance. These icy paintings, if you take them at their surface value only, are certainly not Renoir. Sheeler is not a colorist, at least he does not count on color for his major effects. Design is his distinction.

After the normal amount of experimental still lifes had been accomplished, studies of the nude followed in due course though, significantly, he was only interested in the human figure as parts of it were revealed, an arm, a breast in an offhand pose. He turned to a yacht's sails bellying in the wind or the contours of farm buildings which more held his eye.

One of his first earlier successes was an abstract drawing of a barn, a barn revealed in its essentials without background of any sort. From there on he has chosen, led by an inscrutable logic, to reveal such studies of barns, with necessary variations, in all their aspects.

It all came from an intense interest in the mechanical world pressing about him. He wanted to recognize and assert its every detail in which he saw, along with its identity, a symmetry to match that of ancient buildings. That he has used the camera obscura to aid him in making his record was inevitable but when he used the camera it was only to emphasize his work as a painter.

Sheeler is a painter first and last with a painter's mind alert to the significance of the age which surrounds him. The emotional power of his work comes also from that. It is hard to believe that a picture such as *Classic Landscape,* which is a representation of the Ford plant at River Rouge, owes its effectiveness to an arrangement of cylinders and planes in the distance, maybe it isn't entirely that but that contributes to it largely. It is, however it comes about, a realization on the part of the artist of man's pitiful weakness and at the same time his fate in the world. These themes are for the major artist. These are the themes which under cover of his art Sheeler has celebrated.

Marsden Hartley: 1940

Not previously published

WHILE THE disc is revolving and the amplifier in the belfry across the street is broadcasting its carillon tones upon this Easter morning brilliant and cold—sounding the old hymns for us to hear, willy-nilly, without graciousness but a very considerable insistence—there's the Amen.

And, there's a show of paintings in New York this week at the Walker Gallery by an international artist of considerable fame who has come home to America, to Maine, to complete his life. Marsden Hartley is painting better today than he ever could have hoped to do formerly and the reason becomes more and more apparent. It is a painter's reason, a basic reason, it has to do with the mind, the body, and the spirit drawn gradually together into one life and finally flowering, once.

That's what pictures, or anything of value, must be: once. It has happened. It has happened here. Here the deed has become vocal, in this small place, in this small space, on this cloth, between those wooden frames. And by this commonness, this thing that might happen anywhere but has by "accident" happened here—at last— AT LAST, becomes universal.

Hartley, approaching old age (that is to say, youth—if he wins!) is just beginning to understand and to show what it means to be a painter—that is to say, a man: the drama of it, the slippery edge along which any man must advance, always dangerously, to a performance which cannot but be dramatic when it succeeds, tragic when it fails.

The gnarledest of paintings can emit purest light—when they finally come through, when they make good, when they close up the broken life such an American as Hartley must have led, to bring into place his native completion.

These are all Maine scenes, *Flowers from Claire Spencer's Garden—Bargaduco Farm, The Lost Felice—For a Seaman's Bethel in the Far North, Mt. Katahdin—Autumn #1, Driftwood on the Bargaduce,* etc., etc. What does it matter? Real they have to be because, unless you paint pure nothing, you paint a place—and in that place you will reveal all places in the world. How else will you paint nothing? And walk out of it whole?

Technically I am not competent to speak as a painter but I can tell vigor, struggle, paint that is put down to be paint and to say whatever paint can say without lying but with knowledge and a man's purpose—which a man must share, all but in the one way, with every other man.

It is important to me to see a man like Marsden Hartley doing what he is doing with a life that grew up where I grew up—without prejudice. Hartley was a sensation in Berlin before the last World War with the prescience of his wild canvases. He is a new sensation today for those with eyes who will see here another, broader and deeper prescience, full of late courage and passion, of a sort of love that's not easy to kill or to understand either for that matter—lying at the base and under a shaken but unmoved world.

21. Marsden Hartley, *The Lost Felice* (1939). Oil on canvas, 40″ × 30″. Collection, Los Angeles County Museum of Art (Mr. and Mrs. William Preston Harrison Collection).

22. Marsden Hartley, *Mount Katahdin, Autumn, No. 1.* Oil on canvas, 30″ × 40″. Sheldon Memorial Art Gallery, University of Nebraska-Lincoln.

23. Marsden Hartley, *Lilies in a Vase* (*c.* 1920). Oil on paper, 27″ × 19⅛″. Collection, The Columbus Gallery of Fine Arts, Columbus, Ohio (Gift of Ferdinand Howald).

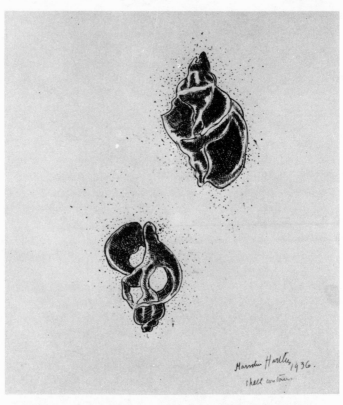

24. Marsden Hartley, *Shell Contours* (1936). Pen and ink, 10″ × 10½″. Collection, Museum of Art of Ogunquit, Maine (Gift of Florence H. Williams, 1967).

Beginnings: Marsden Hartley: 1948

Partially published, Black Mountain Review, 1957

IN ONE WAY I am not at all the man to write of Marsden Hartley. I know nothing of his seagoing ancestors, his down-east background. For that very reason, perhaps, since he spent his life, while I knew him, in an escape from that, seeking as a painter of pictures, to follow a life not as far removed from his hereditary one as might on the surface be indicated, I knew this phase and sympathized with him in it. He was in addition a poet, a writer with a delightful prose style which fascinated me. Besides I had had a father of the same remotely English blood who looked like Hartley, at least to the length of his nose, a nose, Dad used to say like the Duke of Wellington, a Roman nose.

What gets into these men of wholly English Blood that sends them flying out to all corners of the world as soon as they come of age? All of them are endowed with a certain *gaucherie* which the more marks them, I suppose, as men. It was a characteristic which extends even to the clothes they wear. They are men's men even to the clothes they wear. Marsden was no exception. It showed in the very colors he chose to paint with, nuances did not please him, but boldness dominated the palette he used. Such men are driven by curiosities which drive them into awkward positions out of which they have to fight free as best they can. That makes men of them, not without a certain crudeness, and they show it whether on the bridge of a ship or engaging the colors confronting them on a canvas they are painting. (Hartley was a man's man from the very bridge of his nose to the loosely set bones of the rest of his skeleton.)[b] You had to love him to understand him which no woman had it in her heart (or her eyes)[b] to do during his long life, he lived into his middle seventies. He never married but was popular with certain women for all that. (He remained a lonely man his entire life.)[b]

I remember him first as occupying a room, a back room, in an old house on West 15th Street, New York, the old Greenwich Village section, houses on which you'd see occasionally a plaque affixed to the wall saying, for instance, that this is the house where Alexander Hamilton was brought to die following his duel with Aaron Burr at Weehawken. Hartley loved these houses with their associations with colonial times and high ceilings. The rent besides was low though in winter they were cold being heated by an open grate though that was no deterrent to a man from Augusta, Maine, used as anyone was in the last century to primitive heating arrangements.

In the apartment immediately back of his own, the old parlor of the place, a young couple, recently married, or perhaps not, were separated from the lonesome man by the bare thickness of the flimsy partition against which his bed as well as that of the loving couple both abutted. As he lay there through the January nights of a long winter he could hear the very rustle of the bed clothes as they shifted their positions, the straining of the bedsprings and even their subdued conversation close to his ear on the other side of the wall. It was a great torment to him lying there alone. His whole life had been a similar torment which painting alone assuaged.

I always wanted to buy a picture or two from him fresh from his palette (but he had to keep his prices high in order to live)[b], too high for my pocketbook. I admired for years his still lifes (of flowers, particularly his lily pieces, of which he painted many. Finally at an auction at the Anderson gallery, when even his good friend Stieglitz had no longer a place for him in his gallery, I was able to buy a canvas or two—one of them unfinished—but NOT one of the flower pieces I wanted.

Hartley once or twice brought out several carryable canvases for me to select from, at perhaps fifty dollars each, but they were all secondary work and I would have none of them. Meanwhile he was rapidly going broke and would be speaking again of some mythical sister or sisters back home and which I understood to mean or to be the source of a meager patrimony which kept him alive.

The colors and the shapes he painted were for the most part seen close to the eye and positively, even crudely painted, boldly and with aggressive simplicity. Their outlines—perhaps two birches broken off leaning together in the woods—were distinct, dramatically conceived so that it was obvious that it was intended that they should mean an inescapable tragedy to which the canvas pointed—and nothing marginal. A mountain torrent splashing itself to pieces on the rocks was no less dramatically centered—or it might be a boulder standing alone, a split boulder, the halves eternally separated.

Hartley knew Paris, and, more important, the Berlin of just before the First World War and painted there. The torment of those times and the positive assertion of the young German state of these times tormented his soul, the soul of a great artist, so that he painted during this phase abstract furies, close to the eye, pressing as it were on the eye, of great significance and beauty—nothing has superseded or even approached them. I have seen many attempts to equal them with their bold strokes of primary colors, exploding bombs, the arching trajectories of rockets which predicted what the world was destined to see in real life—but nothing as startling or as beautiful as his vision. It was a phenomenon unequaled in the history of art. If for nothing else these paintings of this period mark Marsden Hartley as one of the most powerful figures in American painting.

He made many friendships in those years but seems to have been satisfied to leave the group centered around the French of those years—and one of the most productive and delightful groups that ever came to the fore in France—more or less alone. It is to me at least as if he had said to himself that that sort of thing was not what he was primarily interested in. That was French and he, you could almost hear him say, was American. That is what drew us together. Because it was at that time that I began to know him.

It was as if he deliberately turned his back on Europe, it was the time when I had published my *In the American Grain* and Stieglitz and Djuna Barnes, both close friends of Hartley, had praised it. Hartley was a thinker as well as the other things of which I have been thinking. He was as well a poet and an essayist—when he was strongly moved; that is my authority for saying that his decision to quit Europe for America was a fully conscious one, bred of a powerful conviction that here, more than anywhere else, that reward which he sought was to be found. It is to be emphasized that he was not an uninformed man but had lived in the very vortex of the art life of the period and had looked and seen what that world offered before he rejected it.

He came back, not to the New Mexico and the Florida which he took in his stride, writing and painting many important records of his experience, but to Maine!—to his beginnings, the coast of Maine, its woods and its people, the fisher folk of Newfoundland in which he refound or rediscovered his roots. He wrote his poems, and he was at times a very perceiving and detailed observer and had a poetic gift—not as significant as his wonderful gift with the brush, but a vision which, when taken with his paintings as part of the man, we cannot ignore. Some of his poems are unequaled.

I am thinking of one of his paintings, one of the most tender and sensitively painted of all his canvases, the portrait, a still life, of a pair of woman's gloves lying on a table where she has just thrown them. Nothing could be farther from the Berlin or the Paris of his younger days. The artist has come home and is interested only in that life he had at one time abandoned to go to Cathay, as his ancestors in their China clippers had gone before him. He had looked to see what is to be seen in the world and after he had seen, returned to sum up for his heart what he had found there.

The last phase was, I think, for Hartley not an unhappy one in spite of failing health—at least there were no regrets. He didn't get from the world all that he wanted to get, but who in this world gets that? He could laugh his head off at us or at his own perceptions when he would see completely through the motives of the men around him.)[b]

Marsden Hartley: 1956

Not previously published
HE WAS a New Englander, more than a mere New Englander, he was from Maine, the inhabitants of which have something wild in their blood. Something exotic bred of their Abenaki ancestry. Even if they have no Indian blood in their veins they were never like the rest of us but welcomed the thought of it. The Kennebec and the Penobscot were names common to their thoughts as they were to Hartley's vocabulary.

And yet there are no Yankees that retained the English tradition in their veins as he or they. After all, as we know nowadays, Maine is nearer to England than any other of the states and has a light if not a climate nearest of all the states to theirs. In its isolation far to the north it is truly an island much as is England.

I remember an English family that grew up in the New Jersey suburb of the 1890s next door to us: the Norsworthys. They were United Brethren, the older people, Naomi, Leonard and Howard, the youngest. Once Howard said to me, You little son of a gun! [And I responded with,] You little son of a bitch!—a term, not of endearment, that I had just learned. He was horrified. And that is or represents the atmosphere in which Marsden Hartley was raised.

He was not so much an American as a child of foreign parentage, a wild imagination, bred of clipper sailors, from the coastal isles, unyielding to ordinary confinements—a child of families who knew the woods and fishing on the Grand Banks.

This boy was a born aristocrat, and like many others of the same breed was born to lead a lonely life. He was a tall, raw-boned man with a hawk-like nose, a Roman nose, they call it in England, a man definitely not destined to work in a sweatshop. He had a hawk's eyes too that were a clear blue and saw everything. He was as

gentle as a kitten, and loved cats—as does many a sea-faring man—
and loved to have them near him.

He loved women too but the incongruity between his fierce
looks and gentle ways were on the whole too much for them. He
had to look elsewhere for his comfort—yet one of his early
paintings, *Two Trees,* shows a story not to be forgotten. It is in the
open woods, two white birches occupy the middle ground of the
picture, two young white birches that had been snapped off by a
storm, doubtless an ice storm, one on the left, one on the right,
toward each other! Their tips, touching the earth between them,
almost met. Can that speak of some early tragedy of the heart?
There are some beautiful and aloof Maine women, come of the old
branches, which can still be heard of about Augusta, where Hartley
grew up. Maybe it was one of those.

Nowadays the arts, a career in the arts, is the only release for a
man such as Marsden Hartley to escape to. He was safely in an art
school or had just come from art school and was painting and
writing—they have always gone hand in hand with him—when the
First World War was about to begin. That was his first opportunity. He grasped it with enthusiasm. The Expressionist movement had hit Berlin like a thunder clap. Marsden Hartley was in the
thick of it.

Midas

Now, 1941
A CERTAIN number of refugees from the Death in Europe, revolutionary in the full sense, have met others here who welcome them to this country. Together they propose to continue an advance into the present and to publish a bulletin from time to time of their interests.

In the present emergency, the revolutionary element in thought and in life will continue their concern; to preserve and to elevate everything (anti-political, anti-terrorist,)[b] constructive, aggressive, of radical power in art as in the physical sciences today to its proper place before the mind. (No need to fear it, that it will disturb whatever excellences exist in present plans, rather it fits there perfectly, because, in fact, wherever such excellences exist, it has produced them.)[c] If the concern be painting, to celebrate what new thrusts will stand upon the shoulders of surrealism and to discern a new horizon beyond that; to raise woman from her proposed servitude to the state; to announce the new cure for cancer when it comes; the poem that shall be actually new.

One of the purposes of the Death among us is to terrify the world, to use a destructive ideology to push our culture so far back that it will take a full generation, another crop of flesh and mind, before it can begin to regenerate. Then to thrust another war upon us that will again drive the mind from its advances, this shuttle to go on in perpetuity. We are never to be allowed to catch up, to regain our equilibrium for a permanent arrest of the Destroyer. But we on our part will stay on the heels of the Death, baying and snapping, never giving it a moment's rest, to keep it there at bay. So that at the moment of respite, the instant war has finished its last ravages, its strength spent, *the very next instant*, we may spring forward to carry on the culture—to enhearten and supply the elements of a peace—not where it left off but still further advanced above what it had been formerly. We propose without pretence to publish a bulletin of our activities, if any, and to notice the work of creative agents in other fields.

(For my part in it here am I, a fool, finding myself suddenly amazingly to the point!)[d] War elevates the artist, the builder, the thinker to the peaks of the stars, trebles his significance. In times of peace he is, at best, a humdrum worker not because he must be so but because he is perpetually laboring under weights to inflame and to magnify. But in times of war—helplessly split off in the cyclotron of the times—he becomes inevitably king of men (by contrast)[d]. By his very existence, beyond himself, the elements win new significance, woman blossoms from her imposed shell, man, older than the stones, rears himself and reaches out into the unknown.

(Opposed to the Death the poet's advances cannot but be the passionate news of the moment. The artist especially holds the world of desire upon his shoulders but only when fluent with genius—to warm and engender.)[e]

We address ourselves not to the poet, the scientist, the sociologist separately—rather to the fertile subject itself which we intend to transform and to magnify: not to man so much as man as he is the product of time. Who am I that exist now and existed then? Not merely a man, surely, but far more complex than that, the summation of all men that preceded me and their very genius to push themselves forward—in me! That is where I exist, in that inheritance. Purely of the imagination.

Everything which advances the understanding of this subject, this "thing" which makes new sallies into time—comparable in its movements precisely to geography in the era of Vasco da Gama, the arts in the twelfth century, psychiatry in the later years of the nineteenth century, astrophysics, organic chemistry, French painting since 1850[1]—anything which pushes an advance, a tenable new

---

[1]An interesting sidelight to Williams' ongoing preoccupation with French painting can be found in the transformations of this last phrase: version (b) of the manuscript reads "painting since 1900." In version (e) this has become, as above "French painting since 1850." In the published version, finally, we read: "French painting since 1820."

position into that substance which is not merely "man" but includes also his image in time; in sum, everything which constitutes the province of the poet (who encloses the whole materium and continuum in his concept) in its revolutionary grasp, we coneive as our business.

The poet's designation of what he sees is always and must be always, new! Without willing it he has been forced up by the Death into a high light today, the major significance of his time. For to him as an interpreter (of whatever substance making up the moment)ᵉ there is no equal. He is the drastic clarifier of events. Not biology, chemistry, philosophy, politics, dogma—not one of these is large enough to comprise or contain the whole matrix of creation as it is caught in the concept of the poem. All must look to that finally for its completion—as Einstein has already done and admitted that he has done so.

The poem alone focuses the world. It is practical and comprehensive. For us its characteristics are these, to begin with: It says— or we exist that it may gain a hearing to this effect: We've got to go on because nobody else is going on and America is for the moment an asylum for what we do not intend to let die.

An outstanding character of poetry (along with the arts generally, particularly emphasized today,)ᵉ is that it cannot be the accompaniment of other than an unfettered imagination. It cannot exist other than as revolutionary attribute of a free people— wherever they may be by twos and threes. To limit it is to kill it. You cannot prune it like a peach tree for better effect, or hoard it away as food. It is fruit and flower of the mind. You may, if you please, prune the mind but its flower you cannot touch other than to destroy it for it is the effect of what has passed and is thus unalterable. It comes when the climate permits or it does not materialize. But if it do not appear, then the plant has never blossomed.

That climate which gives it lief to expand is love, as gold, its symbol, is most gold when it is given freely to the beloved.

Love and the arts are inextricably mixed and the one character of love which can be most respected by the poet is precisely that, the lavishing on the beloved of every gift in a man's power to lay at her feet. For poetry does just that: revolutionary in the most pointed sense, it goes to the heart of human desire and lavishes there its gifts.

It is the striking gesture of the arm of a man wherever employed. Chop off the arm, the gesture is taken up by other arms intact. Deny a people its arms in time of persecution, as the people of Spain were, actively or passively, left armless by the great niggardly peoples of the earth, the tragic poetry of it is still unaffected. You can't prune that. You can't destroy gold. Gold may destroy you, for you can't eat it, any more than you can eat the arts. (But to give of the very perfection of life itself is the essence of the poem.)[d] These are the prizes of free men—murderous in intention if thwarted—the prizes of love.

The people of the minds of the poets, the creators, the people of books who conduct our lives—are those most attacked today by the Terror. It is for us to keep their world, the imagination on which they thrive, for them and enhance its advantages in order to preserve ourselves—who are even more imaginary and dependent on them for our "reality" than upon the air we breathe! What sort of creatures are being created now, today muffled in cloths? Is there one thing created by the arts that is distinguished? Point it out! Lear, Oedipus, Quixote, Ahab. We cannot afford otherwise. We eat from them, drink from them. They feed us. The poet creates to believe, to enjoy—destroys to survive. We live only by the arts of our poets.

Modern poetry is a definition, in the radical speech patterns of the day, asserting our development and elevation of thought above that of the ancients.

Not that there are not defects. America as an asylum is in many ways not a good one. Man has been mother to woman so long in America that he has forgotten her function (and his own) in large measure. But the producer is haggard at the termination of his labors. Man somewhat as a consequence has lost his revolutionary character, touching woman and going on from there. (This is an effect not only physical, but,)[e] in America productive also of a matrix of undifferentiated thought, inimical to complete contacts as a general thing—with a throw-back of female elements in the arts and in affairs: anti-revolutionary, complacent, quilted.

The attack upon the basic problem goes on underneath the

shows of the surface one. It is always basically, in all the variations, one with its apex on the moment, in the sciences as well as the arts: one. Thus and only thus may highly divergent appearances coincide, be conceived to unite in a common effort, permitting our friends to come to us. (Thus concepts originating in one milieu may, when the base is the same, unite with those of another.)ᵇ That is, only when the basic problem is conceived as the same can divergences unite and be understood as related to effects of varying orders. And thus only will such a concept as surrealism find a common ground, no matter how antagonistic it may seem to be, to the advance of thought and effort in America where it has no such original basis as existed in France yesterday. That is, only when a profound enough basis is discovered for it here in our own lives on which we can meet others.

That basis is the Midas touch, the alchemy of the mind which cannot be seduced by political urgencies—but makes all into gold (as David Lyle of Paterson, New Jersey, says)ᵇ: the *com* radical; com-bined; com-plex; com-plexion; com-prehensive; reaches out, takes hold. We are united in our hatred of the Terror, the negative, the Death. (But that alone isn't enough—or even a legitimate basis of understanding.)ᵇ

But surrealism is to us evidence of a culture which did not succeed, (we are inclined to say,)ᵉ which heralded disaster. (Nothing of the sort!)ᵉ This is the primary confusion, (this is what the Death speaks of desperately as)ᵉ "degenerate art." Nothing of the sort! As a perception of disintegration it was (and is)ᵉ the "truth." The basis of it as a poem, as creative construction was not even touched by the political accident. (The mind is not a political animal even though man may be.)ᵉ

It is inevitable that, foreign to us, the conception of surrealism must rest upon the same ground which as poets we conceive. Gold is the standard.

However, to create a picture and to appreciate it are two separate things. One is all effort, the other is all paint. One gives, the other takes. To conceive the basis for a movement in art does not create masterwork. We are aware of that too.

It is to advance the researches of the mind, weak as the attack may seem to be—and to unite the divergent good, all of it that can be (united in the cause to combat evil and advance the good)[b]—to blast war's pretence to constructive energy—herald the revolution-ary concepts of the day (,that we speak)[b].

We seek as far as we are American to take in the difficult "foreign," identical with us in the *gold* of it no matter how the ornament is shaped or what may be the purpose to which it seems to be put. To reject the spurious, *i.e.*, War, fake. To reveal the rare and the curious relationships which are the mind's true business.

We deal with the truth which we KNOW. We are NOT in doubt. We interpret *all* GOOD in *any* form and show its revolutionary value even in revolution itself—where it is churned up in the general pell-mell and the virtue of it disguised by accident.

As an example, we should propose looking at history to remove from the discovery of America its character as a search for gold, the stealing of it from the natives and raise up the gold itself, triumphant!

We should try to unite such elementary projects as are repre-sented by the magazine *Minotaur* and *London Letter* with our own Direction! Could anything be more mad? They are as divergent as—the seas. Or as identical!—in the character we imagine of their good. We hunt the gold in all of them—the revolutionary element! and have no interest in the spurious values trivially allocated there. That is the impossible task we have set ourselves to do: to dig under where, hidden in the soil of the mind, divergent excellences may be found stemming from the same pure stem of gold.

For if money is the symbol of collective effort, gold, by its indestructibility by air or acid, its malleability, its color and its sheen, is the symbol toward which money looks in its turn. And there is nothing that can take its place as an uncounterfeitable, readily available, though rare enough, object of value to pass thus symbolically from hand to hand. The old originators didn't select gold arbitrarily to be their standard of exchange. But gold, that is to say "gold," by confusion has come to be taken as identical with money in some languages. We do not fall into that error.

We accept it for granted, then, that the complexion of our minds, Americans and those who come to us with their gold is the same, we who have not yet been attacked directly and those who have newly retreated before the Terror. We know the gold and its identity with the living but have no desire to eat it—only the mad do that.

What are we to do in this complex of difficult understanding? Certainly, if we retreat it is only to lay the ground for a final revolutionary advance: the ideogram of George Washington's retreat across Jersey to win in the end is neither quaint nor untimely in this context.

Attack! that much at least we have learned from modern war. And there is more we can learn from the enemy—tactics universally translatable though we are never deceived by his silly strategy, infantile in conception, the magnificent thought! that if we could pull the wings off all the flies they would not bite us. But action releases energy. We can learn that. War releases energy. Energy can be used to transmute and create. Thus war by releasing energy indirectly serves in the creation of values. Or may be made to serve if we are prepared to seize the advantage from it!

War is a bastard agent. It eats its young, it creates only to mutilate and swallow its own offspring. It fertilizes the body of its continental flesh, the female carcass that it cynically urges to new bursts of labor, with glee, offering a prize (literally!) to its woman that she may exceed herself; then pig-like it crunches her shoats in its jaws while pushing her into the trough, finally eating her also— thus becoming sterile! War feeds on lies of deception, on the confusion of the woman, on pushing indignities upon her and then robbing her piecemeal. She is suppressed, her aphrodisiacs taken away from her and her reproductive wiles crushed to the features of a sausage machine—the sacks of flesh shooting into his gullet as fast as produced. He swallows and belches—while she serves him in his disgusting trade.

Meanwhile and metaphorically, to change the metaphor, the by-products of reproduction and destruction are thrown upon the slag-heap replete with mysteries beyond the imagination of any but a poet to resolve.

The arts of war! There are no arts of war but sterility and deceit. There is no art of shoat swallowing. There are arts but they are only bastardized after their theft by war. The arts create, war destroys. The sciences are! but they have not a single character which war can claim as its own but their undoing.

Make no mistake, war releases energy, so far it is good—but it has no art of its own, no authentic character but mud, exhaustion and heroism which is never more heroic than when it throws its life away for nothing at all—that might not have been had casually from love for the mere asking.

The tradition is that the art of war is to have the most men on the field first. But that's the art of painting, before the onrushing impetus of the idea, when it is ravishing the mind. What's peculiar to war in that? Not a single thing. War has no art to create anything, only to degrade and destroy. But the artist pauses, disciplines the fury and translates it to the eye. War creates nothing but stinking corpses and the perversion that makes leaders. Leaders! sucked out of men, eating others because of their own poverty. There are no arts of war. Everything is stolen there—except the energy released which is not its own and badly used by it.

This must be returned to creative forces by revolution, there is no other way, no other incentive sufficiently violent to overtake it, claim it, and carry it away. It must be returned to the correct complexion of the imagination, which will use it generatively—with a fury war only imitates, secondhand, and at once before it is dissipated completely.

But (and here I speak only for myself) I am myself for fighting physically—perhaps because I have never properly done so. That if there is war with its horrible boredom and sense of futility I am still not for lying down before the Terror. I am not a pacifist. But when I fight and give up my carcass I want it to be correct. I want my mind satisfied as to why I am doing it and what I expect to perish for. I know that I can win nothing that way.

I want it understood that when I fight I do not have to lie and pervert modern knowledge of the physical sciences, biology, philosophy and art to deceive myself into thinking I am "right." On the contrary, I disclose why I am engaged and shall expect to go out thus armed to murder the bastards—knowing that I am more able, more persistent, better armed and prepared in a better cause than they who are my brothers.

Feeling, too, can be progressive, logically developed from a point of departure as well as thought.

But I am old for physical enlistment and should have to see others younger, whom I love, be subject to the injuries. They should hate me and that whole criminal generation which saw the skulls crack from the malignancy of their thought and the disease spread from that over Europe, unless . . . ! A generation which in spite of a few isolated cries watched while the Terror armed itself slowly and carefully and did nothing to counter it. The young should hate us all today, unless that virtue, perceivable in spite of the difficulty in such a manifestation as surrealism, should hatch, by some one or two, its revolutionary purpose. For of such a criminal agglomerate as that generation of which I am a part—only the poet, the creator may survive.

(I myself was chairman in Bergen County, N.J., of a committee for medical aid to Spanish democracy while the Storch Squadron went out with their planes on Easter while the women and children were in the streets—people with whom they had not the slightest quarrel—and blasted them to butchers' meat in the holy Basque city of Guernica "to see how effective the planes and bombs would be." And I stood up in the 8th St. school in Hackensack and warned and begged for a few dollars to send—not guns or ammunition—but bandages, old clothes, surgical instruments—and to their everlasting shame not a single physician in the whole county, Friedian of Edgewater who had already gone to Spain excepted, so much as turned a hair, though I sent a personal card to every one of them.

I say, I come of a criminal generation. I come of a profession that is not used to lying down by disease and watching the patient make counterpoint by her screams to pious mutterings. I come of a profession that goes out to fight—occasionally at considerable risk.

So I cannot urge war with a clear conscience. But what am I to do?)d*

We must recognize war as a releaser of energy! So far it is good. Incredible but inescapable. (Anode and cathode.)d Though in itself it is weak, futile—the result of sloth, foul indolence, the energy it releases should put all peace lovers to shame. For if poetry had been regnant in the time when war was cooking, as an agent war must have appeared in its true colors—cheap, empty, sterile: *ersatz* only for the arts that sluggards *dared* not encounter or follow.

The revolution must capture from the Terror this power it makes available. Only peace as it might be conceived in all its controlled violence can capture this initiative from destruction and build it directly into mechanisms for our use. Now woman is honored and fertilized as creature of the imagination, not merely her carcass doubled or trebled by a kind of fission. War's lies, leeches that they are, sprinkled with salt, let go our flesh and fall off. We must ferret out those lies no matter where the trail leads. We shall be surprised or not, no matter, the objective is to capture the initiative for the creator everywhere, the artist, the scientist—the running animal; undeceive the puppet-makers concerning the true nature of the revolutionary St. Francis—whom they recaptured and subjected to their rule.

Nothing but war *has* made America the battleground of intelligences. These things do not come from nowhere. But war released badly what might have been released well. It released at least what was needed here—and gained, perhaps something for them there. We needed that daring and desperation, that infusion of *information* and experiment which we lacked, they needed more *room* for the cultivation of variants, a more expansive layout, a different locus, a new set of materials on which to use and prove choked projects. If what they would attempt is true under this (any one) circumstance, it need not necessarily be true under all circumstances; but if it is true under two dissimilar circumstances then it is likely to be universally true. War has brought together, by release, divergent intelligences for new trial and opportunity, let us acknowledge it.

But these intelligences and initiatives, it must be clear, have nothing to do with the Death, the Death has been only the dispersing agent. It has released energy, creating nothing. The same thing might have happened to better advantage in times of peace, when life was predominant. But it didn't happen. It was stalled by stupidity. The energy was lacking, but only the energy locked from our use. In desperation now before the Death, life begins to move violently (and we see Calas, Breton, Matta, Onslow-Gordon, Tanguy—agents merely, released for new activity in a fertile basin)[d].

The doing away with the slum districts of London is an excellent thing. War has begun the demolition of the slum districts of London. But this is not an act to be credited to war as an agent but to the release of energies consequent upon war. The necessary destruction could have been better done, more economically, with less collateral waste through the agency of peace but only a violent peace dominated by revolution. The means were locked up in stupidity, war released them.

And here that which has been hog-tied, condescended to, shoved about, and set to watch honors being given to plaster casts, gets a backing that will set it up to new sallies of its own.

(No one need be timid about saluting the anarchist. We're not ninnies. We have no intention of blowing ourselves or anybody else up.)[b] We must know. We must say what we know. We will not be defeated or bemused. But the artist not only knows and reveals, he proves the reliability of his contentions by his works. As with geometry this is the basis of art; the diagram is not didactic. It is fact, proof of the existence of creative man—signed by the creator.

What shall follow surrealism? Picayune question—though there is a way by which the issue can be predicted. But that something equally pregnant must follow it, consequently, we are set to prove, as that nothing could have escaped it, at its major moment, no matter how vitiated that thrust developed to be in some hands. For nothing but surrealism, as it has turned out, preceded, foretold, and so sapped the war of all intellectual strength before it started. And the best of art is always so. Surrealism took all the war's identity, predicted and emasculated it by the same stroke—sucked it dry and was its plain bible to read in—if it hadn't frightened so many.

Thus, plainly, none but the poet holds it in his secret power to tell, in terrific, frightening concentration what the consequences of those forces which make this war its plaything will be. This will be the successor to surrealism.

The idiotic belief that the arts must be put aside for arms—*until* a time of peace (as if they needed coddling and were perishable) must give way to a triple fury of activity, to steal the released energy for constructions.

We proclaim the occasion of our intent to drive the program (of fertility and construction) home.

A living and secret activity, as of fetation, has been undertaken. We do not overlook the fact that nothing but a gnat is born the week following its conception. A time of considerable length must often pass before parturition. But, under cover, the activity is there madly, as at no subsequent period during life, overwhelming changes compressed to a matter of hours—whereas later years will go by in comparative unproductivity. Unless the arts attack by revolution and at once, the offspring of this energy released by war will all be bastards.

In short it is to legitimatize the products of that power released by the Death and induct it into the services of life that the arts are addressed and we are its servants.

There I might end but there is a codicil of specific direction: We are offered the "normal and healthy" as a corrective to our perverse habits, inviting us to "purify" our minds of "degenerate" art, to wean ourselves from its corrupt interests, the degradation inherent in woman and to fall in love instead with "nature"—after all somewhat too palpable and childish a deception. We are to gape heroically at mountains, peer down into mines, whence they would get the materials we are thus induced to dig for our own destruction, and love it! the great "outdoors"!—all such lies carefully ornamented to our tastes, for deadly profit. In truth, the great "outdoors," "joy for health" and all such crap (because a covered lie) we are determined shall give way before the far greater mountains, the far greater depths of the imagination (—to woman— as imagined by such a painter as Paul Delvaux)[d]*.

We have no interest in that "normal" art which is a subterfuge, using "nature" and its flesh to hide the deceptive sterility of a

25. Paul Delvaux, *The Mirror* (1936). Oil on canvas. Destroyed in World War II, reproduced from the *London Bulletin*, No. 3, 1938.

26. Paul Delvaux, *The Phases of the Moon* (1939). Oil on canvas, 55″ × 63″. Collection, The Museum of Modern Art, New York (Purchase).

cringing imagination—asking us to be passionately attached to a cylinder (of hollow steel, mind you!) because of its classic proportions. (Healthy!)[d]

Lies! (It is sterile, it is dead. I will not fall in love with a block of marble or a theorem in "composition" that is out of a book. I am not impressed with measurements and weights. They mean, precisely, Quisling.)[d]* They mean trickery with a purpose to undermine and destroy. (Nothing more ridiculous than to see a figure in military uniform looking at the naked backside of a marble woman in the name of "normal" art.)[d]

It is the Death in whatever form they present it.

(There is relief in such works as those of Paul Delvaux: his gigantic unmeasured women with their heads touching the ceiling, their beribboned bulk in windows dominating in the back of the mind the particular man as he picks apart the secrets of a daisy under a lens. They ride up, powerfully peopling his mind—not with classic measurements and "proofs" but with the dynamic of fertility and—

I salute the paintings of Paul Delvaux.)[d]*

(We need a broad gesture, an example, a flagrant disclosure—a magnificent exaggeration to overwhelm [the Death], a foundation shaking imbecility to put us right, some Rabelaisian monumentation: an ingot of gold such as might be made of the metal in the vaults of Kentucky—a golden bar fifty feet long, twenty-five feet wide and twenty high to be molten in a gigantic pot and poured into the sea)[f] (or molded upon a gigantic death mask of J. P. Morgan. . . . It could be completed—with art—as a bust, a shrine in the middle of Death Valley, solid Gold . . . ! It would be visited and gaped at by millions.)[d]

The Poet in Time of Confusion

Columbia Review, 1941

THE REASON men resort to war is that they fear the implications of peace. But this weakness must be hidden if they are to appear as conquerors. So they try to create confusion in the minds of others, by this to weaken them also and so reduce them: The majority are always ready to surrender their liberties for the promise of security and must be kept confused lest they discover how illusory such promises are likely to be.

To defeat an aggressor our first move must be to defeat the confusion he creates, by which he confesses his inability to proceed without it, and thus see through him.

All must help in this, the artist among others, for which, even, the artist is peculiarly well fitted as we may surmise from the common action, preliminary to his advances, an aggressor takes to destroy if he can that first excellence of the arts, their marvelously complex and superlatively efficient eyes. He can see them hovering over him beyond the possibility of his largest planes to reach, and knows that he will go mad finally before his own face reflected there.

The confusion an aggressor would create to hide behind is like a movie screen on which appear his unfleshed desires, what he would like to have us believe and accept of him. But there is a littered and otherwise empty space back of it, which is himself, where he would not have us go. It is our effort to reach that place of reality which characterizes what we must do, a beam of light into it, to destroy him.

Of what other thing is an artist's life composed than the desire and the ability to look past this screen at any cost? That is what an artist does, that is what he is trained to do. Therefore his great use in deflating all liars. Therefore they burn his books and tear out his pictures—or slyly steal them! That is the reason they so brutally murdered Lorca at Granada, no more than for being, as he was, a poet.

But the artist is not a very strong persuader of the generality of men. On the contrary, he is attacked right and left because the difficulties he proposes, which would make of peace a violent sphere of action, often by revolution, are too much for them. Let him take that to heart then, that he is not a very strong persuader of men and, relieved, seek instead clarity, to be the more unsparing, the more lucid.

To begin with, the artist must acknowledge that he does not get his energy from nothing, a vaccum, but from action, crude action. Whatever war is, because of it energies are enormously released over the world. But if war is permitted to remain dominant these determine us inevitably toward destruction. Energies *are* however released, we must begin by accepting that. War is a focus of action, breaks up sterile combinations. See to it only, I should say to the artist, that you grasp in among these aimless forces and seize what you desire. It is to take and use them in your own way that you have been conditioned. Only released energy can knock us out of our lethargy, set us in motion. But use these energies according to the training not of the warmongers with their lying imagery but with sleepless vigor, as the artist is trained to do for accuracy and spiritual release.

Thus I would say to the poet. Write to correct lies. How? Perpetually as an artist by the passion which is most sensible in you—but with an artist's pitiful conception of the personal moment, to find the precise word and to place it in the line with full awareness of the broad day of your total perceptions. Nothing that prevents this can be good. Anything which predicates what you must say, as a poet, without complete freedom to determine, from the sensible facts, your own conclusions or that attempts to foist a form upon you, outside your choice, in which you must say it, is a lie. Destroy it.

There is only one good art in any age; it is that which uses the sensible terms of that age fully with widest application to its needs for liberation of the whole man.

You can't lie and be a first-rate artist. Therefore, look for inconsistencies in all attempts to destroy the artist and his works and—spot the real liar.

Question everything you see on the gaudy screen; look behind it. Perhaps this man is a great poet, or is he a regressive comment on the art of his day? Perhaps this man is a noteworthy philosopher, or should we say an able perverter of the significances of his terms? That Jew is a great moralist, or rather a bigoted apologist for the tenets of a belated sect. Look at their words, pick them up and try to fit them to a form and line which is consonant with your day. Trust your reactions. They are a sort of truth. Let the imagination rise as to the possible sequences and connotations.

To the artist that is truth which permits all questions to be answered freely in the unrestricted terms of his art.

Let us say that France presented a philosophical-historical correctness of reasoning in the aggregate of her national reaction to the invader—taking all the factors we know into consideration, the national political corruption, the self-seeking of the wealthy families. Take it as a movement in one direction—without trying either to praise or condemn the movement. Take it as a nation moved by one determinant. Try to discover that determinant. Relate it to more recent actions. That nation is now out of the major action. Has the action been perhaps irrelevant? Ask anything.

Are women in public life the source of degeneration and homosexuality the source of genius? Is this the spur? Shall the land of the countries be divided among the peasants or held for their benefits by others? These questions will be answered many times over by economists and governmental agents; do you answer them as a poet? Are the mentally unfit to be removed from the possibility of reproduction by edict of the Board of Health? Or is each succeeding apex of civilization no more than the crest of a wave that inevitably breaks and falls to be renewed again from below from sources we cannot determine? Are we to rescue the ailing in body and reinject their depleted blood into the race? Why do I say "depleted blood," perhaps it contains the indispensable seed of the future? And what will be the result? Or are the Mendelian laws inexorable? Do we even know them? What shall we do?

Will Germany be the better for driving Jewish blood from the veins of the race, (if this indeed be possible), or will such action end in ultimate racial disintegration? Give the mind freedom to weigh. Will Germany, following the present action, go into a decline through such a policy of racial discrimination as historical precedent seems to indicate that it will? Has not the Jewish race, which they would remove, been the catalyzer, bringing every race to its apex of political productivity?

What of the British Empire? Will not those who seek to reshuffle it, ignoring its example, be thereby the greatest sufferers in the end?

These are questions to be laid on the field of battle, but whose answers will not be determined by the victory there. The victory or defeat can be determined only in terms of the questions themselves and the questions answered only in their own terms independent of who is a mere military winner or loser. If we must fight, we shall have to fight, bitter war will go on, but at least not to our confusion. It is the "cure" to the spirit that the arts offer.

And the arts do give an answer, for what the artist does that few give him credit of doing is precisely to act. In the face of complex difficulties he elucidates a position and takes it. He does. He makes; difficult as the interpretations may be. He is a doer, finds the place for the word in the line and puts it there, in that place, be the consequences what they may, and himself in that place also, bodily, if need be.

The work of art is valuable and keeps its universality, through variations of time and locality, by the inability of anyone to put a lie in that form which is accurate to the day and make it live. The subject matter may vary or be dictated but the underlying form cannot be dictated. There it stands defiant of dictation and in that form lies the truth.

The conclusion reached and the fight envisioned, under the inevitable attack, irrational in its nature, the resistance will be no less irrational but it is compulsory. We must fight. We must destroy the screen of lies set to confuse and so undo us. For the conclusion is inevitable that by our eyes we shall prove ourselves better men than those who would block perception. Ours is a faith firmer than theirs by the same token, an invincible purpose to reveal truth casually, day by day, that makes theirs an idle vanity by comparison.

The point is that under stress it is cooling to the mind to turn aside a moment and attempt to draw conclusions in a field removed from the general, the field generalled, let us say, by what is known, somewhat unfortunately, under the name of art. It should be and is, at its best, a field uninfluenced by political imperatives, the taboos and passions of what is known, somewhat unfortunately, as the practical. Art is just as practical and far more to the point, many times, than the maneuvers men of affairs hold up to us as models they would have us live by. Be his reward what it may, the artist holds a weapon against lies in his hands which he must use without faltering.

Axioms

Not previously published, 1943
EVERY twenty years or so the boys have to be brought up short because of what they've forgot.

If you don't think that place is important go ahead and shove it into the mouth of the moon.

The controversy between the Catholic Church and naturalism is unresolvable because it comes of a confusion of terms; it is no controversy at all, see Dora Marsden *et al.* on what constitutes a legitimate question. Whereas naturalism represents the full scientific front, the Catholic Church can by no stretch of the imagination be identified with Christianity, much less religion as a whole.

Place is the only universal. When Eliot in a religious poem, "Ash Wednesday," indicates that place is a limitation he denies the basis of religion.

Speaking of pictures and their showing, An American Place[1] is a much more acute designation under which to exhibit them here than The Modern Museum, a name which entirely misses the point as to what is presented (and why certain pictures are painted)[b].

Writing is not a means as Auden mistakenly believes, man is the means, writing is the word.

As to the use of the term American when attached to a work of

[1]The name of the gallery Stieglitz ran from 1929 to his death in 1946.

175

art, I confess it is of no importance unless it is intended to signify that excellence has no particular locale.

The use of new scenes and new terms in a work of art such as South American poems, let us say, is of perennial value if by shifting, that is to say, eliminating what we are used to, the undying truth of that which lies beneath is the better revealed.

To discover what value lies in a man there is nothing like death, which removes his location; the law is a universal one.

Place, rightly understood, means any place, but it must be a place, some place, a particular place, and whatever place the abstractionist finds, he finds, if it has been touched by human hands, that it also has a name. It is this name only which is usable by the artist.

What of Alfred Stieglitz?

Not previously published, 1946
WHAT SHOULD I desire when I am dead? Nothing whatever. For death according to all authorities is the end of desire. And he who would excommunicate me, I excommunicate him. Therefore, there are no longer any restrictions, let them write anything of me that they can—if they want to write anything of me; the only prejudices they are not any longer to consider are my own: *carte blanche*. Let them please their own prejudices: S as B or b as s or as you please— x. Go on, amuse yourself—until the bottom falls out of the market. You will get advices from the inside, that the new altar may not languish in the building.

If the terms are meaningless, then the equation means only the equation. Oh yeah? But if the bomb works what does that mean so far as the terms of the equation are concerned? Precisely what was meant at the beginning: nothing. As far as I had any acquaintance with Stieglitz this represents his philosophy and why art was to him supreme—at a price. That's where I stuck. Not that it wasn't a good barrier to the public but it kept too many people out. That and his eternal talking. I got sick of it.

As far as I'm concerned the time to talk about a man is when he is alive, not dead. What are you talking about, a lot of pictures locked in a private closet? I hope Stieglitz's death means they'll get out and into circulation at a reasonable price so I can buy one here and there—I couldn't before Stieglitz died. Did he expect me to ask for a picture at a private price? Nothing doing. He locked the pictures up, put bars around them that he could remain their master. Now the bars are down and a good thing, he lived long enough. Too long; he'd stopped caring about people.

The pictures needed to be separated from Stieglitz to win their own life and to be appraised in the open. He sat there gloating over

177

them like a miser. Like a spider he built his net to attract those he wished to browbeat or entrap, using the pictures as a come-on. That's a lousy attitude to take. I got sick of it. He acted, toward the end, like some American expatriate poet trading in the more tenuous refinements of the soul. Too bad it was paint on canvas to make it so handy for impounding.

So he had his way and more power to him if that's what he wanted, but under the crimson and orchidaceous surfaces I think he was a damned good horse trader. That's his value to me. I despise the aura of holiness, I like a good camera man. But Stieglitz had the peculiar misfortune (being a small man) to want to keep about himself only those he felt he had under his domination. Marin just didn't care, let's not go into the matter of the others. But Marsden Hartley got kicked out early because he just damned well wouldn't take it. He did all right by himself.

One of Stieglitz's favorite stories was of the two doors over one of which was written, "This way to see God!" and over the other, "This way to hear a lecture about God!" The crowd was going in at the second door. Stieglitz was beyond the other.

He was a good merchant and his pretence to poverty was just part of the buildup. Sure, he didn't care if he starved but he damned well didn't starve—he was surrounded by wealth, the wealth he needed and got. It was real wealth as opposed to the good old solid cash the big-building boys had (remember the equation?) and what in hell are they ever going to do with it but turn it into murder, blood and human meat—even the meat of their own sons and eat it. They don't know what else to do with it. They make wars and that's all they *can* make. Stieglitz knew values better than that. He was for peace, for pictures for the great wealth of the world. But he'd be God damned if he was going to let those bastards have it. They could damn well pay for every smell of it they could get. It didn't make any difference to him whether or not they came to his gallery. There wasn't one big enough for them to shove it up into as far as he was concerned.

But what in hell did he have to compete with them for? He had a heavy chin and a love for the big money. He was out for big game and THEY DIDN'T LICK HIM. He cared like hell for the fact that they didn't lick him. He wanted to be God and in his little shitty hole of an office building he was God. He was the only god any decent person in his right unsold mind could ever take seriously. He liked all that sort of crap.

So there was Stieglitz, the Jew. What did that mean to him? Nothing whatever—except a hard drive into the guts of the living bastards he had to battle—unseen up there on the 17th floor. He belonged to New York City and he should (as he knew) have been given power, POWER. No! No power. They wouldn't give him power. The Museum of Modern Art wouldn't give him power. That hurt him and he wouldn't play. There you are again.

You damned well can't be mild in this game of values. The money-bloody-boys who buy and sell lives on The Street (and don't for a split second realize the way they're sold out in their own rights) aren't mild. They take their women where they find them for the cash they can spill—they order their literature and the tough (sloppy sentimental) big hearts write it for them with swish and smash. So why should a Stieglitz have been mild and forgiving? He forgave no one but fought them down to the wire with his last breath.

That part of the guy I admired, from the ground up. He was clear-sighted. He didn't know everything about painting, as he thought he did—and what the hell do we expect more than that a man should be wise *in his day?* Stieglitz knew his stuff when he had to, and did, finally, I think, through the kindness and devotion of several disciples attain to a certain comfort at the end. I didn't like his "side" but as an intelligence, as a profound prophet of real values as opposed to the murderous falsity of cash over everything else, as a pioneer photographer, as a friend, as a lover of peace, and as a fighter, principally, I deeply honor his memory.

Woman as Operator

Women: A Collaboration of Artists and Writers, 1948
WOMAN AS operator—in primary colors, the correct address—does not lose her sex to the man who is sex more than the mind loses its depth to reason in the man who is thought. She continues down into the midbrain below the possibility of his deepest masculine approaches. Meanwhile the man is consumed and turned, simultaneously, into ideas *in his own head,* impregnated by penetration to new lows, the perpetual wheel.

I don't know how you could make a painting presenting man without including woman. But woman, somehow, lends herself to painting in her own right as man does not. Somehow the painting IS woman. Or might be.

Man on the contrary is at the best *The Card Players* or *Cardinal Don Fernando Niño de Guevara* or *Sarasate.* But woman doesn't have to be so particularized. With her, somehow, an intimate relationship blends itself into the material (paint). You'd make man noble or strong or a soldier or fat but woman even tho' it be *An Old Woman Cutting Her Nails* (painted on the back of another painting) makes no such pretences.

There's really nothing much to man aside from what he does, what he knows, what he desires or makes. Take those things away and you have no man. But woman, that's something else again. It appears even at the height of voluptuous enjoyment as something unassailable. There's nothing to be done with it. To a man the more loving and willing she is and the more she gives herself, the more remote she becomes to him.

What is he to do? Impregnate her? Kill her? Avoid her? You see, it all amounts to the same thing: do what he will she remains in spite of his greatest doing or not doing the same thing, woman, woman in the abstract, something without a face, something beyond his

27. Romare Bearden, *Women with an Oracle* (1947). Oil on canvas. Courtesy of the artist, reproduced from *Women: A Collaboration of Artists and Writers* (Samuel Kootz, New York, 1948).

28. Paul Cézanne, *The Card Players*. Oil on canvas, 25½″ × 32″. Collection, The Metropolitan Museum of Art, New York (Bequest of Stephen C. Clark, 1960).

power—something that (according to his nature) he can abstract, generalize upon, devise means for elucidating but

Women know this impossibility of a meeting between the sexes better than men do. There are two hard spheres, half of them green and the others yellow.

The swooning voluptuousness of woman that she enjoys at the apex of yielding comes out in the end, for her, as a celebration of philosophic reality—whereas for man it turns up as a confession of philosophic nonentity. Therefore man has to be identified (to save himself) as this or that, thinker, laborer. So he goes on painting all his life, "developing his art" as they say. Women merely grow old.

Woman is never destroyed by man but always by the child. But by "keeping" the garden or the house or the flock she postpones her final and inevitable annihilation longer than can a man other than man as artist, "in his dreams." Self-portraits are almost entirely the products of men. Mme. Le Brun posing as a man is no exception.

The problem of painting figures on a canvas is a difficult one that grows more difficult when the identity of a certain man calls for representation. But it is necessary to draw the man if you are to do a portrait. How can you do it at the present state of painting? The very fact of modern painting defies representation. What, to be sure, are you going to represent when apart from the act nothing is present? The face? Surely *not*. His mind? His *mind?* The great mind of a Franklin Delano Roosevelt? Who is cynical enough to think he could paint a man's mind as a portrait? You might as well try to paint the speed of a hurricane or the stillness of a desert.

But modern painting can, I believe, paint woman. When she stands on her feet, any woman, it is woman standing on her feet whereas if it is a man you immediately say, What man? Therefore it is obvious to the painter, who has to put things on canvas, that they be basic and not merely incidental. Somehow a man always looks affected in a picture (except as clown) whereas woman always looks serious.

You see at once in looking at casual pictures representing women in the contemporary scene how unwomanlike they are—the women in ads and travel pictures. They are baffling because they represent, actually, female men even tho' the intention was to show women. And to complement them—it is all that can be done—they are usually set off against male women. Arabesques of this sort can be very charming especially when they are used for decoration—but with discretion! Not obsession.

And so an exhibition with "woman" as its theme is not only legitimate and important today but timely. In fact it is far beyond the time today for a readjustment of the sense in such matters or we shall entirely lose all sense in our day of woman. It would not be untimely to leave our economy in such things to some committee for the selection of Miss America, 1948, but one would have to be a Negro to get the point, something we can't all boast.

To represent a woman as operator, as Bearden does, you have to realize her relationship to painting, which is different from man's relationship to painting. Every portrait of some woman comes out as woman; every portrait of man comes out as some man—or nothing. Even Leonardo couldn't escape this. You may ask, Why do not our painters follow Titian? They might but it would only represent "Titian." There's nothing in that direction. A man has to shut out almost all things believed to be woman today to paint woman.

Imagine showing a prostitute at her trade, naked, in any position you like, French postcards: it could be any wife, in a painting, unless you labeled it. Unpleasant, to say the least, but very popular—making up the whole field of the industrial and many other less suspect conceptions. That's man's conception of woman, not a painter's. It has, fortunately, nothing to do with a representation of woman as operator. In fact I can well understand that the painter, the present-day painter, will have to continue to avoid voluptuousness in woman for a long time to come.

For voluptuousness is very deceiving and can very frequently look much like the gaudy backside of a baboon which is made after all to sit on as well as to defy and attract. Painters are not interested in jokes or at least do not often base their designs on them.

All women sit on their faces. A few are noble, a very few. The painter proceeds accordingly.

With woman there's something under the surface which we've been blind to, something profound, basic. We need, perhaps more than anything else today, to discover woman; we need badly to discover woman in her intimate (unmasculine) nature—maybe when we do we'll have no more wars, incidentally, but no more wars. Such a show as this, almost flippant, certainly "wrong" as it may seem, at least avoids the more malicious flippancy which masquerades as "woman" today. Such a picture as Bearden's (taken with the others, good and bad), if it can link the basic conception of woman I have sketched with an art that is in the condition painting is in today, becomes important.

As between nations and men, woman is the universal solvent. (Why do we not hear more of women, as women, not taking the parts of men, in Russia today? They are suppressed lest they act to dissolve our differences.) It is altogether fitting at such a time that her traits (no face) be celebrated—by the artist who alone among men resembles her.

A Letter, Touching the Comintern, upon Censorship in the Arts

The Tiger's Eye, 1948

LIKE Father Riccordo Lombardi in Italy when he says that there is much in the Communist doctrine of which he approves, (the equalization of wealth between the rich and poor), so I admit, there is much justice in the insistency by Communism upon a literature based upon a "peoples' good."

Let us not at this point go off into polemics: Who shall determine who shall do what? Shall there be a censorship and by whom, government or a board of professionals or otherwise? There is always a censorship, individual or by some collective agency, governing every work of art; some sort of criterion is forever being applied one way or another. Omitting any further comment upon that, let me rather go direct to an attempt at an evaluation of what is desirable, what is worth censoring, what the censorship, in brief, masks and would uncover.

The objective of all censorship is a value of some sort. All censorship, public and private, is an attempt at reclaiming values. In other words, what are we censoring *for?* The Comintern insists that art should arise from the people, its purpose being to elevate the popular good to distinction. What's wrong with that?—remember we are discussing not methods but values.

Everything is wrong with it, you'll say. What about Dylan Thomas? What about Valéry? What about Ezra Pound? What about——? Should their work be suborned by an ignorant censorship? Unthinkable in an intelligent social-economic environment where any art at all is expected to develop and thrive. Might one not say rather that all art should be suppressed under those circumstances as, in fact, is strictly the case where censorship is misdirected?

Let's put it another way: An artist has no choice in his materials—

no more than has a chemist. We *can't* write like so and so and so and so, we can only write according to the compulsions of the *Zeitgeist* of our day following the concatenation of events which is known to us as real in our time. Only when we do this can what we turn out be good; only then is it not cheatery, "popular" in the worst sense and so a lie. Thus we have arrived already at a certain "good."

Now it isn't everyone who can do this. One isn't up to it. This can be done only by the man skilled in his trade. There is a certain "front," a certain edge against which the chemist, the physiologist, the Comintern in its own belief, is waging war: the present as it faces "the future." I shall comment further upon that in a moment.

The advancement or at least the adjustment of the mind (for what else is it?) toward this reality of the times is what the Comintern teaches—and in that (still leaving out of the discussion the means they have chosen for achieving this) everyone agrees. At least I assume that the world does generally agree in this.

I say that this "front" like the front of a cold wave, an advancing army or the conflux of human knowledge itself, is not wholly a matter of human choice. It is also not a matter that can always be foreseen. But it is a matter that concerns us all, collectively. There I am in complete agreement with the Comintern.

But that works both ways; if it concerns us all, collectively, then it must, obviously, govern us as individuals. No man, I insist, can be wiser than his times. I don't say he can not bring about his will in his day or that he may not see "ahead further" than anyone else in his time. I will even insist, and this is important, that it is only the individual who can advance "beyond his day," formulate the thoughts about him, remake the world. In no other way can this come about.

But what he is formulating, which is equally important, is only the general reality, the "front," the level, to which he along with all the others is bound to come to equalize the tensions of his day. He can't do anything more.

Darwin was bound to "discover" the elements with which the *Zeitgeist* had confronted his world (he certainly couldn't have discovered anything else) which he shared in common with all others—a reality before which yesterday was a cipher.

No one questions this in the natural sciences, of course, or fails to see the connection between abstract and abstruse physics and the ultimate success in atomic fission. But when it comes to the arts, controversy becomes violent; the government steps in—church government or social-political government and otherwise.

"Individual freedom" is chanted, the word "stupidity" is hurled like a time bomb at political minds trying to tell the artist what he must do.

Who shall be the censor, by what criterion? In other words, shall we be governed? Absolute freedom is the artist's birthright as it is the physicist's if the "front," what we may call the advancement of knowledge, is to be valued. If the people generally are to be advanced, we are saying, the artist must be free. Right.

And saying this we have to continue by concluding that the Comintern is his enemy—not only that, but that they are defeating their own design, that is, that they are defeating the advancement among their people of the general "front," not necessarily in this case of knowledge, but of reality—in some measure, the truth. That is a pretty serious accusation. But let us look at it for a moment:

We say that when the Comintern admonishes the artist to quit certain tendencies and adopt others it is an enemy of the people. But is this always true? What are we dealing with? Values. It is always possible that in a blundering way they may even be right; not that they know, perhaps, what they're talking about, how can they, being politicians and not artists? But, still they might be right.

How? They just might be able, by chance, to redirect the artist to the "front" when perhaps he has strayed away from it. It is, at least, an interesting possibility.

Where then can the artist have strayed? To say, away from the people, from knowledge, isn't satisfactory. But away from reality, from the direct requirements of his times, must contain, at least, a modicum of sense. And where could he have strayed? Into what morass? Surely nowhere but into the past or the future.

The future is mere fantasy, it does not exist. What we call the future is always the present, unrecognized. But the past! That is where the danger lies. The past doesn't exist any more than does the future. It too is a fantasy, a dream, but a dream that has terrific power over us; and it is always for us a defeat of reality when we permit it to have the government of our lives today. I say this, that it is the past that is the power we have most to fear.

But the past is tradition. Oh, the past is the Academic! It is the denial that the arts arise direct from the people, from the Common Front. It is the assertion that the arts are propagated like the tapeworm from its own segments, that literature begets literature from age to age and people to people.

Wrong, self-destructive as we know the censorship to be as practiced by the Comintern, yet, let us acknowledge, that it is not the worst censorship which it is possible for the arts to suffer. Let us acknowledge that some sort of censorship is always operant in the arts but that the past is our worst enemy.

"So we wander aimlessly in the irretrievable past or distant Utopias; but the fleeting moment we cannot grasp." I hope that with time and a better understanding of the world, we shall find a more useful directive for our lives than the crude censorship of which we are speaking can possibly afford us. But for the moment I must concede that it is not entirely bad.

Nicolas Calas's Illumination of the Significance of Hieronymus Bosch's The Garden of Delights

Not previously published, 1951

I AM NOT a specialist in the works of Hieronymus Bosch nor medieval art generally. I am, however, an artist of some experience, facing the tasks which concern all artists of whatever time or category in placing their creations before an impersonal, even an antagonistic, eye. I have been asked to give an opinion upon a text by Nicolas Calas, a writer, dealing with *The Garden of Delights,* a fifteenth-century painting, a triptych, by Hieronymus Bosch. At great length Calas anatomizes and develops the meaning of that painting, explaining its reason for being as well as the detailed significances of its various parts.

After reading the text and studying the hundred or more plates, black and white or colored, which accompany it, I have come to the following conclusions:

Calas has set out to prove that the overall intention of the painting is to present an exposure (resentful against impiety) of the disastrous effects of heresies current in that day, the folly of man, as against the teachings of St. Gregory and St. Augustine especially, the solid ground of the true church. To this end, as a painter [Bosch] distorts and inverts his images (from the normal. Everything is upside down,)[b] thus marking them as untrue against every right understanding of what is orthodox. At the same time he has hidden his meaning from the simpleminded, reserving it, a riddle to be solved, for those with insight into the teachings of the saints. Only those will know the full truth of the work and how it should be interpreted.

Calas has discovered that Bosch's complex arrangements can be explicitly understood, can be unified, by referring them to a source, the writings of St. Gregory and St. Augustine. It is his belief that when these texts are studied, as he has done, step by step, the whole meaning of *The Garden of Delights* becomes clear. Furthermore, and this is the full justification for spending so much time on what might seem a piece of irrelevant pedantry, that it becomes alive with meaning, a powerful dissertation on the human spirit, of as great a significance today (in a troubled world)[b] as ever it was in the time of its painting (, the fifteenth-century world that Bosch suffered and fought)[b]. And that, by the method of the thought, as revealed by the painter, the work vies with contemporary work. In short, by laying the method of the work bare, Bosch is made to appear, in the light of contemporary understanding, one of the timeless, towering masters of the art.

Bosch's canvas is crowded with figures. Looking for the origins of the creatures and objects with which Bosch has filled his picture, all of them, with overwhelming uniformity, are, as Calas has found, not only mentioned, but discussed at length in Augustine and Gregory, especially in the former's *Letter to Leander,* and in Gregory's comments on the Psalms. They arise from these texts to the last detail. So that Bosch, by poring over them, knowing them by heart as a beloved reference, could have and indeed did derive [from them] the images he turned into the interrelated creatures and objects of his composition. Calas [gives a] point by point exposition of each figure presented, found specifically mentioned in the multiple texts—everything that is on the canvas, from the two-legged dog to the giraffe (the one exception): the mitre fallen, on which the "sparrow" sits, the unicorn, the flight of blackbirds, the two palm trees, the fish floating in the sky, the bridleless riders in the great carrousel of the center panel, the blind elephant. We are convinced that the distorted mountain-edifices, the gold, the pink, and the blue, are indeed each a church, a house of perverted worship. The peculiarly placed glass columns that support nothing, the clear and the opaque (as through a glass, darkly) all have a complex meaning that Calas painstakingly develops and makes convincingly clear. The owl stares from the cavern at the base of the fountain behind Christ's figure in Eden, the false Eden, it must be understood. And then, in the right panel, the Inferno, the granaries are afire. The figures rise directly out of Gregory and Augustine, a clinching argument in establishing the correctness of Calas's primary assumptions.

Pictorially earlier renderings of similar forms in various of Bosch's and others' compositions, drawings, and paintings such as the *Epiphany* in the Prado, the "Haywagon" triptych, and the *Temptation of St. Anthony*, reinforce the justice of his conclusions. All the birds in this false Eden represent sinners, all is addressed in the words of Gregory to "those who already know how to take the leaps of contemplation [, how to] ascend the lofty summits of the Divine sentences, as the tops of mountains."

Nothing much is recorded of the life of Hieronymus Bosch; I will not attempt to speak of it. But his paintings other than the one under scrutiny give some light upon his mode of thought. His large single figure compositions *The Cure of Folly, The Prodigal Son, The Crown of Thorns,* show the mastery of his treatment of the human face. His own portrait among them shows him to be shrewd, a keen observer of human character, as in his well-known *The Juggler,* revealing man and woman as they are, realistically presented. He lays them before us—for our understanding—as a painter, showing himself to be a thinker of great force, a great user of the portrait as the means to an end—symbols to bespeak his mind.

That the picture under study is a polemical one, a parable, becomes apparent when we pay heed to the way these faces appear: aside from the large figure in the right panel of the triptych, far larger than any other in the entire painting, the faces of the damned (which the whole painting presents) are without expression. They are emotionless, passionless, caught in a trance, neither enjoying nor suffering, cerebral, as in an exercise, as if pawns, terms in a polemic, a dissertation pictorially presented. That one figure alone, turned back at us from the far end of what seems the shell-like relic of a dead horse, a millstone balanced upon his head, a half revealed smile, shows any recognizable human character. The rest are like the illuminations in old books, in the *Bible Moralisée,* marginal to the lesson. There is strictly speaking no pleasure in this Garden of Delights.

29. Hieronymous Bosch, *The Garden of Earthly Delights* (right panel detail, head). Oil on wood, 220 cm. × 97 cm. Collection, Prado, Madrid.

30. Hieronymous Bosch, *The Garden of Earthly Delights* (left panel).

31. Hieronymous Bosch, *The Garden of Earthly Delights* (left panel details, Christ and Eve).

32. Jan van Eyck, *Giovanni Arnolfini and his Bride*. Oil on canvas.
Reproduced by courtesy of the Trustees, The National Gallery, London.

That one face—startling enough—is his own: in hell. Calas speaks of it as a confession.

There are in the picture also no children; nothing of the young save only a litter of pigs.

In view of the foregoing it is my opinion that in this study Nicolas Calas, in spite of certain objections which will be discussed in a moment, has irrefutably established his main point: that the picture is derived directly from Augustine's and Gregory's texts. To establish the thesis he has driven it home by inescapable arguments: a discovery of the motives that drove Hieronymus Bosch to his picture, *The Garden of Delights,* establishing his work on solid ground by the study of the painting itself, its contemporary parallels, and associating them with the texts of Augustine and Gregory.

But if there is still any doubt of this, the most wonderful and convincing proof of the correctness of Calas's theme *and method of presenting* it is his study of the foreground of the left panel, the *Fountain of Life* and the group before it, the figures of Adam and Eve together with Christ in the Garden of Eden.

That this is indeed a heretical Eden cannot now be mistaken. The position of Adam's foot, in relation to Christ's foot as having "slipped," the marriage between Christ and Eve, as their hands are joined, are interesting enough. But when we are led into a closer study of the scene's details, under a magnifying glass, we find the heretical Christ's hair to be composed of snakes and his eyelids and very lips, which Eve seeks to approach, to be a tangle of worms. By these revelations we are startled into a still fuller realization of the truth of Calas's contentions.

Under Eve's lower lip, parodying perhaps the shadow under Eve's lip in Van Eyck's *Adoration of the Lamb,* is a hole. And looking close, "watching" her ankle is a nail, opposite which, the member being pierced, bored into as though it were wood, is the head of a demon showing through.

Calas believes this whole juxtaposition of Christ and the unclean maiden, Eve, to be related to the position of the figures in another contemporary work: the Arnolfini portrait by Van Eyck, which is

" 'a portrait of . . . a man and a woman represented in the act of contracting marriage.' Christ and Eve join hands in a way suggesting a parody of the joining of hands of the Arnolfini."

Calas continues: "Even if Bosch held Van Eyck in high esteem, he must have deplored the negligence with which this mundane court painter treated religious ceremonial." This whole passage should be read in detail to get the full weight of Calas's meaning and the justification for the task he has undertaken. Even Eve's hair as it cascades down her back is an amplification of the tassel beside the bride in the Arnolfini portrait.

But now comes the most interesting question of all: the consideration of Calas's point of view, its "inaccuracies" bred of his method of investigation and what is to be understood from it, as well as what it has contributed to our understanding.

To me it seems that Calas's text is to be taken as a true revelation (time having been annihilated by the jump from the last day of creation, the seventh, to the Apocalypse, the eighth) of the working of Bosch's mind—paralleling the contemporary, the working of Calas's mind today. This is a new way of appraising the illustrious past.

Calas's presentation is the work of a mind that puts itself on a par with Bosch, as though he too were contemporary and his picture, which before he painted it had its "creation" already extant in his consciousness, were a contemporary phenomenon—as it cannot but be—something alive today. Such a view gives the text new authority. It is no longer an explanation in which the present day attempts to put itself into conditions of the past which it cannot know and so stultifies itself. It is rather an evocation in which the present mind brings the past up to today and makes it work before our eyes. It is an eye cast into Bosch's mind, true enough, but it is also our eyes and mind which we lend to the past that it may live again as we watch it performing, alive before us. Calas lends Bosch his faculties and bids him speak. It makes Bosch come alive and though we can't always be sure (the process would defeat itself if this were true) by releasing itself unrestrainedly it achieves a new insight—provided the premises are correct, which I am convinced they are.

By Calas's use of the method it wins to itself my unqualified support. It can't hold back without itself pretending to be wiser or more astute or a greater painter than Bosch himself—which would be absurd. And so by these assumptions, out of sheer intellectual modesty, not looseness of treatment, it must let itself go completely, not hold back: it cannot afford to be maimed by the thought that Bosch *couldn't* have gone so far. He could and *perhaps* did: one must envision everything even remotely suggested to get at the *full* truth.

In short, Bosch presents in his picture *The Garden of Delights* the image of how a contemporary mind, with all its shiftings of the subconscious, in dreams, in the throes of composition, works.

Thus Calas makes Bosch's mind work as if it were a contemporary mind (and we know the mind has always worked the same): he gives Bosch a contemporaneity we cannot ignore.

It is *not* stated that Bosch coldly and laboriously built up the intricate pattern Calas describes; this is what confuses the self-limiting experts who are staidly correct in rejecting some of Calas's more difficult deductions. They don't see, at the same time, how Calas's approach enlarges and enriches the field. They don't see the rationale of his *method.* It is *not* their method. He proceeds on a different premise: Bosch is not dead, rather this painting of his shows him to be very much alive today as he was when he painted *The Garden of Delights,* feverish with intense convictions.

That the experts have their classical methods of "proof" does not invalidate a different method, Calas's method, which is inclusive of all the resources of the mind, the modern mind. Their method is exclusive, a conscious narrowing of the attention which, at its worst, maims it, restricts knowledge to the narrow confines of the past which Bosch, a man of genius, was able to transcend.

Knowing that Bosch had conned Augustine and Gregory by heart, and [knowing] therefore the pertinent contents of his mind, knowing with what texts he was familiar and knowing from contemporary evidence how the minds of all painters have worked—and Bosch was gifted with an acute and acerb intelligence—it is *convincing* that it would work in that way while painting the work under discussion. It would *not* work with the scholarly exclusiveness of the modern scholar. Bosch's paintings were designed to face a wider world, a deeper world which his tortured forms make plain.

Given, in short, a mind filled with such reading as Calas has revealed to us and given an intelligence such as Bosch undoubtedly possessed, sitting down to paint, it is convincing that it is just in the way shown that the images he puts down would arise to the eye.

As I read Calas's exposition I come on moments of direct clarity, close association between the explained painting and Augustine's or Gregory's text. Then there are deductions by Calas justified tentatively by reobservation of the various figures—sometimes under the magnifying glass. Of these I have spoken. To my eyes they are justified to the last detail. I do not say that they all carry equal conviction (and neither does Calas), but I do say that from what is undoubtedly true of Bosch's intention the more remote interpretations *may* justifiably be made. And in these more remote inferences (such as the "wooden" leg of the figure of Eve and her "broken" arm) Bosch's mind, the painter's mind, is laid bare, revealing a truer method of approach to the painting's meaning than a more restricted method could ever do. It is the way an alert mind, given the conditions, would work and *probably* did work.

It is from the probability that Calas takes his élan (, his justification)[b]. So that, [starting with] a contemporary mind, [and building on his own assumptions,] Calas makes Bosch appear to have assumed as much, [makes Bosch's mind become] convincingly operative. He breathes, he lives and so *must have* thought and acted in that way because he *couldn't* have thought and acted otherwise. He must, with Van Eyck's work in mind (as it cannot but have been), have thought those thoughts; thinking of the *Adoration of the Lamb,* he must have chosen those inverted images to voice his objections.

(And therefore he did. The overwhelming assumption facing a liberated energy such as his is that the process came about as Calas said it did, his statements are true.)*

The argument is *not* clear, it is obscure. The origins of the Church itself are mysterious; therefore in any subsequent apology for the Church (including attacks upon its heretics) the element of mystery, of obscurity constitutes a part. If Calas's text were an explanation only it would become tiresome, a mere scholastic excercise. But if it is a detection of light, the laying bare of a living flame, never out, if it is an evocation of an inner (continuous) meaning, it is worth all our pains, all our efforts to keep that flame alive, to rescue it from desuetude (, for it is that flame which is the inner meaning of our lives. It is contemporary—and that is the core of Calas's justification in undertaking the work at all—it is contemporary, it is alive, it is ourselves—into whom Bosch is projected)[b]. That has been the end of Calas's passionate application. To have adopted any other mode of approach than the one he has chosen would have been to deny a major part of Bosch's truth.

To sum up, in this masterful presentation toward the meaning of Hieronymus Bosch's *The Garden of Delights,* [Calas] makes a fifteenth-century intelligence come vividly alive for us with contemproary richness of understanding so that we may approach it in the expectation of winning new rewards: (a fearless thinker, an alert pair of eyes, you get the sense of a Bosch who wouldn't be abashed by anything he would find in the present world, but could face and stay on top of any contingency of thought or manners.)[a] Evocation is the word we must apply, evocation of the painting's apocalyptic power. Men do not die if their attack is kept alive by their works, hence the masters secreted their meanings in their paintings to have them live, if chance favored them, forever. And the "longer" their meaning the longer they might expect to live—to the last day, the eighth day of Creation as Calas has pointed out. All men who have seen into their lives to this day, to the end, and so written or painted, will continue to hold a secret meaning worth seeking for us such as Bosch has hidden among his forms.

Thus Nicolas Calas, by illuminating Bosch's life through his painting, has made him alive among us, made him apocalyptic, enriched us by the knowledge of a great "contemporary."

The Portrait: Emanuel Romano

I.

Form, 1966

I HAVE BEEN watching the building of a portrait for which I was the sitter. I do not mean that I watched the painting, the putting on of the colors, though I could see the movements, even hear the rasp of the brush at times. I mean I have seen the picture grow in the mind of Emanuel Romano who is painting it. I have seen him struggle to realize what he wanted to put down to depict my face.

(And I watched myself as I cautiously revealed what I knew of myself to him. How is a painter to achieve what he puts upon the canvas if the sitter has no belief in him, if he does not feel that the man has the power to see what is before him? The sitter will give no more than he must. It is not human to expect it. If he does not find the painter able to seize what is there the sitter will not give it.)[a]

It is a struggle between the painter and the subject. The artist must get through to the ground underneath—the basic meaning. Shall the terms be abstractions? Or shall one paint a surface, a still life of a face, devoting his whole art to that? Or shall one make a painting that is a reproduction of the picture in the artist's mind? Together the artist and the sitter combine, one putting up his actual face and the other his abilities, to produce this miraculous image.

That, I think, is what Emanuel Romano is striving for: a face which he has chosen, which he has wanted to take into his mind for the mind to work upon it its chemistry.

We read not to gain, or not *primarily* to gain, knowledge of what we are reading—for we read fiction as readily as we read history or philosophy—but to gain clarity of mind. We read to rescue ourselves from the befuddlement in which we exist between express commitments of our attention.

(Anything: love, the hunt, are the same, anything that gives our senses a particular occupation; the getting of money, games of all sorts. We waken startled from it when such a vision has passed. For what is knowledge compared to a full possession of our senses, when all our faculties are welded toward the accomplishment of a given end and we come face to face with our position in the world?)[a]

Something of that sort occurs when we give ourselves to a painting. There, before us, at its best, we see a concentrate of our lives, a gist which absorbs us, vividly, in all its colors. We become lost in it.

And of all paintings the portrait is the most complex, and the most satisfying. Modern painters have been baffled by it. They have been afraid of the horrible word "representational"; they have run screaming into the abstract, forgetting that all painting is representational, even the most abstract, the most subjective, the most distorted. The only question that can present itself is: What do you choose to represent?

The (stale)[a] concept of what a portrait is has been at fault. It is not simple. (In the making of a portrait lies the painter's greatest challenge—but he has to know WHAT he's painting. The range of answers to that question will open a new field into which the next phase of the art will extend. The portrait is the new field,)[a] it will strain all the resources available to the greatest skills in the art to resolve that.

It must be understood, before going further, what has occurred in painting during the past seventy-five years: During that time (the resources of painting,)[a] the means of seeing and placing colors and shapes upon the canvas have been enormously expanded (, mainly by the French school)[a]. Every avenue open to human ingenuity has been explored. (Today there is no school that one need follow. There is no longer any closed circuit to painting. Today, knowing the resources, anyone can do anything. Cézanne was a great realist—Van Gogh did something else—I pick them at random. They all added to the breaking of the bounds. Light was let in.)[a] It was a true French Revolution. The modern masters, mainly the French, have given us painting, painting itself free from all restrictions. They said to us in effect: There it is. Now see what you can do with it.

For a while the painters chose to paint "subjectively." Influenced by Freud they discovered the subconscious and represented it on their canvases. The scribblings of children five years old were discovered to be "revealing." But the time must come when such a lode is exhausted. Such a time has now arrived.

Painters are asking themselves: Where shall I go next? Shall I return to realism—the public at least would be happier? There is nothing else left for me—I'm sick of my own guts. (Tripe is good eating when well-garnished but—it's still tripe. I want something else. Where shall I go now? Abstraction? The Arabs tried that and finally broke down and did the lions of the famous fountain—which we cherish. Abstractions are only representations of a naive sort. Finally they will find out—I hope I'll be one of the first to discover it, they say—how limited they are. They are limited, exhausted before they begin—but it had to be done.)[a] Ceramics has been their answer.

Painting is looking desperately for an extensive field into which to loose itself that it may run free. To sum it up: 1. The great discoverers of the past seventy-five years have opened up the field, making their discoveries in the art available to all (, today a man can do anything)[a]. 2. The subjectivist field has been exhausted (by the recent investigators)[a]—it was a mere side-pocket. 3. We stand facing a new continent to which the portrait (, among a sea of still lifes, each of which has contributed its bit,)[a] gives the hint for a future. It is a tremendous continent whither our caravels Monet, Cézanne, Braque, (Rouault,)[a] have brought us safely to port.

II.

(THE STRESS is no longer on the distortions of the mind, we have gone beyond that, there are no more discoveries to be made there;)[a] the stress now is upon varieties of experience. (A competent artist can now paint anything he wants to.)[a] The stress now is upon the thing which the artist's mind creates when it sees before it the unworked contours of a face. What the artist will paint is his creation, the hidden work of his own imagination; what he is—painted in the subtly modified contours of the sitter's face. It is his own face in the terms of another face.

The artist is always and forever painting only one thing: a self-portrait.

(And that is what we look for in any work of art: the artist. In whatever work he has done we look only for him, the genius—if he is a genius—the creator himself. We seek in his "greatness" our own greatness. Who would not be painted by a master? Who being a master would stop at painting a side of beef if he would? He himself is there in that side of beef.)[a]

Discovery is the word. (Emanuel Romano is seeking, in the face he attacks, for the man, the woman, into which he can release his own distractions.[1] It is a new art, that of the portrait,)[a] it is a new territory, new all over again today. The modern artist has had to rediscover it (, after the crudities of the distortion era—which was however along the right track of discovery)[a]—a new object—his own imaginary image in the terms of the subject before him. Himself—in all its multiple implications.

(It approaches in resort the province of the poem. Technically the great painters of the recent past have liberated the art completely, nowadays one can do anything but now, as Romano is demonstrating, mere manual ability is nothing, better to take up ceramics.

This leaves open the oldest field of all—the imagination. We in our day cannot be bound by our mere internal anatomy, it is all limited, as final as our own external anatomy. It is novel, or was novel to us for a while, but it has no further significance.

We are also tired of the art of the kindergarten. It is charming with its ears growing out of stumps. Men used to practice that—drawing upon the stories of satyrs with goats' legs and men's shoulders, upon the Minotaur. But it is limited. It is finished after three passes and a lunge.)[a]

Thus we return to the oldest field of all—the imagination. It is

---

[1]In version (b) Williams crosses out the word "distractions" and substitutes "abilities."

the imagination, in terms of the flesh, which we have neglected while perfecting our techniques; the imagination working subtly with the flesh, representing extraordinary co-minglings between two images:—the painter and the sitter. It is a world of unrealized proportions. It is a drawing together such as that between Van Gogh and the *Potato Eaters*—a man facing other men and representing on the canvas himself as modified by those others so inexplicably placed before him evoking his distress, his disappointments, (his starved miscegeny and)[a] his love. It is that that he must paint . . . the internal contours of that other face . . . facing his own (, the artist himself—modified by his love)[a].

III.

AND SO, taking the hint from the portrait, which is not, as it happens, Romano's major interest as a painter, it is this approach which characterizes what I have admired otherwise of his work.

I am not interested in painting a portrait, he says. What I want to paint is a head. (He might as well have said, What I want to paint is a mask.) I am not an "artist." So many nincompoops are artists. I am a painter.

That summarizes the new concept of the man who wants to put pigments upon a taut piece of canvas to spell out an effect. It is the end result of a long period of experimentation, all sorts of experimentation with paint upon canvas.

All the good modern paintings, the portrait of Gertrude Stein by Picasso, Cézanne's portrait of Mme. Cézanne, have been experiments. All have been more important as successful experiments than as anything else. Beautiful. Wonderful work. All of it has been distinguished. All of it has given us great freedom and told us nothing more.

But when I look at Rubens, I see a love of the flesh, good food, wine, the bodies of women. He loved it. He lived it. He painted it. El Greco! I see the spirit rising above the death of a man. In the work of Michelangelo, even in his sonnets, you can see the man. His works that he did late in life, of the Christ, only one leg finished—there is tremendous feeling, immense understanding of the figure in every part.

The finest work of Rembrandt, of Titian was painted when they were old. It is to paint the ripeness of knowledge, of understanding, the fullness of the senses to which all this technical mastery is to be applied.

To paint is to struggle to identify one's self with a world in its newest terms. As the means develops (it is like, as it is in fact, a widened vocabulary) one sees what one did not see before. A vocabulary, which seems to apply merely to speech, actually widens the scope of the mind. The modern painter SEES more than his nineteenth-century peer. He is a more understanding man. His range of subjects is immensely broadened.

So Emanuel Romano is going to Italy again within the year to SEE Italy anew, as an experience. And, as he is able, to paint canvases having in them the Italy he has discovered in his own mind, entirely different from anything he has seen there before.

It will be a conjunction of new elements. It is his mode of approach that is important. It is this that has made his recent canvases—of states of mind in the shape of children, of lovers.

IV.

THE ITALIAN painter, De Chirico, who, young, developed an astounding conception, and then in middle age, gave it up and went so far as to sue a gallery for exhibiting it, is an example of great interest to me. He is an artist who developed young and finished. He could go no further. He said all he had to say. Some shoot themselves. Some give up painting as Rimbaud gave up the poem, and ruin themselves out of a purpose to have done with it.

De Chirico out of melancholy, with cold, dry colors, painted robots, the architecture of ruins, the ruins of thought. He took tailors' dummies stitched in the shape of heads. Dead stuffs. But he made of it exciting statements.

But once he had done this, resembling Stravinsky in his early percussive period, he was through.

We look in vain for an answer to why De Chirico quit his magnificent early work—until we come to what is happening to everyone who is painting today. His work had come to the end of its usefulness. It had SAID what it had to say. It was in danger of saying what it no longer meant to say: the skepticism, so beautifully designed, *whose intent was to signify its opposite*—suddenly became malignant. It threatened to seize everyone as it threatened to seize De Chirico in its inhuman mechanisms and pulverize the very bones of his clothes-dummy self. He became alarmed. He had to, while he could, run from it, deny it, destroy it. He must rescue himself while it was yet possible.

He had to rescue himself even at the cost of insignificance. He had built a robot that would destroy him. Does he not typify the dilemma that has recently threatened all art and all artists? Pygmalion and Galatea is a facile legend but it holds only a degrading threat to the man of imagination. He cannot afford to be caught in that trap.

V.

I DO NOT intend to make any categorical statements concerning my friend Emanuel Romano's worth as a painter. I know him only as an inheritor of the immediate past. I have seen no more than perhaps a hundred of his paintings. He is struggling to express something, something which I am trying to identify—in an idiom with which I am only superficially acquainted but which has always fascinated me.

What I am trying to say is that perhaps, I don't know, it may be that the artist, the painter today is trying to find a new place among his fellows, to forge a new link between what is in his head and the world at large.

He is trying, furiously, without mannerism, without accent of any sort that would baffle the beholder, to say that there is a world of pristine colors (clouded by the actual) in his head. A world different from the world we see, an engaging world, a moving world—hidden from our eyes but in which he lives and moves and breathes. This world he loves, to it he dedicates himself day and night—he dreams it, bathes in it, eats it. Before us he stands dumb, looking into our eyes, embarrassed, unable to do more than try to show us that he KNOWS.

He knows it is there. He knows we do not see it—we cannot see it or we should be moved by it.

It is his business to show it to us, to convince our minds of its presence by painting it, placing it before us. It is the world of his imagination. It is the real world, the world that what *we* call real occludes.

The modern painter is a neo-realist, a painter of the real world, which with a gifted mind he deciphers through the murk. That is what the artist must be today—employing what painter's means he may.

VI.

WHAT I AM trying to say is that there has been a sweeping change in attitude among artists toward painting today. A serious concern with the subject which has succeeded the age of experimentation—and the interval during which they did no painting at all. It is typified by—maybe Picasso's *Guernica* was one of the early examples—by Matisse devoting himself to the embellishment of the walls of a Benedictine monastery. The stress has made a complete revolution, THE revolution, the only revolution of which art in its own body is capable, back to Giotto, to the inner vision, to what the artist "sees" and depicts with deepest sincerity AND ALL HIS NEWLY ACQUIRED PROFICIENCIES OF TECHNIQUE.

It is another turn of the wheel, a reembodiment of feeling, of sanctity, of devotion to the human freight that the artist, like all others must bear. It is this new phase, as interpreted in paint, as Giotto, with his great skill and simple faith transcribed his inner vision, the reality of what he saw so movingly during his lifetime.

At last I am coming to this new painters' faith that moves Emanuel Romano, at last I have found a way in which I can speak of a painter directly and sincerely (without trying to compare him with others, but)c of something which moves me in his work. If I had not approached his work thus circuitously I would not have been able to say what I want to say.

Here is an humble approach (, but here is a highly trained and deeply experienced approach)c to the task a painter assumes when he begins to put paint upon canvas. Romano is furiously at work, working night and day (as if there were not time enough in which to get it said) to tell the beholder the secrets of his mind—not of his mind even so much as of the healing images which he alone sees reflected there.

He SEES these colors and these contours. And he knows that if only he can get them out, put them upon the canvas everyone will be healed. He knows it—and he knows the time is short. He must work, work furiously to paint, to lay it bare that others may be blessed—not by his selfishness in wanting them to see HIS painting. That is unimportant.[1] But to see, materialized, what the "reality" of our lives hides.

The real, the truly real that throngs upon his inward view is there within him (as Picasso saw the suffering of the Basques of Guernica, as Matisse sees the monks whose images he is transmitting to the walls of their holy place). So Romano cannot rest a moment in his rush to perform his duty as a man: to show his gift, to exhibit not himself but the praise that is in him.

We can imagine Bach working in this way upon his *St. Matthew's Passion*. But we must not, we must never forget the new, the new techniques which the great artists of the immediate past have taught us. Romano does not forget any of it.

Here is a blossoming of the spirit. I refuse to try to evaluate its achievements. I am not capable of it. I insist only on the authentic identity of the dedication. I believe in that—and where have I acquired it but from the paintings themselves? They are full of honesty, they are often moving, they are always painted with a

---

[1]In both available drafts of this passage, (c) and (d), this sentence reads: "That is important." But in (d) the typescript has been corrected by hand to read "*un*important."

33. Paul Cézanne, *Madame Cézanne in the Conservatory*. Oil on canvas, 36¼″ × 28¾″. Collection, The Metropolitan Museum of Art (Bequest of Stephen C. Clark, 1960).

34. Albrecht Dürer, *Melancholy*. Engraving.

painter's eye for the materials—a light of deep feeling grows out of them.

They are a recent beginning, not a matter merely of virtuosity, but the growth of a painter of trained ability, of a conviction that he has found himself—at midpoint in his life— *"nel mezzo del cammin di nostra vita."* He knows he has not yet half revealed what he wants to say but so overwhelmingly important is what he must exhibit, so humble does he feel before it, that I am convinced that even now, while his work, his real work is just beginning, we can look with delight upon what he has accomplished.

The Broken Vase

Not previously published, 1957

THE FRAGMENTS of passion are to be valued as much as passion itself. Only to look at the work of the Surrealist and Modernist painters, whom everyone in Europe, America, and South America knows, is convincing enough. But the work of the Ultramoderns, if it does not bring on a paroxysm of schizophrenia—the Sigmund Freud disease—calling to mind the disturbed face of a Pollock or a Michaux or an Artaud, should convince us that the images presented by such work are not a whole. They are a [part] of an impossible whole, a fragment, which has surpassed the artists' conception.

It is a record of a terrific struggle on the artist's part to reestablish in the face of a universal schizophrenia, a split personality, or more comprehensively, a fractured personality.

It brings to my mind the recent poems of René Char, *Leaves of Hypnos*—a miscellany, but it serves my purpose. In praise of such poems as it contains his friends have assembled a book of essays called *René Char's Poetry*. Why should they put themselves out? They recognize a new principle among the poems: they are often no more than fragments. Briefly, they are often partial or developing poems caught in the act of "becoming."

What do they represent to the eye but (a fragmentation,)[a] an incompleteness, a partial development (the rest of the image is not yet known), which is the same schizophrenic (image)[a] which every painter at the present time has to face.

Being artists, *i.e.*, (the most)[a] sensible people in any age, these artists, these painters, insist on [seeing] what they see, as any intelligent person would, whole—as far as they can. They refuse to go mad. Given the smallest fragment of an image they will take that as a toehold, clinging to the fragment as "proof" of the whole. It took a long time for painters to learn deliberately to distort their images; El Greco was one of the first in his efforts to portray a spirituality in his saints, something extra-corporeal—they used to resort to halos and other paraphernalia before that, but he invented another language which could be painted.

But with the Surrealists, after Cézanne, the fragmentation became overt. The painter with whom I concern myself now [is] Emanuel Romano. Not that he was the first, but the twist he gave to the imagination has a very direct and simple and convincing appeal to it. When he arrived in Paris recently he saw a city broken apart. Nothing was as it used to be even five years ago. And suddenly he was conscious of a vase, the tragic Paris of his youth, broken into a thousand pieces.

In his canvases we see the broken parts of this image (—we see a canvas of broken parts—)ª much as in Dürer's *Melancholy* of the fifteenth century, a canvas crowded with broken masonry, we see the same. (But this is not the fifteenth century but the twentieth— we have "progressed" so that our works of art—and our conscious-ness of them—have been put on the canvas and the page more torturedly, not directly as in Dürer's simpler world.

But the effect is the same, no matter how disguised: fragmenta-tion, lack of completeness which must characterize man's view and understanding of his world. It may be a picture of "becoming" as in Char:)ª the artist attempts to assemble our lives on the canvas as he has always done. Against today's schizophrenic fracture of the image, Romano's imagination presented a broken vase (, a definite, actual, painting of the parts of a vase placed on the canvas without other interpretation)ª. A vase is a classic symbol of completion, containing all that is precious to life. When that is broken, we die.

Romano's few canvases that I have seen recently are low in tone but rich and varied in their colors (, arranged very simply)ª. In one canvas an effigy of a fish (a rich orange), fills the center of the picture. In another a plaster figure of a little man, a homunculus, is upright—in another lying on his side, the plaster pedestal still attached. In the background is to be seen a figure of which Romano is inordinately fond—one, two, or three dark and plainly colored pyramids.

(Everything is reduced, in the mind, to the simplest proportions. There is no overlaying between the five or six figures that make up the canvas—all of course on the same flat plane.)[a]

The whole picture is made up of the fragments of the broken vase. (It is severely simplified. There is no attempt at humanism or verisimilitude of any sort. Just an "arrangement.")[a] The fragmentation, or schizophrenia, or non-representationalism, or incompletion, is in this case represented by the typical "vase" itself seen in all phases of its disorganization (organization): the vase in all color variation—always low in tone (but harmonious)[a]—passionately subdued, stands split down the middle (still standing erect), a symmetrically arranged pair of them. The canvas, always with the philosophic pyramids at the back, consists of various fragments of the same vase, or the derivatives (sometimes difficult to recognize), always a foursquare arrangement simply arranged.

One thinks inevitably of pieces of sculpture (Romano's father was a famous sculptor in Israel). The work of the Englishman Moore comes to mind again. Nothing is whole, but as in Moore the normal (relation of the)[a] parts of the image is maintained so that the eye would see beyond—looped so that the eye sees perhaps the shrubbery of a park through a shoulder or belly.

Fragmentation is at the heart of it, the vase is split open so the background shows between the separate parts. Curious sickle-like objects, lying prone or on their sides—not upside down as they might have been with Chagall—(occupy the spaces between)[a]: a still further fragmentation of the simple key object.

(The note of fragmentation, incompletion—backed by the pyramids of permanence in the background—completes the composition, giving the philosophic thought of the whole its validity—yet it retains its pictorial validity [as well])[a].

I began by saying that the fragments of passion are to be valued as much as passion itself. Romano appears to me to be a man whom passion has worn, a silent man who has no voice but the paint with which he sobs alone. He was grown older since he painted his clowns—sometimes without a body, just two dancing legs springing from a neck in a dunce's cap. It may be significant that the habiliments of [woman], her breasts and legs—in bed or out—are absent now.

That also is part of the age's fragmentation—as it is part of the schizophrenic picture—that men and women cohabit with their own sex, unproductively, as in the days of Socrates and Sappho. It is reflected in the fragmentation of the present image affected by our painters.

The American Spirit in Art

Proceedings of the American Academy of Arts and Letters, 1952
IN ART as in politics, in spite of our faults, the time-drift favors America. Have we the courage, the honesty, and the patience to grasp our opportunities? (We are today the direct inheritors of the ages.)ᶜ The best of modern benefits are rooted in us; when we walk into the medieval past we walk (, in all the world,)ᶜ away from America; when an impasse in modern art is encountered the clarification of it is found in the path of our advance, close to hand in our familiar environment. This is my theme; we may lose our lives in pursuit of it.

At random take the matter of obscurantism in the arts. What's the answer? I believe it's just our failure to catch up with what is going on. The whole plant may have to be retooled before we can go into production again. Any American can understand that. For there are two forms of obscurity which we must face, either in the words or the thought. (That in the words is temporary—but the obscurity that lies in the thought is permanent, is incurable, it cannot be written out. We all for humanity's sake wish for a universal language. In *Finnegans Wake* Joyce practiced it. Is that so impossible to comprehend?)ᵈ But the obscurantism of the mystics (, no matter how simply or ornately it may be stated,)ᵈ is beyond solution. (The modern way is Joyce's way as any American, if he worked it out, must one day discover.

We are puzzled and bewildered by the apparently inexplicable emergence in our day of the abstractionists in the pictorial arts— sometimes one art is further advanced than another, music, writing; the development is uneven. Maybe we'll have a perfume that is abstractionist in essence one day smelling as if we'd stepped in something—and there will be those who adore it—but if we take it as a phase in the inevitable time-drift that overtakes all human enterprises we can at least understand it.

Abstractionism in painting? Let me try to trace its modern development, a self-limiting phase destined to add a greater resource, a greater availability, a broader use of materials, a greater luster to the art, just as the modern concept of the poetic line and the new measure or new way of measuring would make available new materials for the poem. I shall try to make these points clearer as I go on.

Thus, for the moment, I have presented two phenomena clouded with misunderstanding, the new poem and the abstract picture.)d The obscurity of the modern poem as well as abstraction in the pictorial arts are however both the children(, the natural or inevitable effects,)d of that time-drift which has brought our culture pattern, what we call America, to the fore. We have only to devote ourselves to them to realize their possibilities and make them ours. (I propose to clarify them in the light of that understanding. Both the modern poem and the abstract in painting, though we are not the first to practice the latter, lead integrally into what we most are and must be.)c

After a brief excursion into the philosophical background I shall again take up the proposal that the abstract in painting was inevitable for us and that the modern poem must be our typical resort. In painting we at least can see that abstraction is the end result of something that began to emerge with Cézanne, (himself, in the structure of his thought, a late product of that seventeenth century where we ourselves originated: Cézanne)d whose concern it was to make color carry much of the burden of his argument.

(America, both North and South, had a culture *that* was indigenous and highly developed, the corn culture, today all but extinct. One of its bibles, the *Popul Vuh*, exists still in German and Spanish translation. Without saying more of it, since I am not sufficiently acquainted with the subject, the only use I wish to make of the reference is to use it as a jumping-off place toward a definition of all art.)d

Art is a repository for the perplexities of mind which surround us on all sides. It is not, like religion and philosophy, a proposed dissolution of our difficulties. It is the repository where we lay them away. The poem is not bred of the wisdom of the ages, it comes of the ripeness of the ages. The work of art gives the concerns of man a tactile reality, it does not dissipate them. It makes the unknown a form which eyes, ears, nose, mouth, and fingers can experience; even nothingness at the hands of the artist becomes a thing, "a thing of beauty" if you will.

Art has nothing to do with religion or philosophy. Works of art are "things." We can take them into our homes and eat them, one way or another, if we want to. The intangibles become ours to experience and enjoy.

Speaking to the high school pupils of my suburb I told them: Our heads are oysters. Take the oyster: A grain of sand enters its secret domain, in other words, between its shells. The poor oyster (living perhaps in Greenwich Village) unable, for cosmic reasons, such as not being able to spit it out, to get rid of its torment, frets over it, rolling it back and forth until, miracle of miracles, it makes of it a beautiful thing, a pearl! That is the artist at work.

Take again the poor Indian, puzzled by his plight; some years the corn is good, some years bad; sometimes the rain comes, sometimes not. He has made a clay pot to carry water from the river to his adobe hut. That's the first act. But then, puzzled with the why of his universe, he doodles over it, makes a smudge which, repeated, makes a design. He rims the neck of his pot with a series of angled hooks and, for some extraordinary reason, he is relieved in his deepest soul. He can say: I am—because there is my mark.

Art raises the dignity of man. It allows him to say, *I am,* in concrete terms. It defines his environment. As Emerson put it (to our shame we have never adequately heeded his words): "A national literature consummates and crowns the greatness of a people. The best actions, indeed, and the greatest virtues, are scarcely possible, till the inspiring force of literature is felt." For only by a multiplication of the gestures of art does any man show himself to be fully alive upon the earth (, does any culture pattern grow to be distinguished)c*.

The artist is the most important individual known to the world.

He is not an accessory, not a decoration, not a plaything. His work is supremely necessary, proved by the urgency with which we insist on preserving it. Man will not let it die. The very inner casings of Egyptian sarcophagi, made of paper sheets, are un-gummed in the improbable hope that a shred of papyrus found there may contain even a few words from a poem by Sappho. If England is destroyed by Russian bombs it will hardly be a matter of importance to history so long as the works of Shakespeare be not lost.

The artist gives, or records, the intimate character of a race in the face of the Unknown. He looks at the priest and the philosopher; the one takes us over the edge of the world into a place after death, the other gives us reasons. But the artist drives us to believe that we are alive (something worth saving) now, here—as others have lived in days past—or as others, we hope, have lived in the past, of whom we are jealous that they may have known and experienced more than we. We too, we may say, having an art of our own, having a corn dance, are alive! Lacking it (or its equivalent) we cannot say that we are more than mere money grubbers and parasites to the generating female. Mere repetitions of inferior models.

There have been periods of ourstanding culture, when men stood up and acted and spoke as superior beings, originated works that branded them as having existed to the full in their time. Such periods occur once every 500 years or so—all other periods are preparations for those apogees. Who will be next? Athens, Rome, Paris, London—perhaps Tenochtitlán. No use going into that. I wish merely to point out that each of these periods was essentially different from every other, as their residual works of art show that they differed one from another—the Greek hexameter from Dante's iambic *terza rima* and Shakespeare's English line—all the way to Walt Whitman's amorphous line of yesterday that is so important to my theme.

I wish to point out that, as with Gothic architecture, the form which the art of any time assumes originated in that time. It was the outcome of a tendency to assert a reality, a certitude, a vivid enjoyment without intellectual limit in that time. (It asserts that the men, the culture pattern of that time was an actuality.)[c]* And, as

with the pearl in the oyster, it originated from the very essence of
the oyster itself—it did not come from the remoteness of the seas
but from that which to the oyster was indigenous, its own shell.

There is, over and beyond all that, a drift of time that wipes out
all cultures and sets others in their places. One dies, another rises,
dies out completely, then, after an interval, the process begins
again. The periods are never continuous. They arise indepen-
dently, they do not imitate each other. The act of recreation, it
appears, has to be entirely new, down to the very bedrock.

Art is a local phenomenon; it is impossible for it to arise
otherwise. The Greek shepherd's hut, with posts holding up the
forepart of the roof, became the Parthenon when the dignity of the
race demanded it. You can see plainly what I infer. (Is it our turn
now, as I believe, or shall we, due to our incompetencies, be put
down in time to come as second-rate?)ᶜ*

This, according to the historian Arnold J. Toynbee, is how our
century will be remembered 300 years hence. He puts it as a
question: "Can we guess what the outstanding feature of our
twentieth century will appear to be in the perspective of 300 years?
No doubt we shall not all guess alike. Some of us will guess that the
present age will be looked back upon as the age of scientific
discovery. Others will expect to see it branded as the age in which
fascist and communist apostates from Christian civilization har-
nessed science to the service of a neo-barbarism. My own guess is
that our age will be remembered chiefly neither for its horrifying
crimes nor for its astonishing inventions, but for its having been the
first age since the dawn of civilization, some five or six thousand
years back, in which people dared think it practicable to make the
benefits of civilization available for the whole human race.

"Perhaps there are two points here which are worth underlining:
This vision of a good life for all is a new one, and—whatever our
success or our failure may be in the attempt to translate this vision
into reality—this new social objective has probably come to stay.
That the ideal of welfare for all is new is surely true; for, as far as I
can see, [and this is the point on which I base my whole argument]
it is no older than the seventeenth century West European

settlments on the East Coast of North America that have grown into the United States. [This overwhelming conclusion whose implications ramify into the whole field of our thinking, has an electric effect upon our lives if we can only keep to it and follow through.][1]

" . . . So long as this aim continues to be practical politics, mankind is certain, however many times we may fail, to go on making one attempt after another to reach the goal. When once the odious inequality that has hitherto been a distinguishing mark of civilization has ceased to be taken for granted as something inevitable, it becomes inhuman (and philosophically unthinkable) to go on putting up with it—and still more inhuman to try to perpetuate this inequality deliberately."

(When the West European settlers arrived on the East Coast of North America to form their colonies—that have grown into the United States—they faced two things: a physical world of tremendous resources which they would learn to exploit to the astonishment of the world, and a new vision, far richer than anything the land itself offered, which has baffled them to the present day.)c

That new vision—rich and varied as is its political history, which I can only mention in passing—has been the backbone of our literature and so of all our art.

From that clear directive we diverge right and left. Following it we go forward to patterns bred of a cultural initiative hitherto untried, turning from it we fall back upon the more comfortable medieval patterns of privilege (and our literature will perish)c. It is of extreme importance that we make up our minds which of these two modes we follow, for (the implications of our cultural concepts are new and basic.)d On this single point America stands to gain or lose all.

(Our first comers while their bodies went forward into the wilderness turned back in their minds to Europe. It was often necessary for their sanity that they should do so. As wealth increased after the first burst of affirmation during the Revolution,

---

[1]This square-bracketed material, and that in the previous sentence, represents interjections by Williams into the quotation.

and the intellectual and spiritual gradations between individuals became more and more apparent, the intellectual trend back to Europe and the past grew in its appeal. The novels of Henry James featured this seeking of European distinction by the heiresses of America. He himself, for complex reasons which don't need to be stressed, fled to the intellectual comforts of Victorian England. It is understandable, it was even admirable in him. He was a distinguished citizen of our republic of letters and a great artist.

But he left another world behind. He abandoned it. Perhaps his nerves were such that he had to abandon it to develop his talents and survive. There have been other distinguished examples in our own day, perhaps some of our best writers. ((You can't take anything from them because they turned their backs on us. It is part of our heritage that we should do what we please.))* It isn't that they have turned their backs on US that should make us either admire them or get our backs up against them. It is, however, that they have turned their backs on the tremendous opportunity of our letters to follow a pioneering mind into the implications of our new cultural opportunity . . . that is the fault.

They have followed the easier way. They have chosen to ally themselves with an established, an old, a ripe, a rewarding legend whose forms—and that is where the point of it all lies—are hallowed, whose dignity is established, whose honor is overwhelming. They have chosen to fix themselves to that. We have to understand it. It is to some natures almost irresistible.

We have no body of literature here we can look up to and back into which we can comfortably sink. We have only an objective. Our cultured classes which have established our universities have wanted to fasten themselves to Europe. They have built their schools not only upon European models but the teaching in them is based on established European patterns of thought. The accident that our language is called "English" has frozen our entire thinking upon literature into a mode which is wholly of ((a past exclusive of America—which was not even discovered when it was laid down.))[1]

[1]After striking this passage in double parentheses, Williams ended the sentence by substituting "wholly of the past."

So that any who does not adhere, in the forms prescribed for his writing, to an antique pattern is badly at a loss. ((This is not spoken with any feeling of animosity.))* This we must accept. The natural desire is to rush to praise that which clings, which returns to the old modes. That is what we trust, that gives us assurance, relieves our insecurity as we say today. We WANT to ally ourselves with the past and so our runaway writers are doing the popular thing.

The writer who is bent upon the native adventure—though adventure isn't the right word—seeks insecurity. He *is* insecure, and must remain so until he can ride over the fixed, stabilized configurations of the great past—which ensnare in their meshes so much that is evil. But he is dedicated to the unknown.

The American writer has two courses open to him: either to seek what security and comfort there is for him in past configurations of learning, or to follow his great constructive genius into his own world, to raise that to such distinction that it will shine in the galaxies of historical cultures of the world as something incomparably great.

Fifty years is a small matter, it will be hard to say after fifty years whether we have gone forward or slipped back, but the way is clearly indicated. Our major highway is ahead, not back, and when we begin to realize how much depends upon our going forward I do not believe that we shall fail.)d

What we are seeking is the least common denominator in the means of expression: in painting, color, reft of all other reference; in the poem, the unaccented line, capable of accepting every shade of revolutionary significance.

It is not a choice that can be made merely to suit our convenience, it hinges upon an essentially different moral and historical outlook. (And what applies to literature applies to all art.)c*

The unwinding of time has posed for us—and by "us" I mean the New World—the old problem: to survive or perish, to seek out new forms and ground ourselves for a new ascent to the first rank in art or to fail. We cannot use forms that are second hand. We cannot use the iambic pentameter after Shakespeare for any major work. We simply cannot—except at the cost of extinction.

What then must we use? Who can tell? But that is where Toynbee's statements can be helpful. The basic idea which underlies our art must be, for better or worse, that which Toynbee has isolated for us: abundance, that is, permission, for all. And it is in the *structure* of our works that this must show. We must embody the principle of abundance, of total availability of materials, freest association in the measure, in *that* to differ from the poem of all previous time. It will be that sort of thing, if we succeed, that shall give us our supreme distinction.

Let's see how it works. I'll start with an anecdote: Alanson Hartpence, who used to be with the Daniel Gallery, once, during his boss's absence, had one of the gallery's best patrons there looking at a picture. The estimable lady admired one of the paintings and seemed about to buy it—or at least she was leaning that way.

But Mr. Hartpence, she said, what is all this down here in this left-hand lower corner?

(I have told this story often before but it bears repeating.)

That, said Hartpence, leaning closer to inspect the place, that, Madame, he said, straightening and looking at her, that is paint.

He lost the sale.

But that is the exact place where for us the virus first bit in. That is the exact place where for us modern art began. For that is the essence of Cézanne, the first break in the medieval defences—and the old walls started to crumble. It is exactly there that we began to say that it is no longer what you paint or what you write about that counts but how you do it: how you lay on the pigment, how you place the words to make a picture or a poem.

From that through cubism, Matisse, to Motherwell, the ultimate step is one gesture. And it is important because it says that you don't paint a picture or write a poem *about* anything, you *make* a picture or a poem of *any*thing. You see how that comes from Toynbee's discovery. Abundance for *all*.

You've finally abandoned all medieval and classic criteria. You do not select subjects any more; to classify poems or pictures by their subject matter is today a little childish. It is in the structure of the poem or painting that excellence exists and that is unlimited, the least common denominator.

As men and women of a distinguished society[1] we can do no less than applaud such as take advantage of this new opportunity. It is one of the excitements of art and all thought that we do not know what savannas, what elemental forests, what seas of the white whale we shall next be called upon to penetrate. The arts are one of the richest fields that still and will always lie open to man.

Of such a one as Motherwell, the abstractionist, who says that the whole occupation of painting is a matter of the relationship between pigment and the surface to which it is applied, to such a man we cannot but offer a hearty welcome. We should be glad that someone has turned up among us to work out that (thankless) historical process. It does not exclude other processes though it does constitute a criticism of them and will prove, in the end, an enlargement upon them to the benefit of the total process of painting.

May we not here improvise to say, of abstract painting, that there is one further step awaiting it before its extinction: when it is being done by the blind.

As to the modern poem, my own field, the line is our battlefield. Walt Whitman was our pioneer but not our master. But I know, for myself, that what he began we have no choice but to finish as we may. Oh, it would make a book—I could talk all night. The old line, the medieval masterbeat, as I call it in my private vocabulary, is the place where, to meet Toynbee's abundance, we have to let in the air—as well as the mob! The line must be broken down before it is built up anew, on a broader basis, according to another measure.

How shall we deploy the poetic line, having abandoned the old way of measuring which the selective feudal spirit dictated? Accent, as we have known it, must go. Accent is the selective maneuver; we are fed up with it. In all probability we shall have to measure the line by elapsed time, as did the Greeks. But we must *measure* it—perhaps relativity will come in here—we must measure

---

[1]The members of the American Institute of Arts and Letters, to whom this paper was first presented.

it, there is no such thing as free verse, there is only verse in transition from one measure to another, from one position to another. Not to measure a gesture or an object is intolerable to a man of spirit. Verse is measure. We must measure it—but it has to be a new measure.

Whitman saw it when he said that classic poems are like the columns of a Greek temple but modern verse is like the waves of the sea. That's as far as he got, but he was in direct line with the meaning.

Thus, as I say, the American artist, in a new mode, is favored by the time-drift toward outstanding, perhaps revolutionary achievement—in which he may lead his world to a healing knowledge of its present state. He alone, it appears, is so favored. It is the lag of old fetters which incapacitates the others. You see what a mess the Russians make of it when they try (through Marx) to imitate us. Instead of freedom they found themselves on the denial of freedom; instead of giving their writers a free rein to develop what they, as a nation, are in need of, they castrate them, leaving us conceptually (if not in practice) supreme. (The lag of the middle ages is too much for them, to make the necessary readjustments they are, to all intents and purposes, impotent.)[c]

Notes on Movements, Artists, and Issues

I. The Visitors

Not previously published, c. 1944

DON'T KICK at the Surrealists, of course they are frustrated. Who isn't? But! they are not frustrated when they write, paint, carve. That's the thing that concerns the artist. They, digging out a non-frustration, put their work into actuality, producing the distinct outlines of defeat in actual words, colors, contours. By that they are pure artists in the true tradition of their various professions. They deal with objectification of the unreal, in other words, with that which is beyond the frustration—which has in fact, created it a church, a government, a farm bureau—or mere propagation in its own right.

They are degenerate, insane and worst of all tiresome. For them to be called pornographic is nothing at all. You don't call a rabbi a sadist because he performs circumcisions. The Surrealists take their impetus largely from Freud. Well, most men take it from their fathers and mothers, unthinking, in much the same way.

Certainly there are fools among them, no doubt many of them are senile idiots—when they say, for instance that photography is not an art then go on to speak of their "best" photographs. But these things are self-evident and need not be a red herring to lead us off the proper track.

A new impetus is needed, it is especially needed during frustration. Surrealism may well be, or need not be, an important phase of the arts but that it is a justifiable and, at the moment, an important one for certain people in these times, I firmly believe.

They, in their abasement, may very well prove the means to lead some other, hidden facet, through to the light. It has happened before.

II. Theory of Excellence in the Arts

Not previously published, c. 1948

I THINK it takes many generations of local culture to produce great excellence in the arts—and so, in literature. The long periods between the great names and the bunching of great names and the evidence of them in works seems, superficially at least, to indicate this. Throwing the emphasis on the meaning, local, the evidence of history—on the past—seems again preponderant in that most peaks of culture have occurred in various places at various times.

And the progress is extremely complex. A certain sector of the workers remain in the locality and perfect the vocabulary, so to speak, give the things, the sensual objects of which all the arts consist accurate and appropriate names—whether this be a plastic form, a musical sequence, or whatever it may be. While others will travel, live aside in other places, still retaining their primary connection with the locality which is the energizing focus for them.

The process as a whole remains, however, the direct effect of a locality—which proves itself by attracting to its radiating center proselytes from other sources which either melt into it or partake of its abundance. French painting has been noteworthy in this. But it is an extreme importance of the theory and its most helpful aspect and use, to realize that it is not possible to transport French painting, for instance to another locality, or to "infect" that locality with French painting. One is absorbed by it and becomes French— as far as possible—or takes from it whatever he can to enrich his own local development. This is difficult, requiring great wit and diplomatic understanding.

For—as has been said many times—"all art is local," that is it is the effect of sensuality, the employment of sensual apperceptions by which to record and compose. And all sense must, to be accurate, apply itself to that which it sees, smells, touches—its locality. But, it might be said, one can see, touch, smell everywhere. True, but not without willingly or unwillingly relating the individual sense to a total meaning which is the aggregate of all the seeing, touching, smelling of any focus of life—the more or less defined "locality" where the sensual perceptions of that part of the world reach its temporal greatest intensity.

It is not possible, in other words, to have excellence without a development from the base, in a culture, a belief held by a group in a certain place, which through work becomes more and more adapted to that place to embody it in sensual expression. It cannot be imported, it would not be applicable or understandable, it must be made where it is to be out of what exists there—otherwise it will not have the time dimension or the breadth of base to resist lateral pressure and include the *whole* of the expression *possible* to that place.

After an effective perfection, such an expression is at the end of its effectiveness. Then it is the difficult task of another energy to take it apart.

III. Picasso Breaks Faces

The General Magazine and Historical Chronicle, 1950
LAST WINTER in Paris seven pictures were shown in the Picasso exhibition, all representing an attack upon the human figure—limbs, body, and face, an attack showing the struggle that continued unabated throughout the "occupation years" in France. Picasso's struggles are taking place in my blood—and not as a Spaniard but as a man facing a common world.

What is a face? What has it always been even to the remotest savagery? A battleground. Slash it with sharp instruments, rub ashes into the wound to make a keloid; daub it with clays, paint it with berry juices. This thing that terrifies us, this face upon which we lay so much stress is something they have always wanted to deform, by hair, by shaving, by every possible means. Why? TO REMOVE FROM IT THE TERROR OF DEATH BY MAKING OF IT A WORK OF ART.

Unless we do that, we are living still in the age of barbarism. This Picasso understands better than anyone living in the world today. He is a Hercules holding us back from destruction. He is not the only hero, but he is one of the greatest now alive. Do we understand that? The confusion of the past has been that "character," the character of the face, even in a portrait by a Titian or a Michelangelo, was anchored irretrievably in a meat of set color and contour. In these seven pictures we see a progress in the attack Picasso has been making upon that face. We may humanly disagree with his tactics but with his strategy we cannot disagree. His success has been phenomenal.

Paris attracts genius because it offers a man its body to do with as he will. For that, an artist seeks to give in return his own very blood. Nothing is held back, either way. Picasso, healthy as a pot, Spanish as the sun itself, has been a grateful lover. He is more Catalan than one from that windy north that ran in the veins of El Greco from about Burgos. His figures rest upon the earth, well-bottomed. But they are, for all that, Spanish in that their spirit transcends the flesh. What is a face? What is a torso *(toro)*? Something to kill, that out of it may rise something greater, upon which the whole world hangs breathless. Will it arise? Can it be? Shall we accept the tawdry defamations fed to us as tenet and party or BELIEVE that we can, in fact upon this earth, witness a ghost lift from a body that has been stabbed to the heart?

This is the war that Pablo Picasso wages for us, besieged as we are, in the guise of paint and canvas.

IV. Art and Social Organization

Not previously published, 1950

ALL MONISTIC theories, as they apply to art, are absurd in our day. This is especially true of a theory of arrest, the fixed notion of English prosody, highlighted by sixteenth-century preeminence, unrelated to social, economic, and political variants, as the standard, or even a standard, of measurement for us now.

A work of art is a mechanism at its best applicable to all the complex human relationships of its day as a means of making them workable—under the given conditions. That is to say the factors that make physics, government, economics workable or should make them workable should also be discoverable in the highest pieces of painting, poetry and music in that day. The mechanism should be interchangeable. Only thus can we speak of a work as "good" or "bad." That is the measure. A "good" poem is good as it might be successfully used in the organization of an entire social, political, economic [pattern] of its day—or reorganization.

Thus Mozart died at thirty-four, poverty-stricken because the organization of his music had so far surpassed the political-sociological abilities of those who had the money to support him that they became dissatisfied with him, suspicious, and so let him starve. It must be noted here that the excellence of his music, its "goodness" was related not to the superficial powers of his day, the aristocracy, but to a deeper reality of the times themselves—an area where government and the preliminary studies of abstract science were tending to break down the past.

The Russians are today trying to turn this relationship of the arts to all other human experience about by trying to fix the work of art in an orbit as an adjunct to the political machinery. The relationship between art and politics, since they require a relationship, is thus right in a way. But they have perverted it in fact by limiting the freedom—in the piece of music, in the poem that it may not surpass the plodding political picture, may not, in fact, correct the political fixity which it has always been its function to save from absurdity when it decays. For the arts do not risk as much as the physical organization of a people when danger threatens; their freedom is the saving grace which a society should use for its escape.

To our present day no sixteenth-century fixation is applicable. We need and we must have a more responsive, a more socially responsive art. The art must rest solidly on the social base of its time—which cannot be fixed as all monistic adjuncts must necessarily be in basic structure.

And it is of the basic structure of verse that we are speaking—but responsive *in its nature* to multiple stimuli, since that is the essence of democracy which all theory must approach if true freedom, the lifeblood of art, is to be rescued and resumed.

V. On the Practical Function of Art

Not previously published, c. 1951

UNDER STRESS it is often cooling to the mind to turn aside a moment from the clutter of reported events and attempt to draw conclusions in a field greatly removed from the general, the field generaled, let us say, by what is known somewhat unfortunately as art. It should be and is at its best a field uninfluenced by political imperatives, the taboos and passions of what is known somewhat unfortunately as the practical. Art is just as practical and far more to the point, many times, than the maneuvers men of affairs hold up as models (of the quality of conduct)* they would have us pursue. In fact the powers of art available in the elucidation of our mind's difficulties are very often far more trenchant and comprehensive than those of any other agent enlisted by man for his relief. It is only that the difficult availability of art's hints and pointings, so hard to decipher, makes it seem less practical than is the case. But though this is so, there is a compensatory advantage: because of the remoteness of art's hints and pointings to the unskilled intelligence, unskilled in their interpreting, the texts of art may properly be more concentratedly compact in diagnosis and indications for action, unbent (by trivia than almost any other arm toward our defense and survival.

Works of art, for all these reasons, are susceptible of being agents of the most practical and pure direction for the human understanding—though the guide to their excellence for most must always remain the pleasure, amazing, strangely disturbing, which their appearance induces.)[b]*

(Be that as it may, the artist holds a weapon in his hands which he must use without faltering.)[c]

VI. Alfred Eisenstaedt

Not previously published, 1951
How STRANGE that from staring through a glass of peculiar shape at dictators and kings, generals and statesmen, those who have sought one way or another to rule the world, you have come away so whole a man, so willing still to search, your sense limpid as the lens that stood between you and those creatures of the world, for what further you may find.

It is as if that miracle of glass, built to record without the faintest hint of a lie those frightful images of terror on the sensitive film, had endowed you with its grace of infinite purity, anastigmatic, clear as the sound of a silver bell against all you have seen so accurately limned, fit and even eager to record a poet's fleeting shadow.

VII. Talks and Readings, Hanover etc., April 1952

Not previously published

WE ALL seek for ourselves the richest rewards from life that we can obtain. To most this is represented, as a token at least, by a Cadillac car.

The knowledge of a persistent ancestry satisfies many and gives them a great sense of superiority that keeps their feet warm in bad times.

The religionist is willing, for a consideration which is one of the great drives of the world, to postpone the realization of his life until after death. And it may be that if he puts his trust completely in this he will be happy.

What can a man do with the wealth, the material wealth, he accumulates in a lifetime? However he attacks it he seeks to celebrate the occasion by possessing valuable objects. And often the most valuable are those realizations of the great periods of antiquity when the artist flourished. Painting, sculpture, music, the poem—though seldom the poet—are sought after by wealthy men to give them that security which man most requires in this world for his own sense of permanence.

The blossomy times of the art of all the ages is precisely that which wealth needs, pathetically, to tell what it represents but cannot succinctly express.

Wealth has no better thing to do with itself than to purchase the effects of those periods when the artist achieved certain peaks of realization in his works. The great periods, the great record.

The communists with their brutal concepts seek the same richest rewards from life as anyone else but they fear the artist and so cut themselves off from what he might add.

The artist alone seeks his reward from life in what he himself can make of it.

And since the world is only a world of appearances he knows that nothing will last, everything tends to disappear in the end. In fact great periods come to an end, that is why we cling to their effects so avidly—the great rare periods which show man at his best. (Were we to lose all record of those, we would show ourselves poor indeed.)*

But we must even, when the time comes, destroy it ourselves; man the eternal phoenix—that too is the function of the artist.

The truth is that the artist is seeking to realize, to celebrate and so make, make new, refresh the world and that is the most that he knows. The past must be broken; it must, it is finished. We must make again what was in the past and if we cannot a light goes out.

There is nothing else to do but to keep the world new in man's eyes.

(But our academies seek to perpetuate the English Departments, forgetting that we have not had to do with an English Department in our country for nearly two hundred years.)*

The drive of the arts, hidden in Soviet Russia out of fear of what truly might come of it, is hidden in America because of fear of the onslaughts of our language upon the secret rigidities of the past—which we fear to attack in order to renew ourselves.

The artist knows he is that man who must make the world anew, in which he will live, out of his own mind with his own hand using the appearances which his senses reveal to him. Every work of art is a microcosm of the world to him. Every fiber of his poem is to him a total of his world.

So that the new, the technical qualities of a poem, are his lifeblood to him.

We seek a new measure. Until we can remeasure the line we cannot make a new line. We don't know what we are doing otherwise. Or we do know what we are doing: we are imitating the past. We think we are equaling the past but we are not, we are only copying.

And this is a palpable defeat. It is not easy to invent a poem. When we do, having rediscovered a way of stating a problem in what you might call skeleton form, we have prepared ourselves—to some extent—to undertake other aspects of the new things life offers us.

But if we are not willing to adventure but keep repeating the

35. John Marin, *Tree Forms* (Stonington, Maine, 1919). Watercolor,
16½″ × 13⅜″. Collection, The Metropolitan Museum of Art, New York
(The Alfred Stieglitz Collection, 1949).

36. John Marin, *The Red Sun—Brooklyn Bridge* (1922). Watercolor, 544 cm. × 667 cm. Courtesy of The Art Institute of Chicago (Alfred Stieglitz Collection).

forms with which life engages our attention, rejecting what the poem proposes, we simply go round in the squirrel cage once more.

The arts are a key to the modern world, to all modern worlds. They are the sensitive edge of our perceptions. When we cut them off we sacrifice a weapon or rather a fine instrument which tells us that we are alive, here, and how much we are alive.

Apparently the world cannot get along at its peak without us.

VIII. John Marin

Catalogue of the John Marin Memorial Exhibition, 1955

A SMALL plant, perhaps a weed, certainly a weed, growing from a split stem in a certain patch of ground, that's what we were, one to wax into a painter, Marin, and one into myself. We were born within half a mile of each other and never moved over a few miles apart all our lives. We knew of each other towards the end of our later years, even met and understood each other completely but never grew intimate. Would you expect more of our twin stem? We had business to do, which we shared; to do more would have interfered each with the other's privileges, our opportunities and aspirations which were largely the same in each case. We had confidence, implicit confidence, in each other, for were we not from the same root? It is good economy (since we were not in the same specific field) for each to mind his own business. We thus presented one front to the enemy. I always thought John Marin a flaming expression of the ground from which we both sprang. He was an affirmation of all that I felt of it that comforted me in times of stress, which I needed in my daily life. I could count on him to back me up.

Not that these things are often expressed by us in the world, more's the pity. But in our world, the world in which we live in this part of Jersey, we take such sentiments for granted. It is only at the end that we permit such expressions to gain the upper hand. It is best so. We are told that the anodic opening but especially the cathodic closing of the current, mark the times of greatest stress. Let it be so with me. I am certain that is how, if he were still alive, John Marin would have wanted it: his paintings remain.

IX. Patrocinio Barela

El Crepusculo, 1955

THERE IS no good considering an artist, in this case a sculptor, but absolutely: is he first-rate or not? He may have certain characters more emphasized than others, granted, but the effect of his qualities must at some point reach an outstanding excellence. You cannot compare Barela with Phidias or Inca craftsmen or the African primitive woodworker or even the German Lehnbach[1]—yet for wholehearted depth of purpose his figures have a comment to make on the age which is like a breath of fresh air, the mountain air of those mesas on which he has lived all his life.

His pieces remind me of Navajo sand painting in their simplicity and primitive fervor—though they are definitely not associated with the old culture. The ritual is more Christian, influenced by the alien race, but the gentleness is not forced, it springs from under the earth from which the corn itself grows and the Indian understands it.

The Indian who has adopted the Christian ritual must find in it a satyric force unsuspected by the white man, a tolerance for his master which he expresses with a smile while working, if he have the soul of an artist, patiently at his craft.

The face for a sculptor presents almost insuperable difficulties. Most modern sculptors skip it entirely or make a mess of it, but Barela in a simple way faces the problem frankly and not without a plastic subtlety that is convincing.

X. Henry Niese

Broadsheet, 1957

THE BEST of men try to burst from the womb, while the best of women try to hold them there—until the proper time. It is a man we are speaking of at the present time. A man will not and cannot tolerate the past whether it be in his own revered father or the whole generation contained in him. He cannot submit himself to

---

[1]Williams probably meant to refer to the German sculptor Wilhelm Lehmbruck.

those disciplines. He must seek a new way. Thus the painters, to escape confinement, record in their canvases a new way of life as well as a new way of painting it.

I have noticed, in seeing the previews at the movies, that they are far more exciting than the finished pictures. That is because we see them graphically, unburdened by the banal story. Abstract painting has missed the point, we are not so much interested in those cerebral exercises, as in freeing the real from its boring implications: we want to recognize our lives but not the tiresome scenes and fellows which and whom we know all too well.

Henry Niese shows us not the confinements of a particular scene but the seeking and actual shapes and colors of a world he beholds liberated for us not in an essential total of any sort but: a view under a truck, a vivid green, a black hillside, unrelated to a finished mode of any sort, whether it be a texture, a man's backside, an old mop, a view from a country porch—repeating nothing and failing to repeat nothing essential to our satisfaction. The composition escapes (and is seized!) regardless of what it encloses.

XI. Whitman's Leaves of Grass and Photography

This version not previously published, 1960

WHEN I first caught sight of the photographs that had in turn sprung from a revised understanding of Whitman's *Leaves of Grass*[1] I was swept off my feet. It made the poem come alive for me as it were for the first time. It needed the breadth of such a poem, the minutiae of such a poem in its comprehensive all-seeingness to in some way compete with it. The photographic process was predestined, I realized, to have waited for just this moment for its realization.

As photograph after photograph was uncovered for me to spend my eyes upon I realized for the first time how much we are losing in the movies. I have long realized its triviality compared with for instance a painting—but also a still. You can see nothing until the

---

[1] *The Illustrated Leaves of Grass,* ed. Howard Chapnick (New York, 1971), (see "Sources," p. 267).

eye is stopped in its track and it can take its own time, at leisure, to penetrate into the depths of the picture—to turn about in the full sense of Whitman's phrase to stretch "and play at my ease."

This the Ziff-Davis photographs were accomplishing before my eyes, it amounted to a new technique which made the flickering movie presentation an impertinence. From the depth of the eyes of a Tennessee mountain woman, slightly averted, an old woman horribly distorted in the prevalent cartoon caricatures which everyone is familiar with (, a cartoon which you will recognize, feeling denigrated even when you most miss the meaning of the word, before which you guffaw and go away feeling confused and lost recognizing nothing to your own disgrace. This is a shot such as Whitman's poems make possible for us, we shockingly realize: From an old woman's eyes)[b] —to the mechanical details of a machine in charging motion.

We all need time to pause and contemplate. We are dying for it. Literally dying for it. These magnificent photographs, the stills for which we have been long waiting give us this time again, we can pause and look around, as this mountain woman has been long doing as seen in the depth of her eyes. Look and you can see what Whitman saw in them and recorded in his poems—which the photograph picks up for us.

They are well-chosen photographs, wide in the comprehensive sweep of their variety. But I must return again to the unique character of the mind and the eyes—to pause and contemplate, by their very technical excellence as examples of the art of photography—to go backward till we realize how our lives have cheated us. Every photograph is a reaffirmation of life's permanence into which you may step to discover new details of flower and cloud, new details of icy barnyard snow swept under a lowering sky—as Whitman saw it, and we in his tracks see it today.

It is the art of the photograph to have stopped us in our tracks almost against our wills, fixed us, not to ridicule us as in the funnies, but to give us back if we have any of it left, that dignity that Whitman has proclaimed for us as human beings.

E.E. Cummings's Paintings and Poems

Arts Digest, 1954

THE PAINTINGS of E.E. Cummings coming from a man better known as a poet you would expect to be genre, topical, more than otherwise, to be characterized as "literary" as were those of the Pre-Raphaelites for instance. That they are not is the difference between the nineteenth and twentieth centuries; we know today that painting is related to paint rather than words and Cummings has emphasized that distinction among us as much as anyone. But unfortunately you have a feeling that all the paintings of this artist could as well have been expressed in a poem, that is why he has remained an amateur—thank God.

I recall a box of strawberries which if they were not addressed completely to the taste were not expressed at all, a Greekish simplicity, you could almost eat them. You do not feel, or should not, like eating a painting but looking at it, devouring it with the *eyes.* I think it is what the paintings literally *say* that is important to Mr. Cummings. That can be of no importance to a painter, only the design—and the color, the same thing, the inarticulate design. And Mr. Cummings is of all things articulate.

It is his virtue, to the very placing of a semicolon or the dotting of an i; let us make the most of it. It marks him as New England bred and a product of its schoolmasterly tradition.

The paintings offer a great variety of subjects but always (not always) on the intimate side, sensitively interpreted, what you would expect of a poet of his verbal dexterity.

Years ago I witnessed an exhibition of Cummings's paintings, it was in a New York gallery. I haven't seen one since. How can I speak of them except from memory? The reproductions which I hold in my hand are misleading. The color is absent. Only the box of strawberries of which I have already spoken (owned now, I am

233

told, by the poet Marianne Moore) holds a still recognizable form. It is a box of strawberries, pure and simple, painted with realistic but poetic insight, the very scent and taste of the berries, even the feel of them in the mouth when crushed by the tongue against the inside of the cheek is there.

A picture of a nude on a bed is no different: she is young. You want to go to bed with her. Even Rubens's women do not give you that feeling. It is not a painting of a nude by Mary Cassatt.

Cummings himself, during his brief abstract period when the line drawing of Charlie Chaplin was made, was caught by the importance of design. But others had gone farther with the mode. He returning on himself from that venture found himself faced by pure paint again and wasn't sufficiently interested in drawing to push the matter further.

He had, or has still, perhaps, the making of a great watercolorist. When he faced his one great opportunity of the sea, he produced, though that is an oil, a small picture said by a competent critic to be, "The finest sea picture of our time." With that optimistic dictum I am in sympathy but have not sufficient experience to completely agree. It is Cummings at his best as a painter and he knew it; he could not go beyond that excellence without giving it more time which he seems disinclined to do, he has other fish to fry.

The paintings of his later years, those of 1950 and after, show by far a greater mastery of the medium whatever it may be. The earlier *paysages,* the still lifes of flowers, even the nude of 1934 are capably done but not remarkable save as the record of a mood. The later pieces however show more confidence, a bolder brush stroke as the artist gains control of them, a freedom which really seems Cummings and what he wants to say. One realizes more and more the relationship between the painting and his poems how one complements the other.

When it comes to the poems (to say nothing of the prose, which is not considered here), Cummings presents us with a far different front from that of which until now I have been speaking. This is the work of a major artist.

The collected poems *(Poems 1923–1954)* which I hold in my hand is an impressive book of 468 airy looking pages with a photograph of the author, full face, on the cover grasping himself, lightly, by the throat. The expression is serious, he is looking directly at you as if he were saying that you do what he has suggested only with more effective purpose. Or you might read the poems, which prayerfully he hopes—if you lack the intelligence to absorb them—may have the indicated effect.

I have had at least five of Cummings's books on my shelves for many years. I did have a sixth but I got so mad at it that in spite of the fact that my wife had made me a present of it at my request I tore it up and burned it; at least it had that much virtue in it and I shall never, in the present mode, cut me into small pieces and feed me to the dogs, "reveal its name." One more book, a handsome one, I keep in my grandmother's trunk in the attic, *ViVa,* happening on it whenever I go there in search of something else. I do not have his first book of poems, *Tulips and Chimneys,* much to my regret.

These are the works of a lyric poet. They could well all be called "songs" for they sing themselves to the ear, for the most part, beautifully; a lyric poet with a weakness for the sonnet which (if you can recognize it) you will find scattered through all the books.

Cummings is celebrated after all for the unconventionality of his punctuation and phrasing. You cannot mistake his page to have been written in anything but the American dialect. The scenes and persons he celebrates, with a dash, are from the life he sees about him. In spite of what they say and what the Red Cross may pretend, soldiers still go to war with "trumpet clap and syphilis."

Anything which forces the eye or the voice to revalue what it contemplates on the page (as in the case of Leonardo or any other artist) is Cummings's meat. For by such maneuvers the attention is tied to what is being said or you might miss it. All very well, you say, what of it? Save that if you continue to read, you have to do PRECISELY what he wants you to do, *i.e.,* use your wits and your eyes CORRECTLY. That is all, save that you will be rewarded for your pains by a vision of loveliness and not be deceived or cheated in any way. He has a New England conscience that can be most exasperating. In fact he is a veritable Puritan with his pornography whenever he is forced to use it.

From *1* x *1 (One Times One):*

nonsun blob a
cold to
skylessness
sticking fire

my are your
are birds our all
and one gone
away the they

leaf of ghosts some
few creep there
here or on
unearth

The above is quoted to make an example of it, for Cummings is said to be difficult, if you can understand one poem you can understand all.

What in the world are you to make of this poem? Because when you are a critic you are definitely not a poet. I'll show you.

It is, definitely, a composition (a conventional composition)—it has to be for the lines are arranged regularly. In fact they are arranged in the form of a quatrain: four lines followed by four lines. That is always something.

Each of these groups of four lines is followed by another to which it is similar. In what is it similar to the one that precedes it? It is like the one that precedes it in the organization of its rhythmical sequence; that is what (musically) it means. Poems are like that.

Therefore it is a poem and not for anything the lines *say*.

It is thrilling thus to have the lines reft of sense and returned to music.

It is marvelous to be so intoxicatedly loosed along the page. We (as all poets feel) are free to cut diagonally across the page as if it were a field of daisies to lie down among them when the sun is shining "to loaf at our ease."

E.E. Cummings, like Bobby Burns, is intoxicated by women as this poem attests and that is what the poem means. But his women must have the manners of quatrains and be governed by that music (not that they must always be that way) if they are to captivate him. That is my criticism of him and of his poem; great virtues.

Over and over he says the same thing, but the meaning gets lost, often, among the punctuation, try as "i" will to make it plain and try as hard as I can "i" cannot make it plainer that it doesn't mean anything what "i" say but what "i" do (on the page) that is the meaning.

Is that plain—and dancing enough?

"The play's the thing" but Cummings is not a playboy, he means what he dances: *da capo al fin.*

Oh! I forgot to say that there have been eight or ten books written since his first book *The Enormous Room,* a book I would have called, but for the French writer, Artaud, a masterpiece. *Tulips and Chimneys* began the poems memorably. We who read that will not forget it. Then came in succession: *XLI Poems; &; is 5; the play—Him; By E.E. Cummings* (no title); *CIOPW; ViVa; Eimi* (prose); *No Thanks; Tom; 1/20; Collected Poems; 50 Poems; 1 x 1;* and the present volume.

Take hope, all ye who enter here, for you will certainly be lost—and amused and fascinated by much beauty. You will not have Virgil for your guide for in fact he would not fit here as Catullus might. I could not speak either for Ariel for the atmosphere smells much too earthy and Cummings himself can be earthy, if you know what I mean.

It reminds me of a story I heard recently about a very shy young woman who when an older woman, whom she had met at a tea, was announcing how embarrassed she felt over her hands being so grimy spoke up:

> I know how you can get them clean.
> How? Inquired the lady.
> Make a pie.

Painting in the American Grain

The Edgar William and Bernice Chrysler Garbisch
Collection of American Primitives

Art News, 1954

How NOT to begin an article on American primitives in painting: You don't begin speaking about Giotto and Fra Angelico or even Bosch or Van Eyck, but of a cat with a bird in his mouth—a cat with a terrifying enormous head, enough to frighten birds, or of a six-foot Indian in a yellow breech clout . . . Washington apart from its official aspect is a quiet, old-fashioned city fit home, the only fit home for a collection of primitives such as this that smacks of the American past . .

As you enter the place [1] —there are a total of 109 paintings of all sizes—the first thing that hits your eyes is the immediacy of the scene I should say the color! They were putting down what they had to put down, what they saw before them. They had reds to use and greens and flesh tints and browns and blues with which they wanted to surround themselves in shapes which they recognized. A beloved infant had died. If only they could bring it to life again! An artist was employed to paint a counterfeit presentment of the scene: as it stood again in the garden by an obelisk near a weeping willow and a cat which arched its back and purred. It would bring comfort to the bereaved parents. That is how the artist painted it.

No matter what the skill or the lack of it, someone, somewhere in Pennsylvania—all trace of the painters that we may identify them has been lost—wanted on his walls a picture of Adam and Eve in the garden before the Fall. There is no serpent here, no sign even of God, just the garden and its bountiful blessings. Wild beasts are at Adam's feet or at least one panther is there. The sky is luminous, this was not painted in a potato cellar, the trees are luxuriant, hoar

---

[1] The National Gallery.

grape clusters hang from the trees and there at their ease sit together our primordial parents naked and unashamed bathed in sunlight. Who shall say the plenty of the New World so evident about them was not the true model that has been recorded—so innocently recorded the beholder in whom no rancor has as yet intruded.

A head, a head of a young woman in its title designated as *Blue Eyes* caught my eye at once because of the simplicity and convincing dignity of the profile. The hair was black and chopped off short to hang straight at the neck line. The complexion was clear, there was a faint smile to the lips, the look, off to the right, was direct but feature of the thing was for me not the blue eyes but the enormous round chin perfectly in proportion that dominated the face and the whole picture. No one can say that chin was not real and that it was put down to be anything than what it was. It is a world not a chin that is depicted.

A record, something to stand against, a shield for their protection, the savage world with which they were surrounded. Color, color that ran, mostly, to the very edge of the canvas as if they were afraid that something would be left out, covered the whole of their surfaces. One of my first views of the whole show, the big room, was of the *Sisters in Red.* Both my wife and eye were amazed. They were talking to us. The older girl, not more than six, had dark hair and looking at us directly was the most serious, even slightly annoyed. The younger sister, holding a flower basket, was a blond with wavy hair, wore an alert, a daring expression of complete self-assurance, the mark of a typical second-child complex, that made her to me a living individual. I fell in love with her—and with my wife all over again for she too was a second child. The brilliant red dresses from which decently projected the snow-white pantalettes ironed no doubt that morning and dainty slippers completed an arresting picture.

A picture of the burning of Charlestown by the British with Boston untouched across the harbor once again emphasized for me the importance for these people of the recording of events. Titles in this case were superimposed upon the canvas, Charlestown on one side and Boston on the other and between them, incongruously,

Bunker Hill. Smoke was billowing to a sky already filled with masses of round clouds that rose above the flame and smoke in the distance.

Intimate scenes of rural life, a scene showing a side view of four cows and two horses, the barn and beyond that a house—a clapboard house, painted white, which completed the scene, aside from three young trees. An obvious pride of possession and of the care which are owed such things.

There is a different pride, which we see in a grouping that fills one canvas, again to the very edge, called *The Plantation*. Apparently it is near the sea, for a full-rigged ship occupies the foreground. Above rises a hill. The theme is formally treated and not without some skill by the artist. The perspective is elementary. Clusters of grapes larger than the ship's sails come in from the right meeting two trees, one on each side, that reach the sky framing the plantation house, with its garden, in the center distance toward the picture's upper edge. Birds are flying about, and down the hill nearer the foreground, linked by paths, are the farm buildings and at the water's edge a warehouse.

A portrait of a woman past middle life arrested me by the hollow-cheeked majesty of its pose. A plain white bonnet, from which the two white strings which lie symmetrically on either side of her flat breasts above her hands complete the oval, complete the whole. A single tree, formally pruned and cut off so only partially shown completes the picture. This portrait is accompanied by a similar one of her husband. They are serious individuals. The principal interest for me apart from the impression they give of their pride and reticence is the colors the unknown artist has used in drawing them. Nowhere except in El Greco have I seen green so used in the shadows about the face.

You will find here another of Hicks's *Peaceable Kingdoms* but that hardly needs further comment at this late date. The same for *Penn's Treaty with the Indians*.

Henry James said, It is a complex thing to be an American. Unconscious of such an analysis of their situation, these artists as well as their sitters reacted to it nevertheless directly. They

37. Unknown American artist, *The Cat* (*c.* 1840). Collection, Edgar William and Bernice Chrysler Garbisch.

38. American school, *Blue Eyes* (*c.* 1840). Wood oval, 18″ × 12¾″.
Collection, National Gallery of Art, Washington, D. C. (Gift of Edgar
William and Bernice Chrysler Garbisch, 1953).

39. Unknown American artist, *The Plantation* (*c.* 1825). Oil on wood, 19⅛″ × 29½″. Collection, The Metropolitan Museum of Art, New York (Gift of Edgar William and Bernice Chrysler Garbisch, 1963).

40. American school, *The Sargent Family* (*c.* 1800). Canvas, 38⅜″ × 50⅜″. Collection, National Gallery of Art, Washington, D. C. (Gift of Edgar William and Bernice Chrysler Garbisch, 1953).

41. Unknown American artist, *Catalynje Post* (*c.* 1730). Collection, Edgar William and Bernice Chrysler Garbisch.

scarcely knew why they yearned for the things they desired but to get them they strained every nerve.

The style of all these paintings is direct. Purposeful. The artist was called upon to put down a presence that the man or woman for whom the picture was painted wanted to see and remember, the world otherwise was for the moment put aside. That dictated the realistic details of the situation and also what was to be excluded. The selection of significant detail was outstanding.

The kind of people that called for the paintings determined their quality. They were in demand of something to stand against the crudeness that surrounded them. As Wallace Stevens put it:

> I placed a jar in Tennessee,
> And round it was, upon a hill.
> It made the slovenly wilderness
> Surround that hill.
>
> The wilderness rose up to it,
> And sprawled around, no longer wild.

These were talented, creative painters. They had to be. They had no one to copy from. They were free as the wind, limited only by their technical abilities and driven by the demands of their clients. The very difficulties, technical difficulties, they had to face in getting their images down only added to the intensity of their efforts and to the directness of the results. It gave them a style of their own, as a group they had a realistic style direct and practical as Benjamin Franklin. Nothing was to daunt them.

The circumstances surrounding the painting of Abraham Clark and his children, 1820, are known. Mr. Clark had just lost his beloved wife. He had gone into his garden with his six small children to read for them from the Bible. There he instructed the artist to paint him with the remainder of his family about him. The father, in profile, his thumb in the Bible no doubt at the passage from which he had been reading, sat to the right under the trees. The boys closely grouped, the baby on the knee of the oldest bareheaded before him. They all look alike, an obvious family. All are serious as befits the occasion. One leans his elbow against a tree. Their colorful faces stand out no doubt, in the clear light of the Resurrection upon the forested and carefully painted background. The fifth son—apparently they were all boys—carries a pet hen carefully in his arm. We are deeply moved by it all.

Across the room in the big gallery is a large portrait of a young woman, Catalynje Post, 1730, wearing a flowered apron. She has a white lace cap on her head. Her arms are bare halfway to the wrists. She wears a low-necked dress and a necklace of pearls. Her hands crudely painted, are placed one at the waist upon the hem of the colored apron, the other at the throat playing with an ornament which her fingers find there. A four-petaled flower and some carefully placed roses are seen occupying spaces in the background. But the feature of the ensemble is the slippered feet, standing at right angles one to another flat before the eye, they have high heels and pointed toes and must have been the pride of their possessor. The artist had difficulty with the nose which is presented full face or almost full face, his struggle to master the difficulty has not prevented him however, from presenting the picture or showing a realistic portrait of a young woman.

There are still lifes which I wish there were room to comment on. Fruit, in one case a watermelon with its red flesh, attracts the eye and the palate. One group symmetrically arranged on an oblong table, recognizable as of Shaker make, particularly fascinated me. Curtains hang, always symmetrically, across the top. At either side are plates, painted flat, with fruit knives. A bowl, it might be that of which Wallace Stevens speaks, is filled in the exact center of the picture making of it an obvious decoration, with melons, grapes, apples, perhaps an orange, peaches, and pears.

It was the intensity of their vision, coupled with their isolation in the wilderness, that caused them one and all to place and have placed on the canvas veritable capsules, surrounded by a line of color, to hold them off from a world which was most about them. They were eminently objective, their paintings remained always things. They drew a line and the more clearly that line was drawn, the more vividly, the better. Color is light. Color is what most distinguishes the artist, color was what these people wanted to brighten the walls of their houses, color to the last inch of the canvas.

It was so with the portrait painted in 1800 of the Sargent family, artist unknown, the gayest and one of the largest pictures in the exhibition. It is the portrait of a cocky little man, in an enormous—to make him look tall—beaver hat (you can't tell me that the artist was not completely wise to the situation) surrounded by his wife and little daughters in white and flouncy dresses. The wife is sitting, sideface, with a new baby in her arms. The room is suffused with light. A toy spaniel frisks joyfully upon the rag rug, the canaries are singing joyfully—at least one of them is—in their cages between the pictures on the gaily papered walls. The paneled door is open. Every corner of the painting is distinct and bathed in light. It is a picture of a successful man.

There are in the same room two pictures, among the earliest of those shown, 1780, two large canvases of men heavily clad and in top hats, coursing hounds in the half-light of dawn and near sundown: the *Start* and *End of the Hunt*. True to the facts the light in both cases is dim which presented practical difficulties to the artist. These pictures are among the most crudely painted of those shown but the record they present is filled for all that with something nostalgic and particularly moving. It brings to mind, as it was meant to do, another day which even then was fast vanishing. The artist was faced by the facts and the difficulties they made for him but he faced them in the only way he knew, head on.

There is also in the same room a picture, undated, entitled *The Coon Hunt*. That, too, presented a scene which must have been familiar to the men of that time. It is moonlight. Half the party, carrying a lighted lantern, are approaching through a forest of partly felled trees. The quarry is on a high limb above their heads. The dogs are bounding into the air at the tree's base. The other half of the party is resting.

It is all part of their lives that they had to see re-enacted before them to make it real to them so that they could relive it and re-enjoy it and it must be depicted by the artist so that it could be recognized—awkward as he may be.

In the middle room, apart from two Rembrandt-like portraits of an aging burgher and his comfortable and smiling wife, among the best painted pictures in the exhibition, are two of the most interesting imaginative pictures of all. I don't quite know what they meant but suspect that the intention is to represent the travels of a man who has seen much of the world, has made money, perhaps retired from his labors and come home to rest and enjoy his memories. Each of the pictures presents, one overtly, a volcano in the distance, in the background a range of high mountains, perhaps the Andes, before a foreground crowded with all the appurtenances of a commercial civilization of those times, bathed to the minutest detail, in the fullest light. The artist means, as he was no doubt instructed to do, to have you see into every part of his canvas; cities, factories, virtual palaces, railroad trains, alas, giving out smoke, rivers with waterfalls are to be seen prominently displayed. It is a pride of wealth which must have decorated a great house now all forgotten.

Many more such pictures showing the lives of our people in the late eighteenth and early nineteenth century are shown in this noteworthy collection of our unknown artists' work. I must not forget to mention a picture labeled *Twenty-Two Houses and a Church* depicting just that. Only the outlines of the buildings covering several acres are shown with their surrounding fences painted white except in the foreground where a darker color is used—the only art aside from the spacing of the buildings displayed. Light, as in all the primitives, is everywhere. Not a single human figure is to be seen in the village, the buildings alone are recorded. The paintings have a definite style of their own, a forthrightness, a candor and and a practical skill not to be gainsaid, that gives them a marked distinction separate from European schools of painting with which they had not the time or the opportunity to acquaint themselves. So that, collectively, they represent not individual paintings so much as a yearning in the new country for some sort of an expression of the world which they represent.

It was a beginning world, a re-beginning world, and a hopeful one. The men, women, and children who made it up were ignorant of the forces that governed it and what they had to face. They wanted to see themselves and be recorded against a surrounding wilderness of which they themselves were the only recognizable aspect. They were lonely. They were of the country, the only country which they or their artists knew and so represented.

This is a collection of paintings, lovingly assembled by a couple, Mr. and Mrs. Garbisch, for their home on the eastern shore of Maryland. They found almost at once that the scope of what they had to choose from far exceeded their plans. They are called "American Primitives," the work of gifted artists whose names are for the most part lost in the shuffle of history.

Brancusi

Arts, 1955

CONSTANTIN BRANCUSI, sculptor, is a Rumanian by birth living as all the world knows in Paris. This is an exhibition of some of his major works. [1]

The *Adam and Eve* (wood) is one of his characteristic pieces. Here is a story that tells much of his methods with his materials, it is the history of an afterthought, revealing the man as he drives on to a conclusion. The *Adam and Eve,* one of the summative pieces of his prime was first conceived by him as two statues—contrasting the sexes, hacked out to exemplify their contrasting anatomies and the significance of the relationship. One is the mother who nourishes the child and through that the continuance of all life. But what of the man? He supplies apart from the spark itself the sinews that hold him before all, erect, on whom the woman relies for her support.

Thinking of the two pieces perhaps with dissatisfaction, apart, Brancusi after he had first exhibited them or perhaps at the very time, his mind itself painfully divided—not knowing what to do to relieve his unrest, had an inspiration!

Returning the pieces to his studio he took a wooden peg and placing the Eve on his Adam's head he fastened her there. A unit! He had made them one which he had always wanted only *didn't know* how. His mind had been slow to act but when at last he saw how the thing should go, he moved with complete conviction, calming himself and presenting himself, an artist, to the world in all his crudity and primitive strength by that simple deed.

This exhibition should be witnessed with those few pieces currently at the Museum of Modern Art, as a unit. There are works

[1]The Brancusi Retrospective exhibition at the Solomon R. Guggenheim Museum, October 26, 1955, to January 8, 1956.

in wood, stone, and polished metal, a fair showing from Brancusi's major work over a lifetime. It is not to be described as abstract art, the figures are presented without distortion, in a natural relationship of their anatomic parts reduced to the essentials. In an early piece, *Ancient Figure* (stone), two arms being in the presentation graphically redundant, one is made to carry the burden of the presentation.

This by the way is an interesting piece. It shows many of the traits of having been conceived early in the artist's career, when he was interested in fragments of ancient statues recovered from the fields about his natal region where he must have observed them in his youth. In this statue there are parts which have been broken off and lost: a heel, part of the forehead and the face—but the essential thing is that it remains sculpturally whole for all that: two monolithic figures, one turned toward the rock, one half away. Later the elimination of the inessential progressed further but in this the details of the anatomy are still discernible. He must have learned much from this early piece. To rely on the accidental for distinction, as on the broken segment of an ancient statue, is not a gesture which Brancusi could long tolerate. There was only the consciously intended, trimmed to the bare essentials, to be seen in his later pieces.

(Being essentially from the hills, a shepherd, Brancusi is concerned mainly with the land and the sky.)*y** The man, now well over seventy, living alone, as he has always lived, in his studio has become famous for his broiled steaks cooked by himself at his own fire which he himself serves as though he were a shepherd at night on one of his native hillsides under the stars. A white collie named "Polaire" used to be his constant companion reinforcing the impression of a shepherd which with his shaggy head of hair, broad shoulders, and habitual reserve he seemed to his friends to be. But he is not as his friends clearly understand to be taken advantage of. I remember him speaking of the small merchants of his quarter when he first moved in, how they looked him over, especially the women, but when they found out his mettle, they became his friends.

When he was young he was a pupil of the sculptor Rodin. After a time he saw how their paths, the older man with his ideas and sentiments which Brancusi did not share and had no interest in, diverted. His ideas were simpler, in their essentials more primitive, more related to the materials with which he, a workman, a sculptor, had to do. It is to bring out of a hunk of wood or stone what is hidden there, by force of what he sees, not a placing on it of an extraneous idea, that forced the sculptor's hand.

Brancusi wanted to lay calming hands on the rock itself, to force the materials to obey his will—that is why his eye sees in his chunks of wood so many revelations. The pieces here from the monumental *Arch* and *The Bench* (wood) are completely revealing. It is strange to see a sculptured head by Modigliani, who began his career in the field and who influenced Brancusi at one time. Modigliani's head is smoothly molded showing as it does much virtuosity in the handling—Brancusi, at about this time, was showing much more interest in the total, massive effect. He was leaving the finish often untouched, broken off fragments, as in *Ancient Figure* already spoken of. He would not be contained by the mere lines of a drawing.

The *Arch* and *Bench* show this tendency admirably. They seem to have been constructed of driftwood, showing the effects of severe weather, the fragmentation and even rot, of the elements and the color, the grey color of all drift. These are the only pieces I saw directly designed to rest on the ground, both arches, one to go through the air which they surround and the other, the bench, to support a burden, a human burden, which it lifts, more modestly, up.

The *Arch* might have been called, from the design across its brow, the way it lifts it without other decoration above the earth, "The Rainbow."

The Endless Column is one that gives the same sense of Brancusi's concern with the air about him (, and the sea, which is to appear so strongly later on)*y**. I saw the same theme expressed in his Paris studio but it seemed to be on a larger scale than here (the Modern's piece) and much more effective. It needs bulk to give it the thrust that is called for—this is perhaps an earlier version. It appears with an alternate swell and narrowing of a quadrilateral column up from

(*Left*) 42. Constantin Brancusi, *Adam and Eve* (1921). Chestnut and oak; limestone base. Collection, The Solomon R. Guggenheim Museum, New York. (*Right*) 43. Constantin Brancusi, *Ancient Seated Figure* (1906–08). Limestone sculpture, 22¼″ high. Courtesy of The Art Institute of Chicago (Ada Turnbull Hertle Fund).

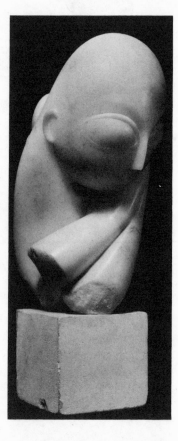

(*Left*) 44. Michelangelo, *The Rebellious Slave.* Marble. Collection, Louvre, Paris. (*Right*) 45. Constantin Brancusi, *Mlle Pogany* (1913). Marble. Collection, Philadelphia Museum of Art (Given by Mrs. Rodolphe M. de Schauensee).

46. Constantin Brancusi, *The Kiss*. Collection, Philadelphia Museum of Art (Louise and Walter Arensberg Collection).

47. Constantin Brancusi, *Princess X* (1916). Polished bronze. Collection, Philadelphia Museum of Art (Louise and Walter Arensberg Collection).

the ground without pedestal, stopping at the ceiling without check as if it were destined to go on indefinitely. It has been carved out of oak or some other strong wood in bold scallops as the beams of some of our colonial ceilings were made using an adze. It is through the air it lifts to an unknown height. The surface of the finish is unessential—in which it differs from the column of a Greek temple.

There are other wood pieces in which I find Brancusi more effective of which I will speak again later. The highly polished surfaces of his great stone *Fish* (Modern Museum) and of the lesser *Fish* (with the reflecting pool) here likewise the *Bird in Space,* marble and metal, and his *Sophisticated Young Lady* call for another view of the sculptor's genius. What in so crude a view, so basic, as his, led him to do it? Was it a feeling of his own futility facing a world foreign to him, an essential peasant, which he must surmount in the only way he knew of, to escape? He lived a bachelor who saw a world of desirable women, often beautiful, about him. The *Fish,* inhabiting an element in which he could not be at home was of this sort—or the *Bird in Space.*

These are of the nature of fundamentals, defeats perhaps but subject to the same treatment as a more familiar world and so, by his art, and his mastery of the essentials of his art, the elimination of the inessential, he could survive. *Mlle Pogany* was an aristocrat, *Nancy Cunard* was an aristocrat, the *Fish* escaping the checks of the land is an aristocrat and the artist, likewise, he Brancusi, being an artist is also an aristocrat and should run with his own kind. Aristocrats are polished, the lines of their anatomies are gracile.

The *Bird in Space* gives an undoubted sense of flight, of the surrounding air, which is difficult for a sculptor to depict with the weight of his materials always before him. Most do not succeed but find their pieces anchored heavily at their feet, even the best of them—the wind in the clothes of the *Nike of Samothrace* or even in Gauden's *General Sherman* are cases in point. But Brancusi did not allow himself the realism that these figures imply—yet he succeeded in his attempt to make the bird fly. We see no wings. It is the balance of the piece; I think a person witnessing it knows without a word instinctively what is intended. I recall a figure representing a

woman's torso, a stone piece, placed solidly on its base that through
some skill in the presentation gives that same sense of elevation. I
wonder how a woman would feel about it.

Speaking of pieces of sculpture solidly anchored on their bases I
want to report presently on one of Brancusi's insistences in making
his pedestals an intricate part of his compositions.

In one of the few "literary" subjects he ever undertook, the
Maiastra (stone), a bird with its mouth open, singing, a fairy tale or
heroic legend from his childhood that perhaps meant much to him,
he expressed it most in the pedestal, a broad stone disk (plaster)
which surrounds the sculptured figure which it supports—as with
an aura of thought. But this is unusual with him, the obsession with
the materials, the direct contact with the wood or the stone or metal
with which his hands are in contact governed his thoughts more.
The direct handling of his materials is one thing that influenced
him, kept his eye from wandering (to non-tactile interests)[y*].
There was also with Brancusi the constant pull toward the center,
to simplify, to eliminate the inessential, to purify, a scientific
impulse to get at the very gist of the matter kept him steady. His
pedestals separate him from a hostile world, isolating his subject
from the inessential, keeping it "sterile" in the surgical sense,
making it something to be considered separately. There is a good
story about this trait in the artist, how furious he was at a patron, an
exhibitor of his, Brancusi's, work—fortunately for us, a Brazilian—
who had placed a piece *sans* pedestal for the public to view. The
artist's remarks are not recorded, but his indignation became plain
enough so that error is not likely to be repeated.

As a draftsman Brancusi is skillful, as might be expected. I will
speak here only of one famous cartoon, that of the *Mlle Pogany*. It
reveals a voluptuous woman with big thighs, the entire figure
realistically shown but even in this phase of his composition the
artist, although he is attracted by the woman and shows it in his
drawing, is concerned most with the proportions and lines of the
figure in the round. Even in the flat drawing it can be felt these are
surfaces that must go beyond graphic representation to be fully
realized. What then does the artist do with his problem? In the first
place he cuts the body off at the neck: enough of that. He is

interested only in the head, a polished woman but a tortured one enslaved by the mind. The figure the artist has seen has the movement, the same movement in it as Michelangelo's slaves, twist upon themselves like the wind of a tornado. Just the fingers of one hand, a concession to the past, are included.

We are witnessing how from the beginning in the cartoon, the sculptor works eliminating details, concentrating slowly (it must have taken years for the finished piece to evolve, not what he had conceived at the first glance, but what in his own mind it had resolved itself to be: a piece of metal which the artist has molded to express forever, as long as a man may live, what he has to say).

The *Prodigal Son* (wood) refutes what I have just stated, that the sculptor's interest has not been concerned with literary subjects. This is not primarily a literary subject at all but a moral one, I will not say a plastic opportunity, but by his handling he has made it so. It reminds me somewhat, the single figure, of the Socrates, the *Socrate,* which he showed me in the Paris studio. I do not mean to contrast the two pieces directly because they are not alike, but they are both of wood and the handling is similar, both witty and both outspoken showing the same tactile quality: Socrates is all mouth, a mouth that goes widely through the entire head so that there can be no question of hiding the brain back of it! Through and through, it holds nothing back (—only the frame of a man, head hollowed out, is retained to show that it is human)^{y*}—the man seen in the frame of his own big mouth. Brancusi's *Prodigal Son* has the same graphic quality though the entire (weary)^{y*} figure of a man, a contrite man is depicted (whereas the head only of the other carries the whole story)^{y*}.

The *Penguins* must have interested the artist mainly because of their shape, how they summarized certain sculptural features, a plastic unity which cannot but have intrigued him. The figures have no other significance.

The *Kiss* (stone) a small tombstone in the Père Lachaise cemetery in Paris, is something else again. It represents two figures, a man and a woman, locked in each other's arms in the final embrace of death, in which they will continue forever united. It is conceived in the very shape of a tombstone of modest size to be inconspicuous as so private an emotion should be. (It is one piece of stone.)*y** The faces are pressed together, fused together, the features blending because they want them to blend into a whole. This must have been a particularly congenial commission for the sculptor to create. It must have engaged his emotions and his mind. It presented a pathetic, an emotional subject but at the same time it satisfied an urge to summarize, to eliminate redundant detail, to make one body out of two, which had always been his aim. To get rid of one body entirely and make the subject unique, single. To have succeeded in that must have been a secret satisfaction of no small proportions. The result represents one of Brancusi's major achievements. (You see nothing but the all essential embrace, lips blended in the kiss, arms about each other's necks, all else is smoothed away, the piece formally finished at the bottom by a pedestal which frames it.)*y**

The New Born is the bare head of a baby, without a neck, in other words an egg showing only a suggestion of what it is destined to be. Again we see Brancusi's fervor for the elimination of inessential detail. The baby is to develop into a man or a woman. That being implied what else need be said—save that this is to be a human being, a brain, the outer case of which has all that has appeared as yet with all its fearful implications.

White Negress (stone) a portrait head, showing that to a sculptor the color of the skin is inessential. The lips are appropriately emphasized. It is a mere detail.

Sculpture for the Hand (stone) is a piece without pedestal that invites touch as much as any rock picked up on a beach where it has been worn by the sea—to an almost symmetrical contour. I cannot believe other than that the sculptor intended that we or anyone should be as quick to detect the divergence from *absolute* symmetry as he. As much might be said of any large pebble. Not having the opportunity to handle the piece, I shall have to forego speaking more of it. It is the sculptural quality of the thing that the artist wants to emphasize and that in this the eye and hand are interchangeable.

But perhaps the most famous, as it is the most spectacular of Brancusi's creations and the piece which has brought him most fame, is *The Princess* (polished brass) with its flagrant implication: it resembles the human phallus. Here Brancusi has blended portraiture and sculptural quality into a subject that has a distinction that has caught the eyes of the world. At the same time he has spoken unashamedly of a distinguished lady's intimate character in a way which cannot give her or the world the slightest offense. On the contrary it can only enhance her fame showing her to be universal in her appeal for us all.

It is a figure of the head and upper breast of a woman with a long and graceful neck, like a swan. It immediately attracts, as the contours inevitably suggest the phallus and testicles of a man. The mind jumps from that to the conclusion of the woman's interest in all men whom she governs and impresses with her charms.

As always with Brancusi, the sculptor's sole interest has been to portray the plastic interest of his subject for him; in that he succeeded brilliantly. It had to be done in polished metal to show the sophisticated character of the subject. It had to be done with the daring that disdained to hide with aristocratic candor a contempt for hiding anything from the view of the world. It would be the nature of his subject to be indifferent to what was thought of her. So the artist, as in the case of Goya in his *Maja Desnuda,* had nothing to conceal and did not. Or if, as in all the arts, reticence is a virtue, the subject is covered in the obscurity of the art itself—baffling to all observers, hidden from recognition under a cloud (of beauty)^y* under which it escapes, as a god on which none can stare with impunity.

To change from (too great)^y* an occupation with the heady liquors of the female form and its implications we have only to look at *Torso of a Young Man* (wood). The powerful legs jut out symmetrically from the immature body as would those of a potential athlete not quite come into his own. The power is there and the threat of the deeds to come but as yet it is recorded as a symmetry which the artist alone, or a mother, can look at with admiration or alarm.

The New Born is another unattached head, as if freshly out of the egg, which concerns the sculptor above the as yet nonexistent body. But in this case it has progressed beyond the first stage: it has developed a vestige of a NOSE and a MOUTH out of which issue *yells,* thus making its presence in the world known and by way of which it is FED! When the artist had plastically conveyed these facts he was through with the problem and quit.

The lesser *Fish* (marble, with mirror), of which I have already spoken, is chiefly notable for its pedestal to which the mirror is attached. The whole with the reflecting surface, doubling the image, with the beveled quadrilateral support narrowing at the waist, makes an attractive decorative unit, something with which Brancusi seldom is concerned.

I have left to the last the further consideration of the much larger *Fish* (polished, green mottled marble) because it is not exhibited here but in the Modern Museum in which it occupies a prominent place as one of the artist's major works. It should unquestionably be seen. Here Brancusi has been at his greatest, eliminating all that is inessential until the pure form comes out in all its simple dignity and conviction as we veritably gasp to witness it.

And finally—*Figure,* the portrait of a young girl (wood), because it so amuses me. This is the picture of a girl before the age of puberty, before sex has hit her. She is ungainly, with skinny but straight legs. She is not alluring but positively ugly, self-conscious and probably miserable—but to the artist who sees how she is put together and has only an interest, with sympathy, in that. One can almost hear Brancusi speaking as he depicts her, possibly naked—with relief that he does not have to consider the woman of it.

Epilogue

The World Contracted to a Recognizable Image

at the small end of an illness
there was a picture
probably Japanese
which filled my eye

an idiotic picture
except it was all I recognized
the wall lived for me in that picture
I clung to it as a fly

Sources

Vortex
Previously unpublished. Undated, but the ms. was undoubtedly written in 1915: Gaudier-Brzeska's "Vortex" (written "from the trenches"), which formed the immediate impetus for Williams's own manifesto, had been published in the second issue of Wyndham Lewis's *Blast*, in July 1915. The paper, typewriter typeface, as well as the purple color of the typewriter ribbon, etc., used for the ms., are identical to those of the ms. of Williams's *Five Philosophical Essays* (see Williams's *The Embodiment of Knowledge*, ed. Loewinsohn, New Directions, 1974), and are of a kind not found among Williams's mss. beyond 1915.

The text printed here is based on ms. C–174 (a) of the bibliography/catalogue of the Williams ms. holdings of the Lockwood Memorial Library of the State University of New York at Buffalo, compiled by Neil E. Baldwin and Steven Meyers. Additional material in parentheses was taken from C–174 (b). N. B.: C–174 (a) in fact consists of: 1. A three-page main version of the ms. (my basic text), 2. An alternate first page which I have designated here as C–174 (c), and 3. Two pages of handwritten notes which I have classified as C–174 (d).

Some Observations on Artists and Critics
I. More Swill: Reprinted as published in *The Little Review*, Vol. VI, No. 6 (October, 1919), 29–30. *II. What Every Artist Knows*, a letter to the editors of *The Freeman*: Reprinted as published in *The Freeman*, Vol. II, No. 45 (January 19, 1921), 449.

Comment on Contact
I. "Contact is issued . . ."* and *II. Further Announcement*: Reprinted as published in *Contact*, No. 1 (December 1920), p. 1 and p. 10.; *III.*

Sample Critical Statement: Reprinted as published in *Contact,* No. 4 (1921), 18–19.

French Painting
Reprinted as published in *The Embodiment of Knowledge,* ed. Ron Loewinsohn (New Directions, 1974), 21–25. Written in 1928 or 1929.

Notes on Art
Previously unpublished. These notes have been taken from Williams's 1927–1928 Journal, Buffalo ms. D–2 (a through e). Much of this Journal found its way into Williams's collections *The Descent of Winter* and *Della Primavera Transportata Al Morale.* The section published here forms page 2 of ms. D–2 (e); a few lines of no immediate relevance to these notes have been omitted here.

Art and Politics: The Editorship of Blast
Previously unpublished. The text printed here is taken from Buffalo ms. C–54, which consists of a page of typewritten notes, which I have designated as C–54 (a), and the main text, C–54 (b). *Blast* was published from September, 1933, to November, 1934. The ms. therefore dates most likely from 1933.

The Neglected Artist
Previously unpublished. The text printed here is based on Buffalo ms. B–74, which consists of eight fragments and versions of varying length (a through h). I have used B–74 (g) as my basic text, since this is clearly the final version reviewed and corrected by Williams. It has an annotation in the upper left-hand corner of the first page, in Williams's handwriting: "3486 words." B–74 (h) is a carbon copy of a typist's (not Williams) "clean copy" of B–74 (g). The original copy of B–74 (h) is at Yale (Yale ms. Za Williams-Millett) and contains an annotation by Williams to an unidentified correspondent (perhaps John C. Thirlwall): "Irrelevant—but there may be a sentence or two here and there of significance. No need to return this." The ms. is undated but internal evidence indicates that it must have been written in 1936: Williams refers to "literary

fellowships to be offered by the Book-of-the-Month Club this year for 'good volumes of poor sale' ." On April 20, 1936, the *New York Times* reported that the Book-of-the-Month Club had announced that it planned to award four fellowships "for good books which have poor sale," during 1936. In the spring of 1936, of course, Williams was indeed "fifty and more": fifty-two, in fact.

Revolutions Revalued: The Attack on Credit Monopoly from a Cultural Viewpoint
Previously unpublished. The text printed here is based on ms. C-9 at Buffalo, which consists of six versions in various stages of completion. I have used C-9 (e) as my basic text and have also consulted ms. C-12 (i) a fragment from Williams's essay "The Basis of Faith in Art," which is in effect a five-page segment of ms. C-9 (f)—pages six through ten—which Williams removed when he decided to use parts of it in "The Basis of Faith in Art." Ms. C-12 (f) of the latter article in fact contains the following note from Williams to himself: "Excerpt the useful parts from the credit speech—as applicable to the artist—revise—have typed in full." Ms. C-9 is dated "July 11, 1936."

An Afternoon with Tchelitchew
First published in *Life and Letters Today,* Vol. XVII, No. 10 (Winter 1937), 55-58. The version published in *Life and Letters Today* and all subsequent reprintings (*i.e.* in *Selected Essays* and *The William Carlos Williams Reader*), follow the text of Buffalo ms. C-3 (d), which is a typist's copy of Williams's rough draft C-3 (a). C-3 (d) contains a few curious and clearly inappropriate emendations in a hand which is decidedly *not* Williams's. These emendations have been followed in the previously printed versions and obstruct the intended meaning of several of Williams's original phrases. (For details see my "Note on the Text," p. 48 above.) I have therefore based the version printed here on Williams's own rough draft C-3 (a), of which C-3 (b) is a carbon copy, thus restoring the wording of several phrases to the meaning originally intended by Williams. The ms. copy of "An Afternoon with

Tchelitchew" at Yale (uncatalogued Mss. Box II) is a typist's copy following Buffalo ms. C–3 (d) and incorporates the inappropriate emendations by the unidentified editor mentioned above.

Cache Cache

Reprinted as published in *View,* second series, No. 2 (May 1942 [Tchelitchew issue]), 17–18. Buffalo ms. C–42 does not contain any significant variations from the printed version. The article is dated Easter Day, 1942, in *View.*

Effie Deans

Previously unpublished. The text printed here follows Buffalo ms. B–31 (b). B–31 (a) is a rough draft without significant variations, and B–31 (c) is a carbon copy of B–31 (a).

My dating of this piece (c. 1937) is purely guesswork, based on unreliable indications such as the appearance and typeface of the ms.

Walker Evans: American Photographs

First published in *The New Republic,* Vol. LXXXVI, No. 1244 (October 12, 1938). The existing mss. of this review at Buffalo and Yale indicate that editorial emendations were introduced in the printed version. One of these emendations was a matter of factual accuracy (the Walker book contains 87 plates instead of 95), but all others represent changes of dubious merit in punctuation and style. Several phrases in Williams's review were omitted in the printed version. I have therefore used Buffalo ms. C–18 (a) as the basis for the version printed here. C–18 (b) is the carbon copy of a typist's version of Williams's rough draft, probably the carbon of the copy sent by Williams to *The New Republic.* The version of the ms. at Yale (Za Williams 248, 249) represents an earlier draft which I have designated as (y).

Charles Sheeler

First published as the introduction to the Museum of Modern Art's catalogue of their Sheeler Retrospective Exhibition in 1939. I have used the printed version (reprinted in *Selected Essays*) as the basis for the text printed here, but have added a considerable amount of material from the twenty-nine fragments and versions which make up Buffalo ms. C–75 (a through z, aa, bb and cc).

Charles Sheeler—Postscript
Reprinted as published in *Art in America,* Vol. XXXXII, No. 3 (October 1954), 214–215, and in the catalogue of the Charles Sheeler Retrospective Exhibition at the UCLA Art Gallery (October 1954), 7–8. The ms. "Charles Sheeler" at Yale (Uncatalogued, Box II) is a copy, by John C. Thirlwall, of this article, as printed in *Art in America.*

Marsden Hartley: 1940
Apparently previously unpublished. It is possible that this short piece, clearly written as a review, was in fact published in a newspaper or magazine of the period, but if it was, it has remained undetected since. The text printed here is an exact copy of the ms. of this title at Yale (Uncatalogued Williams mss., Box II).

Beginnings: Marsden Hartley
The first four paragraphs of this essay, and part of the fifth, were first published in *The Black Mountain Review,* No. 7 (Autumn 1957), 164–166. I have based these first paragraphs on the published text, with the addition of several phrases taken from a Yale ms. entitled "Marsden Hartley," (ms. Za Williams 152) and which I have designated as ms. (b), to distinguish it from the text of the ms. titled "Marsden Hartley: 1940." This ms. forms the basis for the section published in *The Black Mountain Review.* The second part of ms. (b), lopped off by Williams in mid-sentence, has remained unpublished and is printed here for the first time. The ms. was clearly written a number of years before its partial publication in 1957, but, inevitably, after Hartley's death in September 1943. The characteristics of the typescript suggest that the ms. was written sometime between 1946 and 1950.

Marsden Hartley: 1956
Previously unpublished. The text printed here is based on a third ms. at Yale, catalogued with ms. Za Williams 152, also entitled

"Marsden Hartley." This ms. is written on the electric typewriter
Williams acquired after his strokes of the early 1950s. It appears
likely that Williams set out to write a short piece on Hartley for
The Black Mountain Review, using his earlier ms. as a guideline,
then became impatient with his progress and decided instead to use
part of the earlier ms. This accounts for the fragmentary nature of
Hartley ms. (c) and suggests 1956 or early 1957 as the most likely
date of composition.

Midas

A much shortened version of this essay was published in *Now,* Vol.
I, No. 1 (August 1941), 18–24, and was later reprinted in *Selected
Essays.* The text published here is based on Buffalo ms. C–94 (g),
which is the most complete of the ms. versions. Buffalo ms. C–94
consists of nine versions and fragments (a through i) of varying
lengths.

The Poet in Time of Confusion

Reprinted as published in the *Columbia Review and Morningside,*
Vol. XXIII (Autumn 1941), 1–5.

Axioms

Previously unpublished. The text printed here follows Yale ms. Za
"Stieglitz" (Williams's letters to Stieglitz, which include a copy of
the "Axioms.") The single page ms. is signed by Williams and
contains a handwritten note to Stieglitz: "—Haven't seen you
recently but thought you might be interested." The ms. is dated
7/17/43. Ms. C–11 (b) at Buffalo is a carbon copy of the Yale ms.,
also signed and dated by Williams and also containing a handwritten note: "—inspired by the prose commentaries in your last issue."
For an explanation of the disparity between the two handwritten
notes, see p. 30 of my Introduction.

   Ms. C–11 at Buffalo also includes a one-page earlier version of
the "Axioms" with a few insignificant textual variations.

What of Alfred Stieglitz?

Previously unpublished. The text printed here follows Yale ms. Za

Williams 262 a. Williams consistently misspells Stieglitz's name as "Steiglitz" in this ms. For details concerning the circumstances surrounding the composition of this ms., see p. 33 of the Introduction. Yale ms. Za Williams 262 b is a carbon of a typist's copy of Williams's ms., probably the carbon of the version sent by Williams to Dorothy Norman.

Woman as Operator
First published in *Women: A Collaboration of Artists and Writers* (Samuel Kootz Editions, New York, 1948). The text printed here follows Buffalo ms. C-157, which, except for a few details, is identical to the version published in *Women*. For details concerning the composition and publication of this essay see p. 36 of the Introduction.

A Letter, Touching the Comintern, upon Censorship in the Arts
First published in *The Tiger's Eye*, No. 4 (June 1948), 29–31. The text printed here follows the printed version. Yale ms. Za Williams 221, fourth folder, contains a ms. version which is identical to that printed in *The Tiger's Eye*. On page 70 of the issue of *The Tiger's Eye* which contains Williams's "Letter," in a section entitled "Tale of the Contents," there is the following note: "In sending this "Letter" to *The Tiger's Eye*, Dr. Williams wrote of his interest in seeing it in print because of 'the protest it constitutes against the primness of the modern intellectual attitude of so many of our avant-garde (self-styled) magazines. Why do they think one writes? To govern the universe? In a *literary* magazine one deals, one supposes, with literature. The objective is to present questions first of all entertainingly, briefly; to bring up as many facets of disturbing phenomena in the social-political world as possible in a way to make the reader want to THINK. A man isn't expected to solve the problems of his readers along some preconceived editorial policy line, is he?'."

Nicolas Calas's Illumination of the Significance of Hieronymus Bosch's
The Garden of Delights
Previously unpublished. The mss. forming the basis of the text printed here are part of a group of uncatalogued Williams materials

at Yale which were apparently considered for publication in the *Selected Essays* collection, but not used. There are three versions: a handwritten group of notes twenty pages long, which I have designated as text (a); a fragmentary fourteen-page typewritten draft, untitled, but with the superscription "Dear sir:", etc., which I have designated as text (b); and an eighteen-page titled, typewritten version (c), which I have used as the main text for the version printed here. Some of the handwritten fragments are dated 8/24/51 or 8/25/51.

The fact that Williams originally wrote this essay in the form of a letter suggests that he may have been asked by a publisher to comment on an, at that time, as yet unpublished ms. by Nicolas Calas, and that Williams later decided to turn his comments into an essay.

The Portrait: Emanuel Romano

Most of the text of this essay, with an introduction by Mike Weaver, was first published in *Form*, No. 2 (Cambridge, England, September 1966). The basic text I have used here (Yale ms. Za Williams 80, "Emanuel Romano") contains a number of paragraphs not printed in *Form*. I have designated this draft as (d). Furthermore, among the Williams mss. at Yale there is an earlier version of this essay (Za Williams 81), entitled "The Portrait." I have designated this text as draft (a). A separate four-page fragment classified with this text I have designated as draft (b), and a further single-page fragment as draft (c). As Mike Weaver notes, Romano painted his portrait of Williams in September 1951, and the Williams ms. should date from about that same period.

The Broken Vase

Previously unpublished. Yale ms. Za Williams 33, 34, consists of two versions of this essay. The basic text I have used here has four typed pages and is titled "The Broken Vase." I have designated this text as (b). The other version, an earlier one, consists of three typewritten pages and is untitled. I have designated it as (a). These texts, written on Williams's electric typewriter, were probably completed early in 1957. (See Mike Weaver, "Introduction to a Modern Portrait," *Form,* No. 2, p. 21.)

The American Spirit in Art
First published in *Proceedings of the American Academy of Arts and Letters,* Second Series, No. 2 (New York 1952). I have used this published text as the basis for the version printed here. Yale mss. Za Williams 10 and 11 bring together several fragments and versions of this essay: two pages of handwritten notes which I have designated as (a); a one-page typewritten fragment, (b); a fourteen-page early version of the essay, (c); and a five-page later version, including carbons of pages 2, 3, and 4, (d).

Notes on Movements, Artists and Issues
I. The Visitors
Previously unpublished. The text printed here is taken from Buffalo ms. C–146. The title points to the origin of the ms. in the later years of World War II.
II. Theory of Excellence in the Arts
Previously unpublished. The text is taken from Buffalo ms. C–138. The dating of the ms. as c. 1948 is based on the weak evidence of the nature and condition of typeface and typescript.
III. Picasso Breaks Faces
Reprinted as published in *The General Magazine and Historical Chronicle,* Vol. LIII, No. 1 (Autumn 1950), 40–41.
IV. Art and Social Organization
Previously unpublished. The text is taken from an uncatalogued Williams ms. at Yale belonging to a previously mentioned group of materials apparently considered for publication in the *Selected Essays* collection, but not used. This short piece was evidently originally written in response to one of the periodic "opinion polls" which editors of literary magazines like to send to their authors: the article, which is dated "January 9, 1950" is prefaced by the following phrase: "Your approach to a solution of the problem under discussion must lie along the following paths:"—whereupon the article follows, as printed here.

V. On the Practical Function of Art
Previously unpublished. Buffalo ms. C–8 consists of three pages of handwritten and typescript notes of partially overlapping material. I have designated these pages as C–8 (a), (b), and (c). They were clearly meant to be part of a larger ms., from which they were separated, deliberately or by accident. C–8 (a) contains the bracketed, typewritten annotation "final paragraphs," and C–8 (c) is a page numbered "9". My dating of these notes, c. 1951 is based on the very slim evidence of the—for Williams—unusually wide spacing of the lines, which is similar to that of the Calas/Bosch ms., and to that of the Hanover reading (see below).

VI. Alfred Eisenstaedt
Previously unpublished. The text is from Yale ms. Za Williams 221 (fifth folder). Signed and dated August 17, 1951, by Williams. Another typescript of this ms. at Yale, uncatalogued, is a copy made by John C. Thirlwall, probably for possible inclusion in *Selected Essays*. A note by Thirlwall indicates that Williams's remarks were originally written into a copy of a collection of Eisenstaedt's work.

VII. Talks and Readings, Hanover, etc., April 1952
Previously unpublished. The text is from a group of uncatalogued Williams mss. at Yale (Box III). Dated by Williams in the title.

VIII. John Marin
Reprinted as published in the *Catalogue of the John Marin Memorial Exhibition* (Art Galleries, University of California, Los Angeles, 1955).

IX. Patrocinio Barela
First published in *El Crepusculo,* Taos, New Mexico, Vol. VIII, No. 31, Section One (August 4, 1955), 9, and reprinted in *Poetry Taos Annual,* No. 1 (1957). The text printed here is taken from *Poetry Taos.*

X. Henry Niese
First published in January 1957 as part of a broadsheet representing the catalogue of an exhibition of Niese's paintings at the "G" Gallery, 200 East 59th Street, New York. Yale mss. Za Williams 114, 115, and 116 consist of three versions of this statement. I have used the final ms. version, titled "Henry Niese," and signed by Williams. The earliest version of the ms. is a rough draft partially

typed around the initial phrase of another, apparently abandoned earlier text, which reads as follows: "The man in the moon. I will kill 4 squirrels today with my bow and arrows. The squirrels will be put behind the garage. Today is the 29th of december, 1955." It is my guess that Williams was trying out his new electric typewriter and came up with these (interesting) random phrases.

XI. Whitman's Leaves of Grass *and Photography*
This fragment represents an early version of the last five paragraphs of an introductory essay written by Williams for inclusion in a projected selection of Whitman's poetry illustrated by photographs. Williams wrote this introduction in 1960, when the book was first planned, but publication was delayed for many years. The book, with Williams's introduction, has appeared only recently as *The Illustrated Leaves of Grass,* introduction by William Carlos Williams, edited by Howard Chapnick (New York, 1971). Many of the photographs in the published edition, however, do not correspond to those which Williams saw, having been changed, according to Chapnick, "to reflect the changes in contemporary photography over the past decade." I am printing this fragment here, because it is in effect self-contained, comprising Williams's complete commentary on the photographs as such, and because the manuscript pages I have used are considerably different from the commentary actually printed in *The Illustrated Leaves of Grass.* Stylistically much rougher, they strike me as none the less considerably more vigorous, spontaneous, and representative of Williams's response to visual materials, than the paragraphs dealing with the photographs to be found in the obviously heavily edited printed version. My basic text is a two-page typescript among the materials of Yale ms. Za Williams 174, which I have designated as draft (a). Another, single-page, typescript from the same group of materials is a fragment of another version of this ms. I have designated this fragment as draft (b).

E. E. Cummings's Paintings and Poems
Reprinted as published in *Arts Digest,* Vol. XXIX, No. 5 (December 1, 1954), 7–8. The ms. version of this article at Yale is a copy made by John C. Thirlwall.

Painting in the American Grain
First published in *Art News,* Vol. LIII, No. 4 (June–August 1954),
20–23, 62, 78. Reprinted in *Selected Essays,* 329–336. The text
printed here follows a rough draft of this article, entitled "The
Edgar William and Bernice Chrysler Garbisch Collection of
American Primitives" (Yale ms. Za Williams 78). There are
considerable textual problems connected with this essay. The
rough draft, typed by Williams while struggling with the aftereffects of a stroke, contains innumerable typing errors. While this
ms. has a few corrections and additions in Williams's hand, most of
the alterations in the text were clearly *not* made by Williams, but
by someone else, probably John C. Thirlwall. These corrections
are sometimes quite unnecessary and, in fact, occasionally out of
keeping with Williams's own style of writing (at one point, for
example, the word "trees" has been crossed out and the word
"vegetation" substituted, while elsewhere "picture," Williams's
customary word for a painting, has been deleted in favor of
"view"). The other ms. version of this article, also at Yale, is a copy
of the rough draft, as emended by Thirlwall. Both the version
printed in *Art News* and that in *Selected Essays* follow this latter,
emended copy. For the text printed here I have therefore returned
to the rough draft by Williams himself. I have restored the original
text wherever the corrections introduced by the hand other than
Williams's seemed to me unnecessary or inappropriate, or where
they simply represent attempts to "straighten out" stylistic peculiarities otherwise typical of Williams's writing. I have also restored
most of the phrases and words deleted, except where the deletions
were made by Williams himself, since these were mostly false
starts of no particular interest.

Brancusi
First published in *Arts,* Vol. XXX, No. 2 (November 1955), 21–
25. The text printed here follows that of the ms. version at Yale (Za
Williams 32), restoring a few phrases deleted by Williams, and
correcting several faulty transcriptions and some bowdlerizations
introduced in the *Arts* text.